Learning Macromedia® Flash® 8

Suzanne Weixel

PEARSON

Prentice Hall DDC

Upper Saddle River,
New Jersey 07458

Library of Congress Cataloging-in-Publication Data

Weixel, Suzanne.
    Learning Macromedia Flash 8 / Suzanne Weixel.
        p. cm.
    ISBN 0-13-187233-8
    1. Flash (Computer file) 2. Computer Animation. I. Title.
    TR897.7.W49 2007
    006.7'8—dc22

                                    2005056379

Vice President and Publisher: Natalie E. Anderson
Executive Acquisitions Editor, Print: Stephanie Wall
Executive Acquisitions Editor, Media: Richard Keaveny
Executive Editor: Jennifer Frew
Product Development Manager: Eileen Bien Calabro
Editorial Supervisor: Brian Hoehl
Editorial Assistants: Alana Meyers, Kaitlin O'Shaughnessy
Executive Producer: Lisa Strite
Content Development Manager: Cathi Profitko
Senior Media Project Manager: Steve Gagliostro
Senior Marketing Manager: Jason Sakos
Marketing Assistant: Ann Baranov
Sr. Sales Associate: Joseph Pascale
Managing Editor: Lynda J. Castillo
Production Project Manager/Buyer: April Montana
Manufacturing Buyer: Natacha Moore
Production/Editorial Assistant: Sandra K. Bernales
Art Director/Interior Design: Blair Brown
Cover Design: Amy Capuano
Composition: Laserwords
Full-Service Project Management: BookMasters, Inc./Sharon Anderson
Cover Printer: Phoenix Color Corporation
Printer/Binder: Quebecor World Book Services/Dubuque

Pearson Education LTD.
Pearson Education (Singapore), Pte. Ltd.
Pearson Education, Canada, Ltd
Pearson Education—Japan

Pearson Education of Australia PTY. Limited
Pearson Education North Asia Ltd
Pearson Educación de Mexico, S.A. de C.V.
Pearson Education Malaysia, Pte. Ltd

10 9 8 7 6 5 4
ISBN: 0-13-187233-8

TABLE OF CONTENTS

iv

Introduction

Learning Macromedia Flash 8 provides you with the knowledge and experience you need to design and build animations for use on Web pages, in presentations, and as standalone applications.

HOW WE'VE ORGANIZED THE BOOK

Learning Macromedia Flash 8 is made up of five lessons:

Lesson 1

■ **Getting Started with Macromedia Flash 8.** This lesson includes seven exercises designed to introduce you to the program and its workspace. You start with a tour of the Flash on-screen elements, including menus, panels, and the workspace. You will also learn how to start and exit the program. You move on to an exercise that introduces you to the Flash Help program, and then you start to create images using the Flash drawing tools. By the end of the lesson you are able to draw, modify, and transform shapes—the building blocks of all Flash animations.

Lesson 2

■ **Creating an Animation.** From organization to animation, this lesson takes you through the process of building a complete Flash document. You learn how to build an animation using frames and layers. You discover the unique methods Flash offers for keeping file size small, and you get your first taste of animation as you make shapes and objects move across the screen, change color, and transform.

Lesson 3

■ **Enhancing an Animation.** The exercises in this lesson show you how to improve your animations by incorporating sounds, imported graphics, video,

and text. You will learn how to insert actions to control the flow of your animations and to create buttons that your audience can use to navigate through an animation.

Lesson 4

■ **Publishing an Application.** In this lesson, you learn how to prepare a Flash animation for viewing on the World Wide Web, or on a standalone computer. You will learn to test and optimize your movies to ensure the best performance and how to select settings to control the size and quality of the movie when it plays. You will also learn how to export the movie or its components so you can use it in a different program.

Lesson 5

■ **Using Advanced Features.** This lesson covers the advanced features that make it possible for you to create complex animations. You will learn how to make interactive text that viewers can select on-screen, or click to link to a URL. You also learn how to create special effects and mask layers and how to incorporate user interface components such as check boxes in your Flash animations. Exercises on the Movie Explorer and Libraries teach you ways of staying organized even as your animations become more complicated.

Lessons are comprised of short exercises designed for using Macromedia Flash in real-life business settings. Every application exercise is made up of seven key elements:

■ **Software Skills.** Each exercise starts with a brief description of how you would use the features of that exercise in the workplace.

■ **Application Skills.** A scenario is set to put the Flash tools into context.

■ **Terms.** Key terms are included and defined at the start of each exercise, so you can quickly refer back to them. The terms are then highlighted in the text.

■ **Notes.** Concise notes aid in learning the computer concepts.

- **Procedures.** Hands-on mouse and keyboard procedures teach all necessary skills.
- **Application Exercise.** Step-by-step instructions put your skills to work.

New enhanced End-of-Lesson material puts skills to the test.

- **Summary Exercise.** Comprehensive exercises that touch on most skills covered in the lesson. Step-by-step directions guide you through the exercises.
- **Application Exercise.** The level of difficulty starts to ramp up with the application exercises. These summary exercises do not contain detailed steps.

- **On Your Own.** Each exercise concludes with a critical-thinking activity that you can work through on your own. The "On Your Own" sections can be used as additional reinforcement, for practice, or to test skill proficiency.

- **Curriculum Integration Exercise.** Integrate other subject areas into the computer course with the curriculum integration exercises. Topics include math, language arts, social studies, and science.
- **Critical Thinking Exercise.** These challenging exercises are scenario-based—no specific steps are given.

WORKING WITH DATA AND SOLUTION FILES

As you work through the exercises in this book, you'll be creating, opening, and saving files. You should keep the following instructions in mind:

- For many of the exercises you can use the data files provided on the CD-ROM that comes with this book. The data files are used so that you can focus on the skills being introduced.
- When the application exercise includes a file name and a CD icon 🔘, you can open the file provided on CD.

- The Directory of Files on the following page lists the exercise file (from the CD-ROM) you can open to complete each exercise.
- Unless the book instructs otherwise, use the default settings when creating a file.

All the exercises instruct you to save the files created or to save the exercise files under a new name. You should verify the name of the hard disk or network folder to which files should be saved.

WHAT'S ON THE CD

We've included on the CD:

- **Data files** for many of the exercises. This way you don't have to create all the documents from scratch.

COPY DATA FILES 🔘

You can copy data files from the CD-ROM to a hard drive:

1. Open Windows Explorer. (Right-click the `start` button and click **Explore**.)
2. Be sure that the CD is in your CD-ROM drive. Select the CD-ROM drive letter from the All Folders pane of the Explorer window.

3. Click to select the **Data** folder in the Contents of (CD-ROM drive letter) pane of the Explorer window.
4. Drag the folder onto the letter of the drive to which you wish to copy the data files (usually **C:**) in the All Folders pane of the Explorer Window.

DIRECTORY OF DATA FILES ON CD 🖸

Unless otherwise noted, files are in .fla format.
Some .swf files and .html files are optional; students generate them if they test the animation in Flash Player, or publish the animation in HTML.

EXERCISE NO.	FILE NAME	PAGE NO.
Exercise 1	None	
Exercise 2	None	
Exercise 3	None	
Exercise 4	None	
Exercise 5	05PIC	37
Exercise 6	06DATA, 06PIC	41, 42
Exercise 7	None	
Exercise 8	None	
Exercise 9	09DATA	51
Exercise 10	None	
Exercise 11	None	
Exercise 12	12DATA	63
Exercise 13	13PIC	69
Exercise 14	14DATA, 14PIC	74, 76
Exercise 15	15DATA, 15PIC	80, 81
Exercise 16	16DATA	84
Exercise 17	17DATA, 17PIC	87, 88
Exercise 18	None	
Exercise 19	19DATA	96
Exercise 20	20DATA, 20PIC	101, 102
Exercise 21	21DATA	103
Exercise 22	22DATA	105
Exercise 23	None	
Exercise 24	24DATA	110
Exercise 25	25PARK.wmf, 25DOVE.gif, 25BUG.wmf, 25FLY.wmf, 25FLOWERS.jpg	116, 117, 118
Exercise 26	26DATA, 26WINGS.wav, 26TWEET.wav, 26PIC, 26BUGS1.wav, 26BUGS2.wav, 26BUGS3.wav	121, 122
Exercise 27	27DATA, 27PIC	128, 130
Exercise 28	28DATA, 28PIC	132, 134
Exercise 29	29DATA, 29PIC	137, 139
Exercise 30	30DATA, 30PIC	142, 144

EXERCISE NO.	FILE NAME	PAGE NO.
Exercise 31	31DATA, 31PIC	147, 149
Exercise 32	32DATA, 32BAND.mpg, 32DRUM.wmf, 32JOIN.mov	151, 153
Exercise 33	33DATA, STAGE.jpg, CLAP.wav	155
Exercise 34	34DATA	157
Exercise 35	None	
Exercise 36	None	
Exercise 37	37DATA, 37PIC	170, 172
Exercise 38	38DATA, 38PIC	177, 178
Exercise 39	39DATA, 39PIC	180, 181
Exercise 40	40DATA	182
Exercise 41	41DATA	184
Exercise 42	None	
Exercise 43	43DATA	188
Exercise 44	44DATA, 44PIC	194
Exercise 45	45DATA1, 45DATA2, 45PIC	198, 199
Exercise 46	46DATA, 46PIC	201, 203
Exercise 47	47DATA, 47PIC	205, 207
Exercise 48	48DATA, 48CAT.jpg, 48MEOW.wav	210, 211
Exercise 49	49DATA, 49PIC	214, 216
Exercise 50	50DATA, 50PIC	219, 220
Exercise 51	51DATA, 51PIC	222, 224
Exercise 52	52DATA	225
Exercise 53	53DATA	229
Exercise 54	None	
Exercise 55	DOG.jpg, SONG.wav	233

Lesson | 1

Getting Started with Macromedia Flash 8

END OF LESSON
PROJECTS

Exercise 8

- Summary Exercise

Exercise 9

- Application Exercise

Exercise 10

- Curriculum Integration Exercise

Exercise 11

- Critical Thinking Exercise

Skills Covered

- **About Flash**
- **Start Flash and Create a New Document**
- **View the Flash Window**
- **Customize the Flash Window**
- **Exit Flash**

Software Skills Macromedia Flash 8 is a software program designed to let you create applications comprised of sound, shapes, images, and video for use on Web sites and for stand-alone presentations. With Flash, you can create simple applications, such as an animated logo that rotates across the screen, or complex applications, such as an interactive game of Tic Tac Toe. The first step in mastering Flash is to learn some basic Flash concepts and to become familiar with the Flash interface.

Application Skills You are an assistant at Grace Notes, a small stationery boutique. The owner has asked if you would be interested in using Flash to develop content for the store's new Web site. In this exercise, you will learn some basic Flash concepts, start Flash, explore the Flash interface, and then exit Flash.

TERMS

Actions Built-in components you can use to animate or add interactivity to application elements.

Application A Flash document file. Sometimes called a movie.

Attributes Qualities or properties that control the display or behavior or an object or element.

Author To create and edit a Flash application.

Content Objects included in an application.

Dock To affix an element to a specific location onscreen.

File extension A dot followed by three or more characters added to a file name to indicate the file type and the program that is used to open the file.

Flash Player A program used to run Flash applications.

Float To position an element so that it can be moved to any location onscreen.

Frame The basic unit that defines a length of time in a Flash application.

Frame rate The number of animation frames displayed per second.

Gripper In Flash, dotted lines at the left end of a panel's title bar, used to drag the panel.

Layers In Flash, an invisible sheet used to separate objects on a frame.

Pan To shift content right, left, up, or down onscreen.

Panel A window similar to a dialog box in which you select options for modifying the current item.

Pasteboard In Flash, the gray area outside the Stage where you store content that you do not want to display when the file plays.

Playhead A shaded rectangle in the Timeline that indicates the current frame.

Publish To prepare a Flash application for viewing.

Stage In Flash, the rectangular area where you create content and preview a file.

Stream To start playing a file before the file has finished downloading.

Template A sample document that includes settings and content from which you can create a new document.

Timeline The panel where you organize and control content over time using layers and frames. Also, the series of frames for each layer.

Vector-based graphics Pictures that are drawn using lines, shapes, and curves.

Zoom To change the magnification of displayed items to make content appear larger or smaller.

3

NOTES

About Flash

- Use Flash to **author** Flash **applications**, to **publish** applications for use in other programs such as a Web browser, and to play applications on your computer.
- Flash comes in two editions:
  - Flash Basic 8, which is for use by Web designers and people developing interactive and multimedia content, such as audio, video, graphics, and text.
  - Flash Professional 8, which is for use by advanced Web designers and application builders creating large-scale, complex projects. Flash Professional 8 includes all the features of Flash Basic 8, as well as expressiveness tools for optimizing the look and feel of Flash applications, external scripting, and capabilities for handling dynamic data from databases.

    ✓ *This book covers features available in both editions. The illustrations depict Flash Professional 8.*

- A document file that you create, save, and edit with Flash has a .fla **file extension**.
- When you publish the file, it is saved with a .swf file extension. You play .swf files using the **Flash Player** program.
- Flash applications are comprised of a series of **frames**, called a **Timeline**. You insert **content** such as shapes, images, and **actions** on the frames. When you play the application, the frames are displayed in sequence, so that the content appears to change and move.

- This process is similar to creating a flipbook from a simple pad of paper. If you draw a picture on each page in the pad, and then flip the pages quickly, the picture seems to move. A Flash application functions on the same basic principle, with each frame active as a page in the pad of paper.
- Some of Flash's unique features include the following:
  - Flash has a built-in **vector-based graphics** drawing utility that you can use to draw, edit, and modify shapes.
  - You can incorporate interactivity in Flash applications. For example, you can set buttons and images to start actions when clicked, enabling users to access different parts of the application or to start different animations.
  - Flash files download faster and start playing faster than other, similar file types because they are smaller and they are **streamed**, which means they start playing while they are still downloading.

Start Flash and Create a New Document

- To use Flash 8 you must first start it so that it is running on your computer.
- You use Windows to start Flash.
- By default, when you first start Flash, the Start page displays, as shown in the following illustration.

Start Page

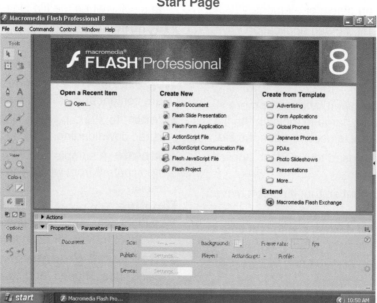

- From the Start page, you can open a recent item, create a new item, create an item from a **template**, or extend Flash to access the Macromedia Flash Exchange Web site.
- The Start page also displays whenever Flash is running with no files open. You can choose to hide the Start page, if desired.
- When the Start page is not displayed, create a new Flash document by using the New dialog box.

View the Flash Window

- A new Flash document file opens with the default interface screen displayed.

   ✓ *If someone has customized the Flash screen on your system, the screen that opens on your computer may not look like the default screen shown in the illustration at the bottom of the page.*

- In addition to typical Windows elements such as a title bar, menu bar, and control buttons, the Flash interface includes the following screen elements.

   ✓ *As in other Windows programs, when you rest the mouse pointer over certain screen elements such as buttons or tools, a ScreenTip displays.*

   - Stage. The rectangular area where you create content and preview the file.

- **Pasteboard.** The gray area outside the Stage, where you store content that you do not want to display when the file plays. This is sometimes called the Work Area.
- **Panels.** Windows similar to dialog boxes in which you select options to control the behavior or appearance of the selected object. The panel name displays on its title bar. A panel may be collapsed to hide its contents or expanded to display its contents.
- Timeline. A special panel in which you organize and control content using **layers** and frames. Elements of the Timeline include the following (see the illustration at the top of page 6):
   - Layers are listed in a column in the left pane of the Timeline.
   - Frames in each layer are listed in a row to the right of the layer name.
   - The Timeline header lists frame numbers.
   - The **playhead** indicates the current frame, which is the frame displayed on the Stage. When an application is playing, the playhead moves from left to right through the Timeline.
   - The Timeline status bar displays the current frame number, the current **frame rate**, and the elapsed time to the current frame.

Flash Screen

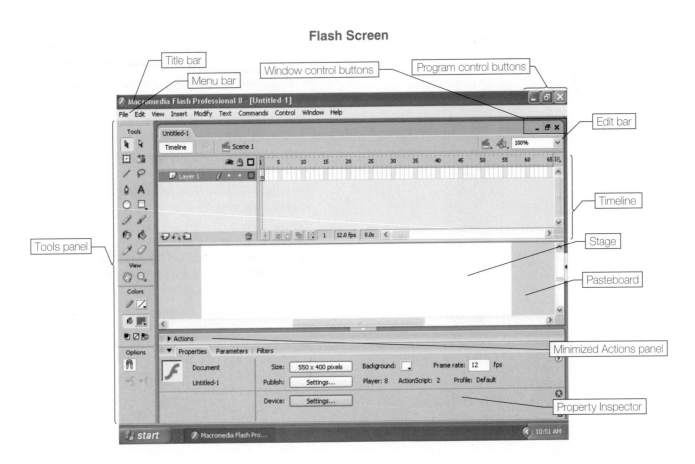

Timeline

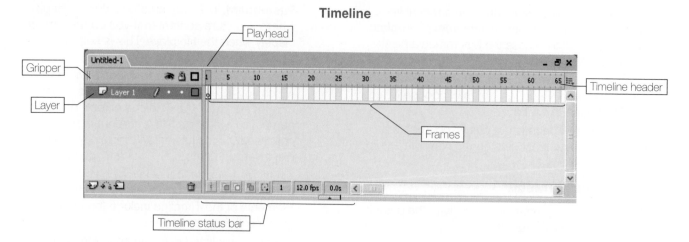

- **Gripper**
- **Layer**
- **Playhead**
- **Frames**
- **Timeline header**
- **Timeline status bar**

- **Tools panel.** A collection of tools you use to draw, paint, select, and modify content, and to change the view of the Stage. The Toolbox has four sections (see the following illustration):
  - **Tools.** Displays tools for drawing, painting, and selecting objects.
  - **View.** Displays tools for **zooming** and **panning** the Stage.
  - **Colors.** Displays tools for modifying the colors of objects.
  - **Options.** Displays tools for modifying the behavior of the selected tool.

Tools Panel

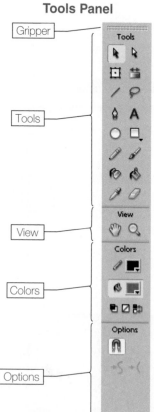

- **Gripper**
- **Tools**
- **View**
- **Colors**
- **Options**

- **Property Inspector.** A panel that displays the most commonly used **attributes** for the currently selected item. You can view and modify the attributes in the Property Inspector.
- **Toolbars.** Flash includes the main toolbar, edit bar, and Controller toolbar, which you can show or hide as needed. By default, only the edit bar displays.

Customize the Flash Window

- Customize the layout of the Flash window workspace by displaying only the panels and toolbars that you need, and by setting the size and position of panels.
- Keeping only the elements you need open is also useful because the Flash window can get crowded.
- Move a panel by dragging the panel **gripper**.
- You can **dock** panels in a specific location, or set them to **float** over the Flash window.
- Collapse a panel to leave it onscreen with its contents hidden; expand the panel to make its contents visible.
- You can also close a panel completely and open it again as needed.
- You can save a customized panel layout so that you can revert to it at any time. Flash comes with one built-in panel layout, called Default. The Default layout displays the collapsed Color panel and the Library panel docked on the right side of the window.
- You can also create a panel group. Grouped panels display as separate tabs in the same panel (see the illustration on page 7); click a tab to make the options for that panel active. When you remove a panel from a group, the ungrouped panel floats onscreen.

Panel Group

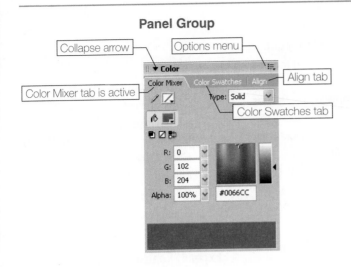

- Collapse arrow
- Options menu
- Color Mixer tab is active
- Align tab
- Color Swatches tab

▣ Some panels are grouped by default. For example, the Color panel includes both the Color Mixer and Color Swatches panels.

Exit Flash

▣ When you are finished using Flash, you exit the Flash program.

▣ If you try to exit Flash without saving your document file, Flash prompts you to do so. You can choose to save or to exit without saving.

▣ If you exit Flash without closing your saved files, Flash closes them automatically.

PROCEDURES

Start Flash

1. Click Windows <kbd>start</kbd> button....................................... 🏁
2. Click **All Programs**.
3. Click **Macromedia**.
4. Click **Macromedia Flash 8**.

   OR

   Double-click **Macromedia Flash 8** icon on Desktop

Create a New Document

1. Start Flash.
2. On the Start page, under Create New, click **Flash Document**.

   OR

   Click **New** button ⬜ on main toolbar.

   OR

1. Click **File**.................... Alt + F
2. Click **New**.......................... N
3. Click **Flash Document**.
4. Click **OK**........................ ↵Enter

Hide the Start Page

1. Click **Edit**.................... Alt + E
2. Click **Preferences**................. F
3. Click **On launch** drop-down arrow.
4. Click **No document**.
5. Click **OK**........................ ↵Enter

Display the Start Page

1. Click **Edit**................... Alt + E
2. Click **Preferences**................. F
3. Click **On launch** drop-down arrow.
4. Click **Show Start Page**.
5. Click **OK**........................ ↵Enter

Show/Hide Timeline (Ctrl+Alt+T)

1. Click **Window**.............. Alt + W

   ✓ A check mark next to the Timeline command indicates that the Timeline is currently displayed.

2. Click **Timeline**...................... M

   OR

   Click **Timeline** button |Timeline| on edit bar.

Resize Timeline

▣ Drag border between Layer pane and Frame pane left or right.

▣ Drag border between Timeline and Stage up or down.

Show/Hide Tools Panel (Ctrl+F2)

1. Click **Window**.............. Alt + W

   ✓ A check mark next to the Tools command indicates that the Tools panel is currently displayed.

2. Click **Tools**........................ L

Show/Hide Property Inspector (Ctrl+F3)

1. Click **Window**.............. Alt + W
2. Click **Properties**.............. P, →

   ✓ A check mark next to the Properties command indicates that the Property Inspector is currently displayed.

3. Click **Properties**.................... P

Show/Hide Other Panels

1. Click **Window**.............. Alt + W
2. Click desired panel name.

   OR

   a. Click **Other Panels**.... R, R, →
   b. Click desired panel name.

   ✓ A check mark next to a panel name indicates that panel is currently displayed.

Hide All Current Panels (F4)

1. Click **Window**.............. Alt + W
2. Click **Hide Panels**............... P, P, ↵Enter

Show All Current Panels (F4)

1. Click **Window**.............. Alt + W
2. Click **Show Panels**............... P, P, ↵Enter

Close Panel

1. Click panel's **Options menu**.
2. Click **Close** *panel name*.

7

✓ *When you see panel name in italics, you should substitute the actual panel name.*

OR

Click **Close Panel Group**.

Close Floating Panel

■ Click panel's **Close** button ☒.

Show/Hide Toolbars

1. Click **Window** .... Alt + W
2. Click **Toolbars** .... O
3. Click desired toolbar name.

   ✓ *A check mark next to a toolbar name indicates that toolbar is currently displayed.*

Move a Docked Panel or Toolbar

1. Position mouse pointer over item's gripper.

   ✓ *The mouse pointer displays a four-headed arrow.*

2. Drag item to desired location.

Move a Floating Panel or Toolbar

■ Drag item's title bar to new location.

   ✓ *Press and hold Ctrl while dragging to keep item from docking.*

   ✓ *Drag item by gripper to dock it in new location.*

Resize a Floating Panel or Toolbar

■ Drag item's border to new size.

Collapse/Expand a Panel

■ Click panel's **collapse** arrow ▾.
   OR
■ Click panel's **expand** arrow ▸.

Group Panels

1. Display first panel to group.
2. Display second panel to group.
3. In second panel, click **Options menu**.
4. On Options menu, click **Group** *panel name* **with**.
5. On submenu, click first panel name.
6. Repeat to group additional panels.

Remove a Panel from a Group

1. Display grouped panel.
2. Click tab for panel to remove.
3. Click **Options menu**.
4. On Options menu, click **Group** *panel name* **with**.
5. On submenu, click **New panel group**.

Save a Workspace Layout

1. Customize workspace as desired.
2. Click **Window** .... Alt + W
3. Click **Workspace Layout** .... W, W, →
4. Click **Save Current** .... S
5. Type name for new layout.
6. Click **OK** .... ↵Enter

Select a Workspace Layout

1. Click **Window** .... Alt + W
2. Click **Workspace Layout** .... W, W, →
3. Click desired layout name.

OR

Click **Default** .... D
to display default layout.

Delete a Workspace Layout

1. Click **Window** .... Alt + W
2. Click **Workspace Layout** .... W, W, →
3. Click **Manage** .... M
4. Click layout to delete.
5. Click **Delete**.
6. Click **Yes** .... ↵Enter
7. Click **OK** .... ↵Enter

Expand/Contract Stage

■ Click arrow at bottom or right of Stage.

   ✓ *Arrows point in when stage is expanded; arrows point out when stage is contracted.*

Show/Hide Pasteboard (Ctrl+Shift+W)

1. Click **View** .... Alt + V
2. Click **Work Area** .... W, W, →

   ✓ *A check mark next to the Work Area command indicates that the Pasteboard is currently displayed.*

Exit Flash

■ Click **Program Close** button ☒.
   OR
1. Click **File** .... Alt + F
2. Click **Exit** X
3. Click **Yes** .. Y to save changes.
   OR
   Click **No** .... N to close without saving.

EXERCISE DIRECTIONS

1. Start Flash.
2. Create a new document.
3. Rest the mouse pointer over any tool in the Tools panel.

   ✓ *A ScreenTip displays the tool name.*

4. Move the mouse pointer over the other tools in the Tools panel, using the ScreenTips to identify the name of each tool.
5. Hide the Tools panel.
6. Display the default workspace layout.
7. Collapse the Library panel.
8. Expand the Color panel.
9. Display the Info panel.
10. If necessary, dock the Info panel between the Library and Color panels.

    ✓ *Remember, you must drag a panel by its gripper to dock it.*

11. Group the Info panel with the Color panel.
12. Make the Color Mixer tab active.
13. Display the main toolbar.
14. Hide the Pasteboard.
15. Dock the Timeline on the left side of the workspace. The Flash window should look similar to the one in Illustration A.
16. Ungroup the Info panel from the Color panel, and then close it.
17. Hide the main toolbar.
18. Display the Tools panel.
19. Dock the Timeline at the top of the workspace.
20. Display the Pasteboard.
21. Close the Color and Library panels.
22. Exit Flash without saving any changes.

Illustration A

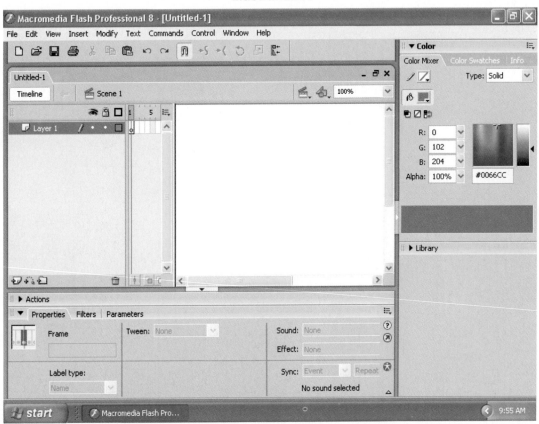

ON YOUR OWN

1. Start Flash and create a new document.
2. Practice showing and hiding different screen elements, including panels, the Timeline, and toolbars.
3. Practice arranging and resizing panels.
4. Practice grouping and ungrouping panels.
5. Save one or more customized layouts.
6. Practice changing to the default layout, and then to your customized layout.
7. Delete your customized layout(s).
8. Revert to the default layout.
9. Exit Flash without saving any changes.

Exercise | 2

Skills Covered

- About the Flash Help System
- Locate a Help Topic
- Modify the Help Panel Display
- Get Help Online

Software Skills Flash 8 provides a variety of ways to get help for using any Flash feature as you work. Use the Flash Help system to locate specific topics or features and access step-by-step instructions for getting started with Flash, or use the Flash Tutorials for in-depth, hands-on lessons on how to build a Flash application. Visit the Macromedia Web site to get tips, ask questions, and access any downloads that may be available.

Application Skills As an assistant at Grace Notes, it is important to learn how to solve problems on your own. In this exercise, you will learn how to use the Help system to answer questions you may have while creating applications with Flash.

TERMS

ActionScript The programming language you use to develop actions in Flash.

Filter To limit options based on selected criteria.

Hyperlink Text or graphics set up to provide a direct connection with a destination location or document. When you click a hyperlink, the destination is displayed.

NOTES

About the Flash Help System

- Use the Help menu to start the Flash Help system, or press F1.
- Flash Help is organized into a series of books that document the basic tools and features available in Flash:
  - *How to Use Help* provides information about the different books in the Help system, and how to use them.
  - *Getting Started with Flash* provides an overview of the Flash program as well as step-by-step instructions covering the basic tasks for creating a Flash application.
  - *Using Flash* includes comprehensive coverage of all Flash features for all levels of users.
  - *Flash Tutorials* are lessons that prompt you through the steps required to complete a specific Flash project. Sample files to use in the tutorials are provided.
  - *Flash Samples* are Flash files that display projects you can create with Flash. There are

descriptions about the features in the files, but no step-by-step instructions are provided.
  - Other books available in the Help system provide documentation for advanced features and development tools such as learning **ActionScript**.

Locate a Help Topic

- When you start the Flash Help system, the Help books are listed in the table of contents in the left pane of the Help panel. Click a book to open it, and then click a page to display the topic in the right pane of the panel. (See the illustration on page 12.)
- A plus sign next to a book indicates that it contains other books or topics. Click the plus sign to expand the table of contents; the plus sign is replaced by a minus sign. Click the minus sign to collapse the table of contents.
- Some topic pages contain **hyperlinks** to other, related topics. Click a hyperlink to display the related topic.

Help Panel

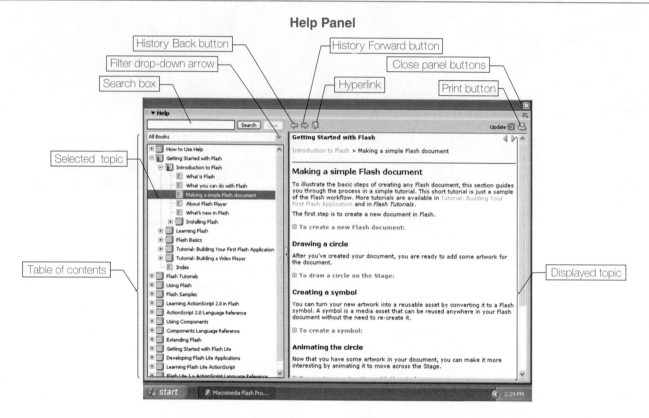

History Back button

History Forward button

Filter drop-down arrow

Close panel buttons

Search box

Hyperlink

Print button

Selected topic

Table of contents

Displayed topic

- Some topic pages display plus signs. Click the plus sign to display additional information, such as step-by-step instructions for completing a task.

- You can use the History Back and History Forward arrows at the top of the Help panel to scroll through the topics you already viewed.

- Use the Search feature to find specific topics.

- **Filter** the books by categories to display only the books you want to search or browse. For example, you can display only the books that include tutorials and samples, or you can display all books.

- Once you find a topic, you can read it onscreen, or print it for future use.

Modify the Help Panel Display

- Manage the Help panel as you manage other panels. For example, you can group it with other panels, or dock it on the side of the Flash window.

  ✓ *Refer to Exercise 1 for information on working with panels.*

- Adjust the width of the panes in the Help panel to show more of the table of contents.

- Hide the table of contents to display more of the topic information.

- Collapse the Help panel to work with Flash features.

- Close the Help panel when you are finished using it.

Get Help Online

- From the Flash Help menu you can access online resources such as the Flash Support Center to locate up-to-date information and support for using Flash.

- Other online Help sources include the Flash LiveDocs feature and the Macromedia Online Forums, as well as tools for developers.

  - LiveDocs provides online access to the Flash Help documents and lets you enter comments about specific topics and read the comments other people have entered.

  - Forums provide the opportunity to discuss Flash features and topics with other Flash users.

- Use the Update Help feature to download updated documentation from Macromedia as it becomes available.

PROCEDURES

Start Flash Help (F1)
1. Click **Help**.....................Alt + H
2. Click **Flash Help**.....................H
   OR
   Click **Getting Started with Flash**.....................G

Display a Help Topic
1. Click **Help**.....................Alt + H
2. Click **Flash Help**.....................H
3. Click book to expand table of contents.
4. Click topic to display Help information.
5. Click hyperlinks to go to related topic.
   OR
   Click plus sign to expand information.

Modify the Help Panel Display
   To Modify the Pane Width
- Drag border between panes left or right.
   To Hide the Table of Contents
- Click **Expand** arrow on border between panes.
   To Show the Table of Contents
- Click **Collapse** arrow on border between panes.

   To Collapse the Help Panel
- Click **Collapse panel** arrow ▼.
   To Expand the Help Panel
- Click **Expand panel** arrow ▶.
   To Close the Help Panel
- Click **Close panel** button ☒.

Scroll Through Help Topics
- Click **History Back** button ⇦ to display previous topic.
- Click **History Forward** button ⇨ to display next topic.

Search for a Help Topic
1. Click **Help**.....................Alt + H
2. Click **Flash Help**.....................H
3. Click in **Search** box.
4. Type topic to find.
5. Click **Search** button Search .
6. Click topic in table of contents.

Clear a Search
- Click **Clear** button Clear .

Filter Help Books
1. Click **Help**.....................Alt + H
2. Click **Flash Help**.....................H
3. Click **filter** drop-down arrow.
4. Click category of books to display.

Print a Help Topic
1. Display topic to print.
2. Click **Print** button 🖶 .
   ✓ *The Print dialog box displays.*
3. Click **Print** to print with default printer settings.

Get Help Online
1. Click **Help**.....................Alt + H
2. Click one of the following:
   - Flash **Support Center**.............S
   - Flash **LiveDocs**.....................L
   - Macromedia Online **Forums** F
3. Log on to the Internet as necessary.
4. Click links to access desired information.

Update Help Documents
1. Click **Help**.....................Alt + H
2. Click **Flash Help**.....................H
3. Click **Download Help Content** button 🔄 .

EXERCISE DIRECTIONS

1. Start Flash and create a new document.
2. Start the Help program.
3. Expand the Using Flash book.
4. Expand the Drawing book.
5. Click the About Flash Drawing and Painting Tools topic.
6. Read the Help information.
7. In the Help information, click the hyperlink to Using Panels and the Property Inspector in Getting Started with Flash.
8. Click the History Back button to return to the previous topic.
9. Click the filter drop-down arrow and then click Features to display only the books that provide information on Flash features.
10. Search for information about Panels.
11. Clear the search and then search for information about Ovals.
12. Click the topic Expressiveness.
13. Hide the table of contents.
14. Read the displayed topic.
15. Display the table of contents.
16. Click the topic Drawing straight lines, ovals, and rectangles.
17. On the topic page, click the plus sign next to the text *To draw a straight line, oval, or rectangle.* Your screen should look similar to the one in Illustration A on page 14.
18. Print the help topic.
19. Set the filter to display all books.
20. Clear the search.
21. Close the Help panel.
22. Exit Flash without saving any changes.

Illustration A

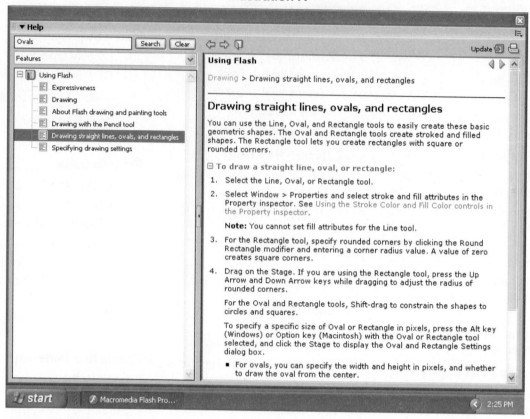

ON YOUR OWN

1. Start Flash and create a new document.
2. Practice using the Help system to locate information about using Flash. For example, locate information about what you can do with Flash, or what is new in Flash 8.
3. Print at least one Help topic.
4. Test a Flash tutorial. For example, try the tutorial about creating a new document.
5. With your instructor's permission, use the LiveDocs feature online to locate Help information for a topic. Note whether anyone has commented on the topic.
6. Exit Flash without saving any changes.

Skills Covered

➔

- Set Document Properties
- Enter Content on the Stage
- Change the Stage View
- Use Undo and Redo

- Save a File
- Close a File
- Open an Existing File
- Print a Drawing

Software Skills You store the content and actions that comprise a Flash application in a Flash document file. Document properties control features such as the size and color of the Stage, and you enter content such as shapes on the Stage. Save the file so that you can open, edit, and publish it. Print a drawing so you can check it or give it to someone else.

Application Skills In order to create a Flash application for the Grace Notes stationery boutique, you must be able to work with Flash document files. In this exercise, you will create a Flash document; set document properties; enter content on the Stage; and save, close, and reopen the document. Finally, you will print the drawing.

TERMS

Background The area of the stage displayed in all frames of an application.

Color palette A display of squares—or *swatches*—of colors. Click a swatch to select that color.

Document properties Settings that define the size, color, and speed of an application file.

Hexadecimal color code A standard alphanumeric value based on a combination of letters and numbers used to identify colors based on their components of red, green, and blue.

Object An item on the stage.

Pixel A single dot used as a unit of measurement and to define images on a screen.

Point A unit of measurement. One point equals 1/72nd of an inch.

Scroll To shift the objects displayed onscreen up, down, left, or right.

Swatch A square of color on a color palette.

Zoom To change the display size of objects onscreen.

NOTES

Set Document Properties

- Before you create content in a Flash document, you should set the **document properties**.
- Document properties affect the entire document and help ensure consistency in the published application.

- In the Property Inspector or the Document Properties dialog box, you can set the frame rate (fps), the size of the Stage, and the color of the **background** (see the illustrations at the top of page 16).

Property Inspector

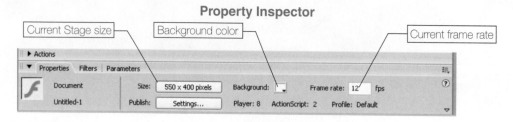

Document Properties Dialog Box

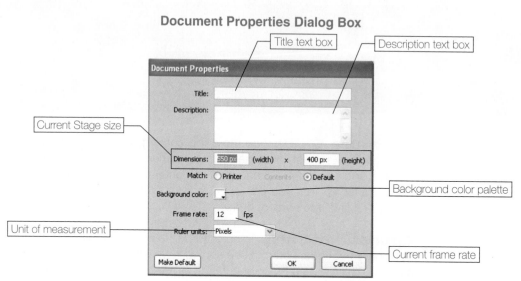

- Frame rate in Flash is measured in frames per second (fps). The default frame rate is 12.

- By default, Stage size is measured in **pixels** (px). The default size of the Stage is 550 × 400 px. The minimum size is 18 × 18 px; the maximum size is 2880 × 2880 px.

- You can select a background color from the **color palette**. The **hexadecimal color code** for the selected color displays in the code box at the top of the palette.

- If you know the hexadecimal color code for the color you want to use, you can enter it in the color palette.

- When you rest the mouse pointer over a **swatch** on the palette, the hexadecimal color code for that color displays in the code box (see the following illustration).

Background Color Palette

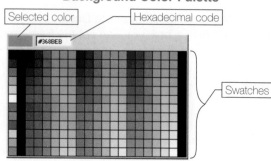

- Use the Document Properties dialog box instead of the Property Inspector if you also want to enter a title and description of the document or change the unit of measurement from pixels to inches, **points**, centimeters, or millimeters.

Enter Content on the Stage

- In Flash, the Stage is the area where you compose the content that displays in individual frames in the application.

- Use the tools in the Tools panel to draw your own **objects** directly on the stage, or import objects such as pictures, sound, video, or text.

- The quality of objects that you draw may depend on your artistic ability. However, anyone can learn to create basic shapes and apply formatting to enhance content in an application.

- To quickly draw an oval, for example, you select the Oval tool ⊙, and then drag on the Stage.

- Flash displays the shape using the default color settings. You learn more about drawing objects in Exercise 4, and about changing colors and other settings in Exercise 5.

Tools for Changing the Screen View

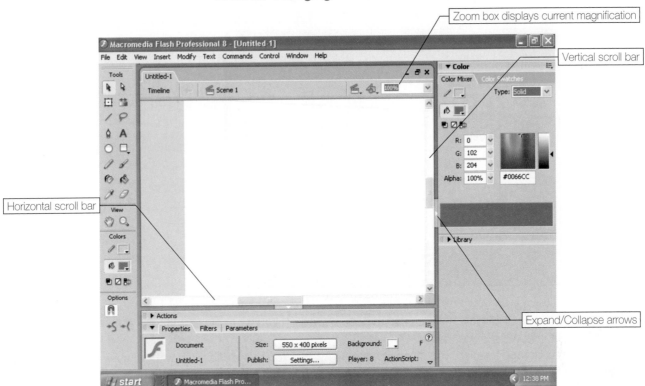

History Panel

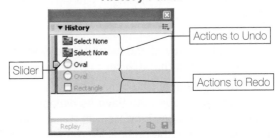

Change the Stage View

■ It may be helpful to close or hide panels you do not need when entering content on the Stage. For example, close the Timeline while drawing objects so that it does not obscure the top of the Stage.

■ You can also use the arrows on the bottom or right side of the Stage to quickly collapse or expand the Stage onscreen (see the illustration above).

■ Adjust the magnification setting of the Stage to **zoom** in or out.

• Increase the magnification to zoom in and get a close-up look at the Stage.

• Decrease the magnification to zoom out.

■ Changing the magnification does not affect the actual size of the objects on the Stage. It affects only the appearance of the objects on your screen.

■ You can also **scroll** the Stage to shift its position onscreen. This is particularly useful when only a portion of the Stage is visible onscreen.

■ Use the Horizontal scroll bar to scroll left or right.

■ Use the Vertical scroll bar to scroll up or down.

Use Undo and Redo

■ Use the Undo command or the History panel to reverse a single action or a series of actions made in error, such as deleting a shape. (See the illustration at the top of the opposite column.)

■ Use the Redo command or the History panel to reverse actions that you undo.

■ If the Undo command or the Undo button is dimmed, there are no actions that can be undone.

■ If the Redo button is dimmed there are no actions that can be redone.

■ Undo and Redo are available only for actions made in the current document in the current session.

Save a File

■ If you want to have a file available for future use, you must save it on a storage device such as a hard disk.

■ When you save a new file, Flash displays the Save As dialog box to prompt you to give the file a name and select the location where you want it stored (see the illustration on page 18).

17

Save As Dialog Box

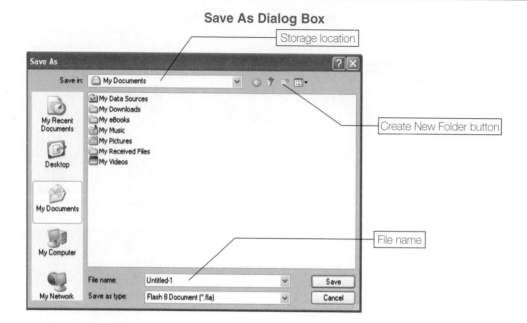

Storage location

Create New Folder button

File name

- Flash automatically adds the .fla file extension to the file name that you enter.

- To specify the storage location, you select the storage device letter. For example, usually you select C: to store the file on your computer's hard disk drive.

- You can store Flash files in a folder on your computer called My Documents, or you can select a different folder. You can also create a new folder for storing your files.

- Once you have saved and named a file, you can use the Save command to save changes to the file.

- To leave the original file unchanged, use the Save As command to open the Save As dialog box again. When you save the file with a new name or in a new location, the original file remains unchanged.

- If you use Undo to delete an object from a file, Flash retains the object in case you want to restore it using Redo. To permanently remove the object and reduce the file size, use the Save and Compact command to save the file.

Close a File

- Close a file when you are finished working with it but still want to continue using Flash.

- If you try to close a file without saving it, Flash prompts you to save.

- You can close a file without saving it if you do not want to keep it for future use, or if you do not want to keep the changes you made since the last time you saved it.

Open an Existing File

- To continue working in a file that has been saved and closed, open it in Flash.

- Recently used Flash documents are listed under Open a Recent Item on the Start page, and on the Open Recent submenu on the File menu.

- Use the Open dialog box to locate and open any stored Flash document file.

Print a Drawing

- You can print a drawing at any time.

- All objects on the Stage and the Pasteboard are printed, in their actual sizes.

- In order to print, your computer must be connected to a printer, and the printer must be turned on and loaded with paper.

PROCEDURES

Set Document Properties

Set Stage Size

1. Create new Flash document.
2. Click **Modify**...............Alt+M
3. Click **Document**......................D

   OR

   In Property Inspector, click **Size** box.

   ✓ *Document Properties dialog box displays, with width value selected.*

4. Type new Stage width.
5. Press **Tab**.........................Tab
6. Type new Stage height.
7. Click **OK**......................Enter

Set Frame Rate

1. Click **Modify**................Alt+M
2. Click **Document**......................D
3. Click **Frame rate**...........Alt+F
4. Type new Frame rate.
5. Click **OK**......................Enter

   OR

1. In Property Inspector, select current Frame rate.
2. Type new Frame rate.

Set Background Color

1. Click **Modify**................Alt+M
2. Click **Document**......................D
3. Click **Background color** palette 🔲.

   OR

   In Property Inspector, click **Background color** palette 🔲.

   ✓ *Mouse pointer changes to an eye dropper.*

4. On color palette, click desired color.

   OR

   a. In Hexadecimal code box, type code for desired color.
   b. Press **Enter**.............Enter
5. Click **OK**......................Enter

Change Ruler Units

1. Click **Modify**................Alt+M
2. Click **Document**......................D

3. Click **Ruler** units...............Alt+R+↓, ↑
4. Click desired unit.
5. Click **OK**.........................Enter

Draw an Oval on the Stage

1. In Tools panel, click **Oval** tool ⭕.......................O
2. Position mouse pointer at desired location on Stage.
3. Click and drag to draw shape.
4. Release mouse button.

   ✓ *See Exercise 4 for complete information on drawing shapes.*

Change the Stage View

Zoom In or Out on an Object

1. Click **Zoom** tool 🔍..............M
2. Under Options in Tools panel, click one of the following:
   - Enlarge tool 🔍 to zoom in.
   - Reduce tool 🔍 to zoom out.
3. Click object on Stage.

Zoom In on an Area

1. Click **Zoom** tool 🔍..............M
2. On Stage, drag around area to enlarge.

Zoom In or Out on the Stage

1. Click **View**...................Alt+V
2. Click one of the following:
   - Zoom **In**...........................I
   - Zoom **Out**.........................O

Set Magnification Percentage

- On edit bar, type desired magnification percentage in Zoom box 150% ▾.

   OR

1. Click **Zoom control** drop-down arrow 150% ▾.

   OR

   a. Click **View**...............Alt+V
   b. Click **Magnification**..............M
2. Click desired percentage:
   - **Fit in Window**...................W
   - **Show Frame**.....................F

- Show **All**......................A
- 25%
- **50%**.........................5
- **100%**........................1
- **200**.........................2
- **400**.........................4
- **800**.........................8

Scroll the Stage

1. Click **Hand** tool ✋..............H
2. Click and drag Stage to desired position.

   OR

- Click **left scroll** arrow ◄ to scroll left.
- Click **right scroll** arrow ► to scroll right.
- Click **up scroll** arrow ▲ to scroll up.
- Click **down scroll** arrow ▼ to scroll down.

Expand/Collapse Stage

- Click **Expand/Collapse** arrow on bottom or right side of Stage.

Undo Previous Actions (Ctrl+Z)

- Click **Undo** button ↶ on main toolbar.

   OR

1. Click **Edit**....................Alt+E
2. Click **Undo**...........................U

   ✓ *Repeat to undo a series of actions.*

Redo Previous Actions (Ctrl+Y)

- Click **Redo** button ↷ on main toolbar.

   OR

1. Click **Edit**....................Alt+E
2. Click **Redo**...........................R

   ✓ *Repeat to redo a series of actions.*

Use the History Panel to Undo or Redo (Ctrl+F10)

1. Click **Window**...............Alt+W
2. Click **Other Panels**........R, R, →
3. Click **History**.......................H
4. Drag slider up to undo previous action.
5. Drag slider down to redo next action.

Save a New File (Ctrl+Shift+S)

1. Click **Save** button 💾 on main toolbar.

   OR

   a. Click **F**ile .... Alt + F
   b. Click **S**ave .... S

2. Click **Save in** drop-down arrow .... Alt + I
3. Select drive and folder.
4. Double-click **File name** text box .... Alt + N
5. Type new file name.
6. Click **S**ave .... Alt + S

Create a New Folder for Storing Files

1. Click **Save** button 💾 on main toolbar.

   OR

   a. Click **F**ile .... Alt + F
   b. Click **S**ave .... S

2. Click **Create New Folder** button 📁.
3. Type new folder name.
4. Click **OK** .... ↵Enter

Save Changes to an Existing File (Ctrl+S)

■ Click **Save** button 💾 on main toolbar.

   OR

   a. Click **F**ile .... Alt + F
   b. Click **S**ave .... S

Save a File with a New Name (Ctrl+Shift+S)

1. Click **F**ile .... Alt + F
2. Click **Save As** .... A
3. Click **Save in** drop-down arrow .... Alt + I
4. Select drive and folder.
5. Double-click **File name** text box .... Alt + N
6. Type new file name.
7. Click **S**ave .... Alt + S

Save and Compact a File

1. Click **F**ile .... Alt + F
2. Click **Save and Compact** M

For a New File

1. Click **Save in** drop-down arrow .... Alt + I
2. Select drive and folder.
3. Double-click **File name** text box .... Alt + N
4. Type new file name.
5. Click **S**ave .... Alt + S

Close a Document (Ctrl+W)

■ Click **Document Close** button ✕.

   ✓ *The File Close button is located above the Timeline Menu Options button.*

   OR

1. Click **F**ile .... Alt + F
2. Click **C**lose C

3. Click **Y**es to save changes ..... Y

   OR

   Click **N**o to close without saving .... N

Open an Existing File (Ctrl+O)

1. Click **Open** button 📂 on main toolbar.

   OR

   a. Click **F**ile .... Alt + F
   b. Click **O**pen .... O

2. Click **Look in** drop-down arrow .... Alt + I
3. Select drive and folder where file is stored.
4. Click file name.
5. Click **O**pen .... Alt + O

Open a Recently Used File

1. Click **F**ile .... Alt + F
2. Click **Open Recent** .... T + →
3. Click file name.

   OR

   Click file name on Start page.

Print a Drawing

1. Click **F**ile .... Alt + F
2. Click **P**rint .... P
3. Click **OK** .... ↵Enter

EXERCISE DIRECTIONS

1. Start Flash.
2. Create a new document.
3. Save the new document with the name **030VAL**.
4. Hide the Timeline.
5. Open the Document Properties dialog box and change the Ruler units to inches.
6. Change the Stage size to 2 inches wide by 2 inches high.
7. Set the Background color to yellow (#FFFF00).

   ✓ *Remember, you can rest the mouse pointer on a color to display its color code.*

8. Change the Frame rate to 10.
9. Set the magnification to 100%.
10. In the Property Inspector, change the Frame rate back to 12.
11. Change the Stage size to 7.25 inches wide by 7.25 inches high.
12. Set the magnification to Show All.
13. Select the Oval tool.
14. Draw an oval in the upper-right corner of the Stage.

   ✓ *Notice that the Property Inspector now displays properties for the oval shape.*

15. Use Undo to remove the shape.
16. Use Redo to display the shape again.
17. Save the changes to the file.

18. Close the file.

19. Open the **030VAL** file.

20. Set the magnification to Fit in Window.

21. Save the file as **030VALS**.

22. Draw a second oval in the lower-left corner of the Stage.

23. Draw a third oval in the lower-right corner of the Stage.

24. Zoom in on the oval in the upper-right corner.

25. Expand the Stage to the bottom of the screen.

26. Scroll down and then scroll left to display the shapes at the bottom of the Stage.

27. Zoom out on the entire Stage.

28. Collapse the Stage to display the Property Inspector.

29. Display the Timeline.

30. Set the zoom to Fit in Window.

31. Display the History panel. If necessary, move the panel so it does not overlap the objects on the Stage.

32. Drag the slider up one action to remove the third oval. Your screen should look similar to the one in Illustration A.

   ✓ *Your screen may not match the illustration exactly, depending on the size and position of the ovals you have drawn. However, the number and general location of the ovals should match, as well as the appearance of the Stage and other screen elements.*

33. Drag the slider down to replace the third oval.

34. Close the History panel.

35. Print the drawing in the **030VALS** file.

36. Close the **030VALS** file, saving all changes.

37. Exit Flash.

Illustration A

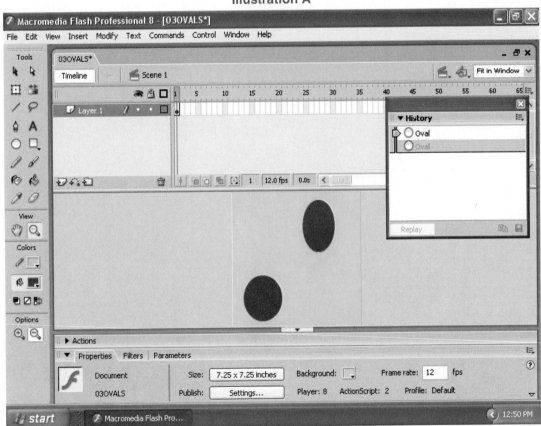

ON YOUR OWN

1. Start Flash and create a new document.
2. Save the document as **03SHAPES**.
3. Set document properties, including the Stage size and the background color.
4. Change the Stage size and background color.
5. Customize the Flash window so that you can see all of the Stage.
6. Draw ovals on the Stage and then use Undo, Redo, and the History panel to remove them, and then to put them back.
7. Practice zooming and scrolling the Stage.
8. Save the changes to the file and then close it.
9. Open the **03SHAPES** file and save it as **03SHAPES2**.
10. Draw one more oval on the Stage and then print the drawing.
11. Return the Flash window to its default display.
12. Close the **03SHAPES2** file, saving all changes.
13. Exit Flash.

Exercise | 4

Skills Covered

- About Graphics
- Draw Basic Shapes
- Select Objects
- Position Objects on the Stage
- Duplicate and Delete Objects

Software Skills Once you have mastered the ability to draw basic shapes with the Flash drawing tools, you will be able to create drawings limited only by your own artistic abilities. The drawing can be animated as part of a Flash application, or used as a static image.

Application Skills The manager at Grace Notes has asked you to draw a picture that can be used on promotional material or on the store's Web site. In this exercise, you will use the tools in the Tools panel to draw ovals, rectangles, and lines. You will also use the Pencil, Pen, and Brush tools. Finally, you will select and position objects on the Stage to create a picture.

TERMS

Bitmap graphics Pictures created using pixels, or colored dots. Also called raster graphics.

Fill The color or pattern used to fill a shape.

Guides Vertical and horizontal lines you drag off a ruler to identify a location on the Stage.

Path A line along which objects can be animated in a Flash application.

Select To mark an object or other element for modification.

Snap To align an object with a fixed location, such as a grid line or another object.

Snap ring A small black ring displayed on the mouse pointer when the Snap to Objects feature is in use. The ring becomes larger when the object is near a snap location.

Stroke The width and appearance of a line used to draw.

Vector graphics Pictures that are drawn using lines, shapes, and curves.

NOTES

About Graphics

- You use Flash's **vector graphics** and type creation features to create and modify drawings in a document.
- Vector graphics use lines, curves, and shapes to define images. The individual lines can be edited, moved, and rearranged.
- When a vector graphic is resized, the lines and shapes retain their original definition and perspective. This means that the graphic can be displayed on output devices of varying resolution without losing any quality.

- Because vector graphics are made of lines and shapes, you can group and ungroup, reorder, and change the color of one or all parts of the picture.
- Vector graphics are saved in the format of the program used to create them. In Flash, they are saved in the .fla files.
- **Bitmap graphics**, by contrast, use colored dots arranged within a grid to define images.
- You edit bitmap images by modifying the dots rather than the lines and curves. When bitmaps are resized, they lose definition and the individual dots that make up the picture may become visible, causing the image to appear fuzzy, or distorted.

23

- Bitmap pictures are often saved in a file format with a .bmp, .png, .jpg, or .gif extension.
- By using vector graphics, Flash can keep files smaller than if other types of graphics are used, and ensure the consistent appearance of Flash applications on different devices.

Draw Basic Shapes

- Use the tools in the Tools panel to draw shapes, lines, and **paths**.
- Many of the tools have options that let you modify the object before or after you draw. The options become available in the Options area of the Tools panel when you select the tool.
- To draw basic geometric shapes, you use the Line , Oval , and Rectangle tools.
  - The Set Corner Radius option , which becomes available when you select the Rectangle tool, lets you draw a rectangle with rounded corners. The larger the corner radius value, the more rounded the corner. The default is 0, which is a 90-degree corner.

- The Pencil tool lets you draw freeform lines and shapes as if drawing with a real pencil. Options for the pencil let you adjust the smoothness of the line.
- Use the Pen tool to draw precise straight or curved lines.
- Use the Brush tool to draw as if painting with a paint brush. Options let you control the size and shape of the brush.
- You draw objects using the current **stroke** and **fill** settings, such as color.
  - ✓ *You learn about changing the stroke and fill settings in Exercise 5.*
- Flash has two drawing models:
  - Merge Drawing model. Default model that automatically merges overlapping shapes. If you move or delete a shape that overlaps another shape, the underlying shape is permanently altered (see the illustration below).

Drawing with the Merge Drawing Model

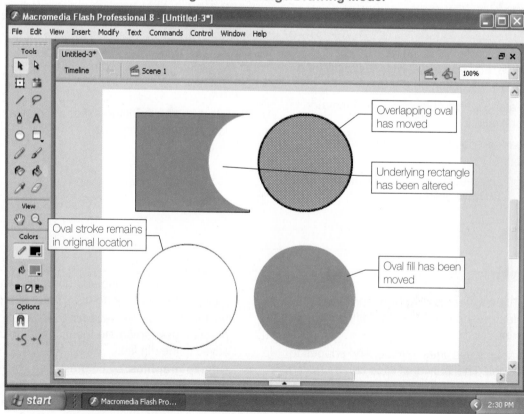

Drawing with the Object Drawing Model

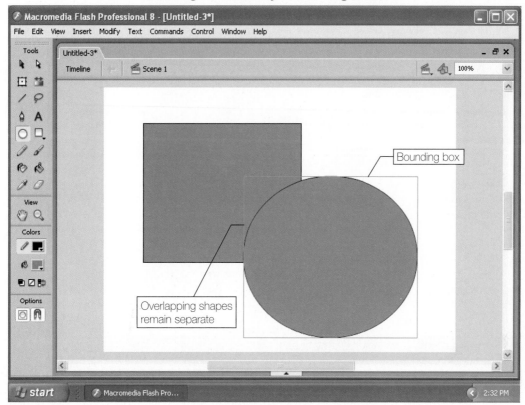

- Object Drawing model. Lets you draw overlapping shapes that do not merge or affect the appearance of other shapes on the Stage (see the illustration above).
- You can combine both drawing models in a single drawing.

Select Objects

- In order to edit or modify an object on the Stage, you must first **select** it.
- Use the Selection tool ![Selection tool] to select one or more objects.
- You can also use the Lasso tool ![Lasso tool] to select objects by drawing either a freehand or a straight-edged selection area. The Lasso tool is useful if the object you want to select is very close to a different object.
- When Merge Drawing is active, Flash applies a dot pattern to highlight selected objects to help you identify them on the Stage.

- When Object Drawing is active, Flash displays a rectangular bounding box around selected objects.
- In addition, when Merge Drawing is active, all lines, shapes, and fills are considered separate objects. You must be sure to select all parts of a drawing that you need.
- For example, if you want to move both the stroke and fill of an oval when Merge Drawing is active, you must be sure to select both the stroke and fill. If you select only the fill, and then move it, the stroke remains in its original location.

Position Objects on the Stage

- You can drag selected objects on the Stage to move them to a new location.
- Flash includes visual elements to help you position objects on the Stage, including horizontal and vertical rulers, a grid, and **guides** (see the illustration at the top of page 26).

Tools for Positioning Objects on the Stage

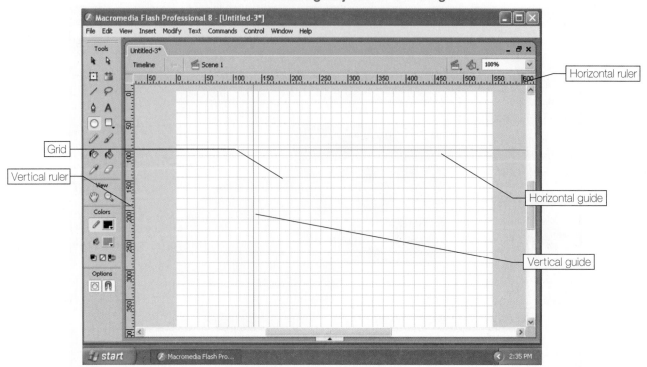

- The unit of measurement on the rulers depends on the unit selected in the Document Properties dialog box.

- By default, the spacing between grid lines is 18 px, or .25", but you can edit the grid to change the spacing. You can also change the color of the grid lines.

- Flash also includes features to help you **snap** objects to a location on the Stage.

- To automatically position objects on the nearest grid lines, make the Snap to Grid feature active.

- By default, the Snap to Objects feature is active so that you can snap an object to the edge of an object already positioned on the Stage.

- The Snap Align feature displays a dotted line when you drag an object to a preset distance relative to the edge of another object or to the Stage boundary (see the illustration below).

Snap Alignment

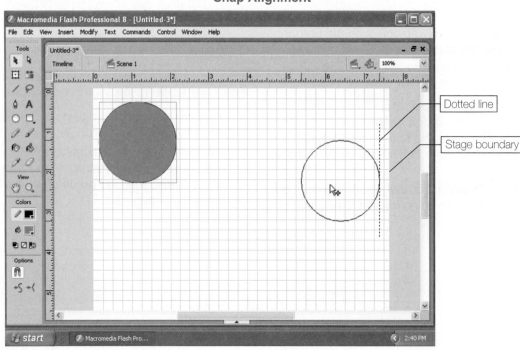

Snap to Grid

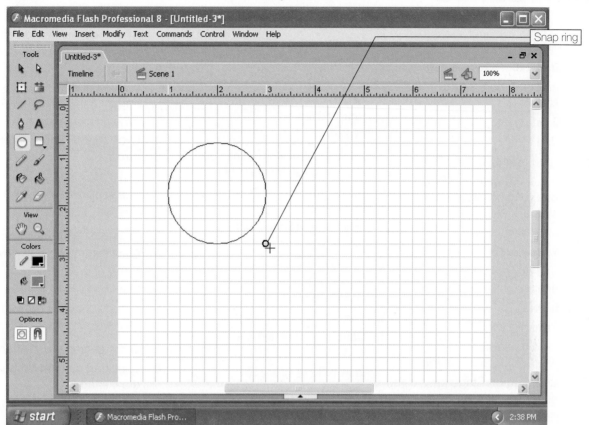

- By default, the dotted line displays when the edge of the object you are dragging is within 18 px of the Stage boundary or within 0 px of an object already on the Stage.
- Snap to Guides automatically snaps an object to a horizontal or vertical guide line.
- When you draw an object with any snap feature active, a **snap ring** displays at the pointer location. When the snap ring increases in size, it means that the object is aligned with the specified location (see the illustration above).
  - For example, with Snap to Objects, the snap ring increases in size when the object aligns with the edge of an existing object, indicating that you can drop the object to align it with the edge of the object already in place.
  - With Snap to Grid, the snap ring increases in size when the object aligns with a grid line.
- With Snap to Guides, the snap ring increases in size when the object aligns with a guide line.
- The position of the pointer on the object provides the reference point for the snap ring. For example, if the snap ring displays in the center of an oval, the center of the oval is the point that snaps to the specified location.

  ✓ *Snap to Pixels is another snapping feature that can be used when the Stage magnification is 400% or higher to snap an object to a specific pixel—or dot—on the Stage.*

Duplicate and Delete Objects

- Use the Duplicate command on the Edit menu to create an exact duplicate of an existing object.
- Delete objects you no longer need from the Stage.

PROCEDURES

Draw Basic Shapes

Draw Oval
1. Click **Oval** tool ⬜ ....O
2. Click and drag on Stage to draw shape.

Draw Circle
1. Click **Oval** tool ⬜ ....O
2. Press and hold **Shift** key..............................⬆Shift
3. Click and drag on Stage to draw shape.

Draw Rectangle
1. Click **Rectangle** tool ⬜ ....R
2. Click and drag on Stage to draw shape.

Draw Square
1. Click **Rectangle** tool ⬜ ....R
2. Press and hold **Shift** key.................................⬆Shift
3. Click and drag on Stage to draw shape.

Draw Rectangle with Rounded Corners
1. Click **Rectangle** tool ⬜ ....R
2. Click **Set Corner Radius** option button ⬜ .
3. Enter corner radius value.
4. Click **OK**.........................⏎Enter
5. Click and drag on Stage to draw shape.

Draw Straight Lines
1. Click **Line** tool ⬜ ....N
2. Click and drag on Stage to draw shape.

Draw Straight Lines at 45-degree Angles
1. Click **Line** tool ⬜ ....N
2. Press and hold **Shift** key..............................⬆Shift
3. Click and drag on Stage to draw shape.

Draw Freeform Lines and Shapes
1. Click **Pencil** tool ⬜ ....Y
2. Click **Smoothness** option button.

   ✓ *The Smoothness option button displays the most recently selected Smoothness option.*

3. Click desired Smoothness option:
   - **Straighten** ⬜ to draw straight lines and shapes.
   - **Smooth** ⬜ to draw smooth curved lines.
   - **Ink** ⬜ to apply no modification; in other words, lines display just as you draw them.
4. Click and drag on Stage to draw shape.

Draw Paths on Straight Line Segments
1. Click **Pen** tool ⬜ ....P
2. Click on Stage at desired starting point.
3. Click at each point as desired.
4. Double-click at last point to end line.

Draw Paths on Curved Line Segments
1. Click **Pen** tool ⬜ ....P
2. Click on Stage at desired starting point.
3. Drag to next desired point.
4. Release mouse button.
5. Repeat stapes 3 and 4.
6. Double-click at last point to end line.

Draw Brush Strokes
1. Click **Brush** tool ⬜ ....B
2. Click **Brush Mode** option button.

   ✓ *The Brush Mode option button displays the most recently selected Brush Mode option.*

3. Click desired Brush Mode option:
   - **Paint Normal** ⬜ to paint over existing lines, fills, and blank areas.
   - **Paint Fills** ⬜ to paint over existing fills and empty areas, but leave lines unchanged.
   - **Paint Behind** ⬜ to paint over blank areas only, leaving lines and fills unchanged.
   - **Paint Selection** ⬜ to paint over selected areas only.
   - **Paint Inside** ⬜ to paint over a fill within a closed shape, leaving the stroke around the fill unchanged.
4. Click **Brush Size** drop-down arrow.

   ✓ *The Brush Size box displays the most recently selected Brush Size option.*

5. Click desired brush size.
6. Click **Brush Shape** drop-down arrow.

   ✓ *The Brush Shape box displays the most recently selected Brush Shape option.*

7. Click desired brush shape.
8. Click and drag on Stage to draw shape.

   ✓ *Press and hold Shift key to draw only horizontal or vertical strokes.*

Turn Object Drawing Model On or Off
1. Select desired drawing tool.
2. Click **Object Drawing** option button ⬜ .

   ✓ *The Object Drawing option button becomes available when the Line, Oval, Rectangle, Pen, Pencil, or Brush tool is selected.*

Select Objects
1. Click **Selection** tool ⬜ V
2. Click object to select.
   OR
   a. Click **Lasso** tool ⬜ L
   b. Click and drag to draw border around object(s) to select.

   ✓ *With the Selection tool, the border will be a rectangle; with the Lasso tool, the border will follow the mouse pointer, like drawing with a pencil.*

3. Release mouse button.

To Select Multiple Objects

1. Click **Selection** tool V
   OR
   Click **Lasso** tool L
2. Select first object.
3. Press and hold **Shift** key .... ⬆Shift
4. Select next object.
5. Repeat until all desired objects are selected.

To Select Both Stroke and Fill of Merge Drawing Shape at the Same Time

■ Double-click in the center of the fill.

To Select All Objects on the Stage

1. Click **Edit** .... Alt+E
2. Click **Select All** L

To Deselect All Selected Objects

■ Click anywhere outside selection.
   OR
1. Click **Edit** .... Alt+E
2. Click **Deselect All** .... E

Show/Hide Rulers (Ctrl+Alt+Shift+R)

1. Click **View** .... Alt+V

   ✓ A check mark next to the Rulers command indicates that rulers are currently displayed.

2. Click **Rulers** .... R

Show/Hide Grid (Ctrl+')

1. Click **View** .... Alt+V
2. Click **Grid** .... D
3. Click **Show Grid** .... D

   ✓ A check mark next to the Show Grid command indicates that the grid is currently displayed.

Edit Grid (Ctrl+Alt+G)

1. Click **View** .... Alt+V
2. Click **Grid** .... D
3. Click **Edit Grid** .... E
4. Do any of the following:
   ● Click **Color palette** and then click desired grid color.
   ● Click **Show grid** check box to show/hide grid.
   ● Click **Snap to grid** check box to automatically align objects with grid.

● Replace value in horizontal spacing box with new value.
● Replace value in vertical spacing box with new value.
● Click **Snap Accuracy** and select new value.
5. Click **OK** .... ⏎Enter

Display Horizontal Guide

1. Display rulers.
2. Position mouse pointer over horizontal ruler.
3. Click and drag down onto Stage.
4. When guide is in desired location, release mouse button.

Display Vertical Guide

1. Display rulers.
2. Position mouse pointer over vertical ruler.
3. Click and drag right onto Stage.
4. When guide is in desired location, release mouse button.

Move a Guide

1. Click **Selection** tool V
2. Drag guide to new location.

Remove a Guide

1. Click **Selection** tool V
2. Drag guide off Stage.

Remove All Guides

1. Click **View** .... Alt+V
2. Click **Guides** .... E
3. Click **Clear Guides** C

Turn Snap to Grid On or Off (Ctrl+Shift+')

1. Click **View** .... Alt+V
2. Click **Snapping** .... S
3. Click **Snap to Grid** .... R

   ✓ A check mark next to the Snap to Grid command indicates that feature is currently on.

Turn Snap to Objects On or Off (Ctrl+Shift+/)

■ Click **Snap to Objects** button on main toolbar or in Tools panel options area.

   ✓ Snap to Objects becomes available as an option in the Tools panel when the Selection, Line, Oval, or Rectangle tool is selected.

   OR
1. Click **View** .... Alt+V
2. Click **Snapping** .... S
3. Click **Snap to Objects** .... O

   ✓ A check mark next to the Snap to Objects command indicates that feature is currently on.

Turn Snap Align On or Off

1. Click **View** .... Alt+V
2. Click **Snapping** .... S
3. Click **Snap Align** .... S

   ✓ A check mark next to the Snap Align command indicates that feature is currently on.

Turn Snap to Guides On or Off (Ctrl+Shift+;)

1. Click **View** .... Alt+V
2. Click **Snapping** .... S
3. Click **Snap to Guides** .... G

   ✓ A check mark next to the Snap to Guides command indicates that feature is currently on.

Duplicate an Object (Ctrl+D)

1. Select object(s) to duplicate.
2. Click **Edit** .... Alt+E
3. Click **Duplicate** .... D

   ✓ The duplicate shape displays overlapping the original.

   OR
1. Select object(s) to duplicate.
2. Press and hold **Ctrl** key ...... Ctrl
3. Drag object to new location.

   ✓ The original object remains in place; the duplicate object is pasted at new location.

Delete an Object

1. Select object(s) to delete.
2. Press **Delete** key .... Del
   OR
   a. Click **Edit** .... Alt+E
   b. Click **Clear** ...... A, A, ⏎Enter

EXERCISE DIRECTIONS

Prepare the Stage

1. Start Flash.
2. Create a new document.
3. Save the new document with the name **04NOTES**.
4. Hide the Timeline.
5. Open the Document Properties dialog box and change the Ruler units to inches.
6. Set the Stage size to 7" wide by 6" high.
7. Display the rulers.
8. Turn off Snap to Objects and make sure Snap to Guides is on.
9. Collapse the Property Inspector.

   ✓ *This gives you more room to work on the Stage.*

10. Set the zoom to Fit in Window.
11. Display a vertical guide 1" from the left boundary of the Stage.
12. Display a vertical guide 1" from the right boundary of the Stage.
13. Display a horizontal guide 1" from the top boundary of the Stage.
14. Display a horizontal guide 1" from the bottom boundary of the Stage.

Draw an Envelope

   ✓ *To see the envelope in the Flash document, refer to Illustration A.*

1. Click the Rectangle tool and then verify that Object Drawing is off. Use the Rectangle tool to draw a rectangle within the guides, 5" wide by 4" high.

   ✓ *The shape is drawn with the default color and stroke settings.*

2. Select the fill in the rectangle.
3. Delete the selected fill.

   ✓ *The stroke should remain on the stage; however, it may be hidden by the guides.*

4. Move the lower horizontal guide up 2", so it aligns with the 3" mark on the vertical ruler.
5. Move the left vertical guide to the right 2.5" so it aligns with the 3.5" mark on the horizontal ruler.

   ✓ *The guides should intersect in the middle of the rectangle.*

6. Use the Line tool to draw a straight, diagonal line from the upper-left corner of the rectangle to the intersection of the guides in the middle of the rectangle.
7. Use the Line tool to draw a straight, diagonal line from the upper-right corner of the rectangle to the intersection of the guides in the middle of the rectangle.
8. Clear all guides. The drawing should look similar to Illustration A.

Illustration A

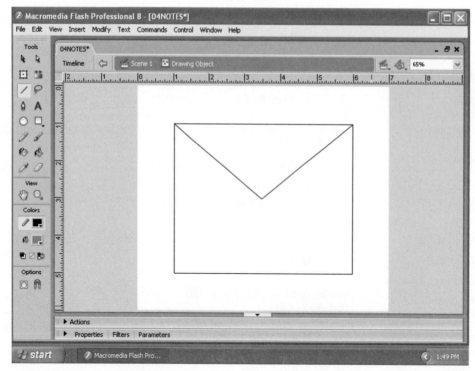

Complete the Picture

1. Display the grid and turn on Snap to Grid.
2. Turn on Object Drawing.
3. Draw a musical staff as follows (refer to Illustration B).
4. Select the Brush tool.
5. Select the Brush Size second from the top.
6. Select the Brush Mode second from the top.
7. Locate the first horizontal grid line from the bottom of the rectangle. Drag along that grid line from left to right to draw a line across the width of the rectangle. You can press and hold Shift as you drag to draw a straight line.
8. Repeat the step to draw three more lines along every other grid line (the third, fifth, and seventh lines from the bottom) moving up the rectangle.
9. Draw a musical note as follows (refer to Illustration B).
10. Use the Oval tool to draw an oval approximately .75" wide and .5" high, positioned so that it is centered on the lowest brushed line at 1.5" on the horizontal ruler (the second grid line from the left). The bottom of the oval should align with the bottom of the rectangle.
11. Select the Pencil tool and set the Smoothness option to Straighten.

12. Draw a 1.25" vertical line up from the center, right edge of the oval.
13. Set the Smoothness option to Smooth.
14. Draw a .5" wavy horizontal line from the top of the vertical line to the right.
15. Repeat the step to draw a second line about .25" below the first.
16. Select the oval, vertical line, and two wavy lines.
17. Duplicate the selection.
18. Move the duplicate up and to the right so the oval is centered on the second brushed line at the 2.5" mark on the horizontal ruler.
19. Duplicate the selection and move the third note up and to the right so the oval is centered on the third brushed line at the 4" mark on the horizontal ruler.
20. Duplicate the selection to create a fourth note, and move it up and to the right so the oval is centered on the third brushed line at the 5" mark on the horizontal ruler.
21. Deselect all objects. The drawing should look similar to Illustration B.
22. Hide the grid.
23. Print the drawing and then close the document, saving all changes.
24. Exit Flash.

Illustration B

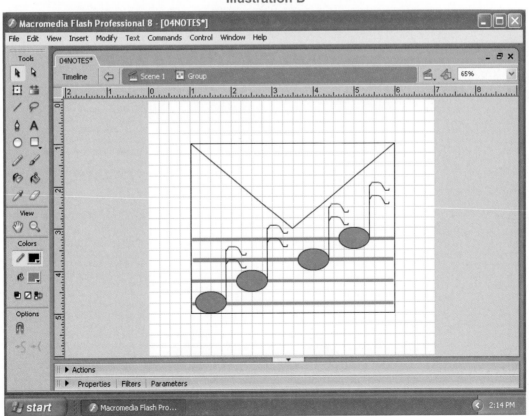

ON YOUR OWN

1. Start Flash and create a new document.
2. Save the document as **04MYPIC**.
3. Practice using the different drawing tools to create shapes and drawings. Remember that you can use Undo and Redo and the History panel.
4. Experiment with Merge Drawing and Object Drawing.
5. When you feel comfortable drawing basic shapes, select and delete all objects from the Stage.
6. Using the drawing tools, draw a simple picture representing something that interests you. For example, if you play soccer, you might draw a soccer ball, or if you like bird watching you could draw a bird. Other simple pictures might include a flower, a face, or a computer monitor.
7. While you work, make use of the available tools for positioning objects on the Stage.
8. When you are satisfied with your drawing, save the changes and then print it.
9. Exit Flash.

Exercise | 5

Skills Covered

- ■ Draw Polygons and Stars
- ■ Modify Strokes
- ■ Modify Fills
- ■ Copy Stroke and Fill Settings

Software Skills Use the PolyStar tool to draw multi-sided shapes and stars. Modify strokes and fills to change the appearance of objects on the Stage. You can change colors and styles to create different effects, including applying gradient fills. Copy stroke and fill settings from one object to another to ensure consistency within the drawing.

Application Skills You work for a consulting company that specializes in fundraising for nonprofit organizations. The theme for an upcoming campaign is Wish Upon a Star, and you must design a logo. In this exercise, you will draw with the PolyStar tool and enhance the shapes using different fill and stroke settings.

TERMS

Gradient Color that shades gradually from a dark hue to a light hue.

Linear gradient A gradient that shades from the starting point to the ending point in a straight line.

Radial gradient A gradient that shades from the starting point to the ending point in a circular pattern.

Stroke height The width of a stroke, usually measured in points.

Stroke style The appearance of a stroke, for example, a solid or dashed line.

NOTES

Draw Polygons and Stars

- ■ Use the PolyStar tool to draw multi-sided shapes such as triangles, pentagons, or octagons.
- ■ By default, the Polygon tool draws a pentagon (five-sided shape), but you can set the number of sides to any value from 3 to 32 in the Tool Settings dialog box (see the following illustration).

PolyStar Tool Settings Dialog Box

- ■ To draw a star, change the shape style to Star. The number of sides setting controls the number of points on the star.

- ■ You can also set the star point size, which determines the depth of each point of the star. The star point size must be between 0 and 1, with the default being .50. Increase the point size to make the depth greater (a wider point), or decrease the point size to make the depth smaller (a sharper point).
- ■ The PolyStar tool shares the same spot in the Tools panel as the Rectangle. Use the drop-down menu to select the tool you need (see the following illustration).

Rectangle Drop-Down Menu

Stroke and Fill Settings in the Property Inspector

Stroke color · Fill color · Stroke height · Stroke style · Click here to show more information

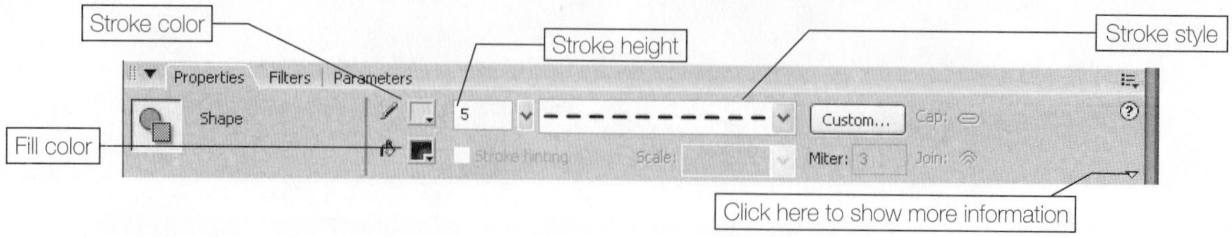

Modify Strokes

■ You can select Stroke settings to change lines and shape outlines of new and existing objects.

■ Stroke options include **stroke height**, **stroke style**, and stroke color.

■ Use the Property Inspector to select stroke settings and preview your selections (see the illustration above).

■ Use the Stroke Color palette in the Colors area of the Tools panel to quickly select a stroke color.

■ You can also select No Color to create a drawing with no outline.

■ To remove a stroke, simple select it and delete it.

■ Use the Ink Bottle tool to quickly change the stroke settings for existing objects. It is particularly useful for changing multiple objects at once.

Modify Fills

■ Modify fills to change the color and style of the area inside a shape.

■ You can select fill settings before you draw a new shape or to change the fill of an existing shape.

■ Fills may be either solid or **gradient**. Gradients are available in either a **linear gradient** or **radial gradient** style.

■ Use the Fill Color palette in the Colors area of the Tools panel or in the Property Inspector to select a fill color (see the illustration below).

■ Select No Color to draw a shape with an outline but no fill.

■ To remove a fill from an existing object, simply select the fill and then delete it.

■ You can also use the Paint Bucket tool to quickly modify the fills of existing objects.

■ With the Paint Bucket, you can also fill areas that are not inside closed shapes, but are defined by lines and strokes on the Stage. If there are gaps in the lines and strokes, you can select a Gap Size option to ensure that Flash fills the desired area, without letting the fill bleed through into adjacent areas.

■ Another method of applying fills is to use the Brush tool with the Brush Mode option set to either Paint Fills, Paint Behind, Paint Selection, or Paint Inside.

✓ *The Brush tool color is determined by Fill color.*

Copy Stroke and Fill Settings

■ Use the Eye Dropper tool to quickly copy stroke and fill settings from one object to another.

■ The Eye Dropper tool is useful if you want to ensure consistency among multiple objects in a drawing.

Fill Color Palette

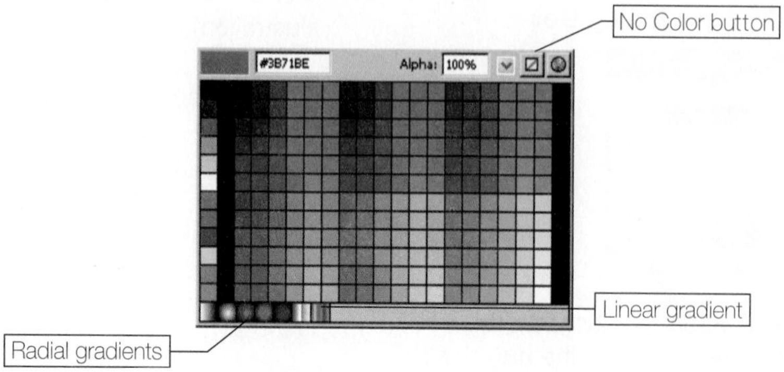

No Color button · Linear gradient · Radial gradients

PROCEDURES

Display PolyStar Tool

1. Click and hold on **Rectangle** tool .
2. Click **PolyStar** tool .

Draw a Polygon

1. Click **PolyStar** tool .
2. Click **Options** in Property Inspector.

   ✓ *If the Options button is not displayed, click the Expand/Collapse arrow in the lower-right corner of the Property Inspector to display more information in the panel.*

3. Click **Style** drop-down arrow.
4. Click **Polygon**.
5. Click **Number of Sides** box.
6. Type desired number of sides.
7. Click **OK**.........................⏎Enter
8. Click on Stage at location where you want to place the center of the shape, and drag out to draw shape.

Draw a Star

1. Click **PolyStar** tool .
2. Click **Options** in Property Inspector.

   ✓ *If the Options button is not displayed, click the Expand/Collapse arrow in the lower-right corner of the Property Inspector to display more information in the panel.*

3. Click **Style** drop-down arrow.
4. Click **Star**.
5. Click **Number of Sides** box.
6. Type desired number of points.
7. Click **Star point size** box.
8. Enter value to set star point depth.

   ✓ *Enter a value between 0 and 1. The higher the value, the wider the point.*

9. Click **OK**.........................⏎Enter

10. Click on Stage at location where you want to place the center of the shape, and drag out to draw shape.

Modify Strokes

Select Stroke Color

1. Click desired drawing tool.

   OR

   Select existing object.

2. Click **Stroke Color** palette .

   ✓ *You may use the Stroke Color palette in the Tools panel or in the Property Inspector.*

3. Click desired color.

   ✓ *Click No Color to apply a transparent stroke.*

Select Stroke Height

1. Click desired drawing tool.

   OR

   Select existing object.

2. Click **Stroke Height** box in Property Inspector.
3. Type desired height.

   OR

1. Click **Stroke Height** drop-down arrow.
2. Drag slider to select desired height.
3. Click a blank area of the screen to close slider, if necessary.

Select Stroke Style

1. Click desired drawing tool.

   OR

   Select existing object.

2. Click **Stroke Style** drop-down arrow in Property Inspector.
3. Click desired style.

Use Ink Bottle Tool

1. Click **Ink Bottle** tool ....Ⓢ
2. Select stroke color.
3. Select stroke height.
4. Select stroke style.
5. Click stroke object on Stage.

Modify Fills

Select Fill Color

1. Click desired drawing tool.

   OR

   Select existing object.

2. Click **Fill Color** palette .

   ✓ *You may use the Fill Color palette in the Tools panel or in the Property Inspector.*

3. Click desired color.

   ✓ *Click No Color to apply a transparent fill.*

Use Paint Bucket

1. Click **Paint Bucket** tool ......Ⓚ
2. Select fill color.
3. Click **Gap Size** option button.

   ✓ *The Gap Size option button displays the most recently selected Gap Size option.*

4. Click desired Gap Size option:
   - Close small gaps
   - Don't close gaps
   - Close medium gaps
   - Close large gaps
5. Click fill object on Stage.

Copy Stroke Settings

1. Click **Eyedropper** tool ....Ⓘ
2. Click stroke object to copy.

   ✓ *Stroke settings display in the Property Inspector and the mouse pointer displays the Ink Bottle.*

3. Click stroke object to format.

Copy Fill Settings

1. Click **Eyedropper** tool ....Ⓘ
2. Click fill object to copy.

   ✓ *Fill settings display in the Property Inspector and the mouse pointer displays the Paint Bucket.*

3. Click fill object to format.

EXERCISE DIRECTIONS

Prepare the Stage

1. Start Flash and create a new document.
2. Save the new document with the name 05STAR.
3. Change the ruler units to inches and set the Stage size to 8" × 6".
4. Display the rulers.
5. Position a vertical guide in the middle of the Stage—4" on the horizontal ruler.
6. Position a horizontal guide in the middle of the Stage—3" on the vertical ruler.
7. Hide the Timeline, if necessary.
8. Display the Property Inspector, if necessary.
9. Set the zoom to Fit in Window.

Draw a Polygon

1. Select the PolyStar tool.

   ✓ *If necessary, display the Rectangle drop-down menu to select the PolyStar tool.*

2. Turn off Object Drawing, if necessary.
3. Click the Options button in the Property Inspector to display the Tool Settings dialog box.

4. Verify that the Style is set to polygon.
5. Set the Number of Sides to 8 and then click OK.
6. Set the Stroke color to dark blue (#000066).
7. Set the Stroke height to 5.
8. Set the Stroke style to dashed (the option below Solid).
9. Set the Fill color to light gray (#CCCCCC).
10. Click in the middle of the Stage—the intersection of the two guides—and drag down and to the right to draw the polygon. Release the mouse button when the top of the shape touches the Stage boundary.
11. Select both the stroke and fill of the shape.

    ✓ *Choose Select All from the Edit menu or use the Selection tool to double-click in the middle of the fill.*

12. Modify the fill color to apply a blue radial gradient.
13. Modify the stroke color to bright yellow (#FFFF00).
14. Deselect all objects. The drawing should look similar to Illustration A.

Illustration A

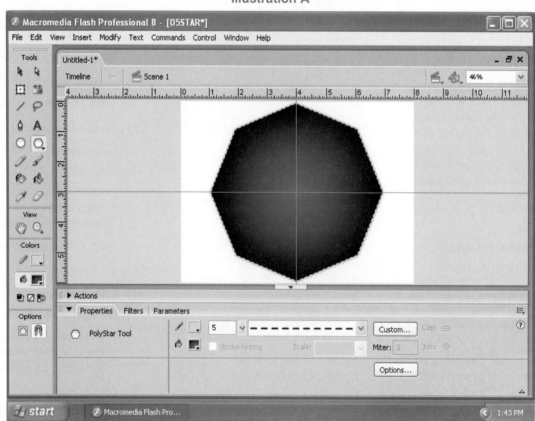

Draw a Star

1. Select the PolyStar tool.
2. Turn on Object Drawing.
3. Set the fill color to bright yellow (#FFFF00).
4. Set the stroke to No Color.
5. Click the Options button in the Property Inspector.
6. Change the Style to star.
7. Set the Number of Sides to 7.
8. Set the Star point size to .40.
9. Click OK.
10. Click in the middle of the Stage—the intersection of the two guides—and drag down and to the right to draw the star. As you drag adjust the rotation so that one point aligns along the vertical guide.
11. Release the mouse button when the star points touch the stroke of the polygon.
12. Copy the stroke from the polygon to the star.
13. Copy the fill from the polygon to the star.
14. Modify the star fill to red radial gradient.
15. Deselect all objects.
16. Hide the guides. Collapse the Property Inspector. The drawing should look similar to Illustration B.
17. Print the drawing and then close the document, saving all changes.
18. Exit Flash.

Illustration B

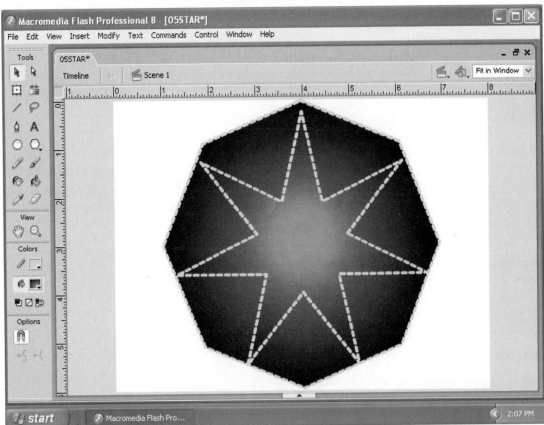

ON YOUR OWN

1. Start Flash and open **04MYPIC**, the document you created in Exercise 4, or open **05PIC**.
2. Save the document as **05MYPIC**.
3. Modify the strokes and fills of the objects in the drawing.
4. Add at least two stars and/or polygons, selecting the stroke and fill settings before you draw the shape.
5. When you are satisfied with your drawing, save the changes and then print it.
6. Exit Flash.

Skills Covered

- **About Transforming Objects**
- **Rotate Objects**
- **Skew Objects**
- **Flip Objects**
- **Scale and Resize Objects**
- **Distort Objects**
- **Reshape Objects**

Software Skills Once you have drawn objects on the Stage, you can use Flash's transform features to modify them to create the precise effects you need. In addition, you will find that the transform features are very useful when you start animating shapes.

Application Skills In this exercise, you will use the transformation tools to enhance the drawing you created for use as the Wish Upon a Star logo.

TERMS

Bounding box A rectangular box that displays around a selected object.

Distort To reshape an object by transforming points, lines, or curves.

Scale To resize an object by a percentage of its original size.

Skew To slant an object on either its horizontal or vertical axis.

Transformation handles Small rectangles around the sides of a bounding box that can be dragged to transform an object.

Transformation point The center point of an object. Sometimes called the registration point or center point.

NOTES

About Transforming Objects

- Use Flash's transformation tools to modify the appearance of an object on the Stage.
- You can rotate, **skew**, **scale**, flip, resize, and **distort** objects.
- When you select the Free Transform tool, all transformation options are available. Alternatively, you may select the specific type of transformation you want to perform.
- When you select an object or objects for transformation, a **bounding box** displays around the selection. **Transformation handles** display around the bounding box and a **transformation point** displays in the center of the selection (see the illustration in the opposite column).

Transformation Tools

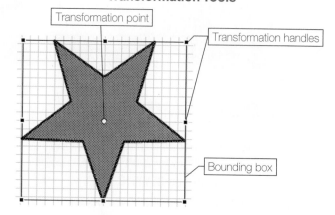

■ The position of the transformation point is determined by the X and Y coordinates, which display in the Info panel or in the Property Inspector. You can move the transformation point by dragging it, or by changing the X and Y settings.

Rotate Objects

■ You can rotate an object around its transformation point.

■ Flash has commands to automatically rotate an object 90 degrees clockwise—to the right—or counterclockwise—to the left.

■ You can also rotate an object by dragging a corner transformation handle. The mouse pointer changes to a circular arrow when it is correctly positioned to rotate an object by dragging (see the following illustration).

Rotate Pointer

↺

■ To rotate an object by a precise amount, use the options in the Transform panel (see the following illustration).

Transform Panel

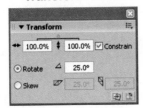

Skew Objects

■ Skew an object by dragging a center transformation handle.

■ Drag the center handle above or below the shape to skew the object horizontally; drag the center handle on either side of the object to skew the object vertically.

■ The mouse pointer changes to two parallel lines when it is correctly positioned to skew an object by dragging (see the following illustration).

Skew Pointer

⇉

■ To skew an object by a precise amount, use the options in the Transform panel.

Flip Objects

■ You can flip objects horizontally or vertically.

■ Flipping does not change an object's position on the Stage relative to other objects.

Scale and Resize Objects

■ Scale an object to adjust its size by a percentage in relation to the object's original size.

■ For example, scale the object to 200% to make it twice its original size; scale it to 50% to make it half its original size.

■ You can change just the height of an object, or just the width.

■ To keep an object in proportion, scale both the height and the width by the same amount, or select the Constrain option in the Transform panel.

■ Drag any transformation handle to scale an object. When the mouse pointer is correctly positioned for scaling, it changes to a two-headed arrow (see the following illustration).

Scaling Pointer

↔

■ Use the options in the Transform panel to scale an object by a precise percentage.

■ You can also resize an object by setting height and/or width dimensions in the Info panel or in the object's Property Inspector.

Distort Objects

■ You can distort the shape of an entire object using the Distort or Envelope option.
  • With the Distort option, you drag the transformation handles to move a corner or edge to reshape the object.
  • With the Envelope option, you may drag points as well as handles to reshape the object.

■ When the mouse pointer is in the correct position for distorting, it changes to a white arrowhead (see the following illustration).

Distort Pointer

▷

Reshape Objects

■ Use the Selection tool to reshape lines and curves created with the Pencil, Brush, Line, Oval, or Rectangle tools.

- When the mouse pointer is resting on a line, it indicates the type of reshaping you can perform:
  - An angle below the pointer indicates that you can move a corner or an end point (see the following illustration).

Reshape Corner Pointer

  - A curve below the pointer indicates that you can adjust the curve of a line segment (see the illustration at the top of the opposite column).

Reshape Curve Pointer

✓ You can also use the Envelope option to distort an object. When you use Envelope, a box displays around all selected objects; drag the points to distort all items within the box.

PROCEDURES

Free Transform

1. Select object.
2. Click **Free Transform** tool [⊞]..........................Q
   OR
   a. Click **Modify**..........Alt+M
   b. Click **Transform**...............T
   c. Click **Free Transform**.........F
3. Position mouse pointer for desired transformation.
4. Drag to transform object.

Rotate and/or Skew

1. Select object.
2. Click **Free Transform** tool [⊞].........................Q
3. Click **Rotate and Skew** option button [↻].
4. Position mouse pointer for desired transformation.
5. Drag to transform object.
   OR
1. Select object.
2. Click **Modify**...............Alt+M
3. Click **Transform**.....................T
4. Click **Rotate and Skew**...........R
5. Position mouse pointer for desired transformation.
6. Drag to transform object.

Rotate an Object 90°

1. Select object.
2. Click **Modify**.............Alt+M
3. Click **Transform**.....................T

4. Do one of the following:
   - Click **Rotate 90° CW**..........[0] to rotate object to the right.
   - Click **Rotate 90° CCW**.........[9] to rotate object to the left.

Rotate a Precise Amount

1. Select object.
2. Display Transform panel.
3. Click **Rotate** option button.
4. Click **Rotation** box.
5. Replace current value with desired rotation angle.
   ✓ Positive numbers rotate to the right; negative numbers rotate to the left.
6. Press **Enter**...................↵Enter

Skew a Precise Amount

1. Select object.
2. Display Transform panel.
3. Click **Skew** option button.
4. Click **Skew Horizontally** box.
5. Replace current value with desired skew angle.
   ✓ Positive numbers skew to the right; negative numbers skew to the left.
6. Click **Skew Vertically** box.
7. Replace current value with desired skew angle.
   ✓ Positive numbers skew up; negative numbers skew down.
8. Press **Enter**...................↵Enter

Scale and Rotate (Ctrl+Alt+S)

1. Select object.
2. Click **Modify**...............Alt+M

3. Click **Transform**.....................T
4. Click **Scale and Rotate**...........C
5. Click **Scale** box...........Alt+S
6. Type percentage by which to scale object.
7. Click **Rotate** box..........Alt+R
8. Type degree by which to rotate object.
9. Click **OK**.......................↵Enter

Scale an Object

1. Select object.
2. Click **Free Transform** tool [⊞]............................Q
3. Click **Scale** option button [⤢].
4. Do one of the following:
   - Drag a corner handle to change height and width at the same time.
   - Drag a side handle to change width.
   - Drag a top or bottom handle to change height.
   OR
1. Select object.
2. Click **Modify**...............Alt+M
3. Click **Transform**.....................T
4. Click **Scale**.........................S
5. Do one of the following:
   - Drag a corner handle to change height and width at the same time.
   - Drag a side handle to change width.
   - Drag a top or bottom handle to change height.

Scale a Precise Amount

1. Select object.
2. Display Transform panel.
3. Click **Constrain** check box to maintain proportions, if desired.
4. Click **Width** box.
5. Replace current value with desired width, as a percentage of original width.
6. Click **Height** box.
7. Replace current value with desired height, as a percentage of original height.
8. Press **Enter** .... ⏎Enter

Resize a Precise Amount

1. Select object.
2. Display Info panel.
   OR
   Display Property Inspector.
3. Click **Width** box.
4. Replace current value with desired width dimension.
5. Click **Height** box.
6. Replace current value with desired height dimension.

7. Press **Enter** .... ⏎Enter

   ✓ The unit of measure depends on the Ruler Units set in the Document Properties dialog box.

Flip an Object

1. Select object.
2. Click **Modify** .... Alt + M
3. Click **Transform** .... T
4. Do one of the following:
   ■ Click **Flip Vertical** V
   ■ Click **Flip Horizontal** .... H

Distort an Object

1. Select object.
2. Click **Free Transform** tool ▣ .... Q
3. Click **Distort** option button ▱.
4. Drag a handle to transform object.
   OR
1. Select object.
2. Click **Modify** .... Alt + M
3. Click **Transform** .... T
4. Click **Distort** .... D
5. Drag a handle to transform object.

Distort Using the Envelope

1. Select object.
2. Click **Free Transform** tool ▣ .... Q
3. Click **Envelope** option button ▱.
4. Drag a point or handle to transform object.
   OR
1. Select object.
2. Click **Modify** .... Alt + M
3. Click **Transform** .... T
4. Click **Envelope** .... E
5. Drag a point or handle to transform object.

Reshape a Line or Curve

1. Click **Selection** tool ▸ V
2. Position mouse pointer for desired transformation.
3. Drag to reshape line or curve.
   ✓ To create a new corner or end point in the middle of an existing line, press and hold Ctrl while you drag.

EXERCISE DIRECTIONS

1. Start Flash.
2. Open ⬤06DATA and save the document as **06STAR**.
3. Set the ruler units to inches, if necessary.
4. Display the rulers and the grid.
5. Hide the Timeline, if necessary, and set the zoom to Show All.
6. Select the star object.
7. Scale the star to 85% of its original size, both horizontally and vertically.
8. Rotate the star 90 degrees counterclockwise.
9. Skew the star -90 degrees horizontally and -110 degrees vertically.
10. Deselect the star.
11. Use the Selection tool to select the fill and stroke of the polygon.
12. Resize the selected objects to 4.75" wide by 4.5" high.
13. Distort the selection by dragging the transformation handle in the upper left of the bounding box to the upper-left corner of the Stage.
14. Deselect the objects.
15. Identify the three star points that do not reach the polygon stroke, and reshape them so they are long enough to touch the stroke.
16. Elongate the remaining four points so they extend beyond the polygon stroke.
17. Close the Transform panel and collapse the Property Inspector. Set the zoom to Show All. The drawing should look similar to Illustration A on page 42.
18. Display the Property Inspector and the Timeline.
19. Hide the grid.
20. Print the drawing and then close the file, saving all changes.
21. Exit Flash.

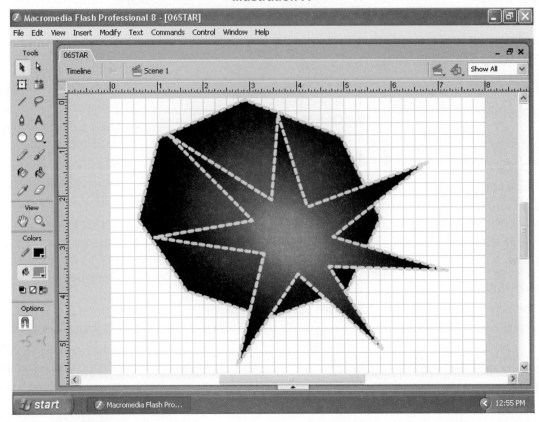

ON YOUR OWN

1. Start Flash and open **05MYPIC**, the document you created in Exercise 5, or open **06PIC**.

2. Save the document as **06MYPIC**.

3. Use the transformation tools to modify and enhance the shapes in the drawing. Alternatively, add new shapes to transform.

   - Rotate and skew one or more objects.
   - Flip one or more objects. For example, you can select all objects in the drawing and flip them horizontally.
   - Reshape lines and curves or distort objects.
   - Resize or scale objects.

4. When you are satisfied with your drawing, print it, and then save the changes.

5. Exit Flash.

Exercise | 7

Skills Covered

- **Understand Segments and Overlaps**
- **Arrange the Stack Order**
- **Group and Ungroup Objects**
- **Use the Eraser**

Software Skills To control the many parts of a vector drawing that you create with Flash, you need to be able to control segments and overlaps. Grouping and ungrouping objects will help you manage your drawings, as will knowing how to erase the objects—or parts of objects—you don't need.

Application Skills The manager responsible for the Wish Upon a Star fundraiser likes the logo you presented, but wants to see another option. In this exercise, you will use segments and overlaps to create a drawing with more interesting effects. You will use the Eraser tool to remove lines and shapes that don't enhance the drawing.

TERMS

Cutout The shape—or absence of a shape—created when an overlapping object is moved away from the object behind it.

Group Multiple objects linked together to create a single object. Also, to create a group.

Overlap An object drawn on top of an existing object.

Segment Part of a line or shape created by an overlapping line or shape.

Ungroup To separate a group into individual objects.

NOTES

Understand Segments and Overlaps

- As discussed in Exercise 4, the default drawing model in Flash is the Merge Drawing model.
- Using the Pencil, Line, Oval, Rectangle, or Brush tool in the Merge Drawing model, when you draw across an existing line or fill, the intersecting lines and fills are divided into **segments**.

  ✓ *Overlapping lines drawn with the Pen tool do not divide into segments.*

- Each segment becomes a separate object that you can select and modify individually (see the illustration on page 44).
- When objects **overlap**, the object drawn on top replaces the existing object.
- If the objects are the same color, they merge to create one single object.
- If objects are different colors, they remain separate, even if they overlap. However, if you move the

top object away, its **cutout** is removed from the bottom object.

- To avoid inadvertently altering overlapping shapes and lines, use the Object Drawing model.

Arrange the Stack Order

- By default, newer objects are stacked on top of existing objects.
- You can arrange the stack order for grouped objects, or for objects drawn using the Drawing Object model in order to move objects forward, backward, behind, or in front of other objects.
- Individual objects drawn using the Merge Drawing model cannot be rearranged.

Group and Ungroup Objects

- **Group** objects together when you want to modify or transform them as one single object.

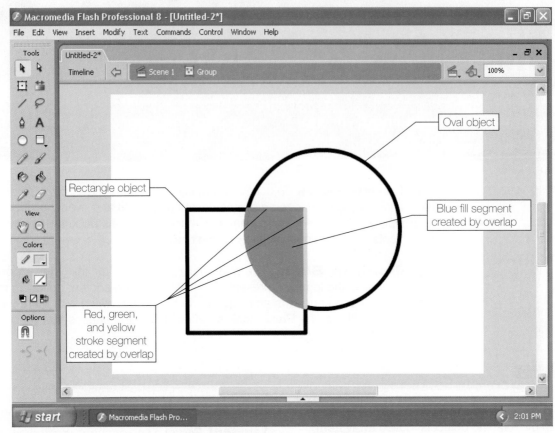

For example, if you draw a face that includes a head, nose, eyes, mouth, and hair, you can group all of the lines and fills comprising the face into a single object so you can quickly select and modify it.

In addition, grouped objects do not create segments or cutouts when they overlap other objects.

A bounding box displays around all objects in a selected group, instead of the highlights used to indicate selected Merge Drawing objects. The group's transformation point also displays (see the illustration on page 45).

You can edit objects within a group without **ungrouping** them using edit mode. In edit mode, only the objects in the group are available for editing; all other objects on the Stage are dimmed.

Use the Eraser

Use the Eraser tool to remove strokes and fills from a drawing.

In normal mode the Eraser removes all objects. You can modify the Eraser to erase only strokes, only fills, only selected fills, or only fills inside a closed shaped.

You can also select a size and shape for the Eraser.

Select a Group or Individual Objects

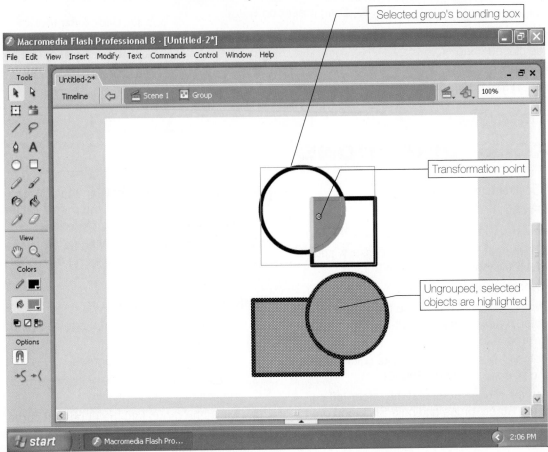

PROCEDURES

Group Objects (Ctrl+G)

1. Select objects to group.
2. Click **M**odify .... Alt + M
3. Click **G**roup .... G

Ungroup Objects (Ctrl+Shift+G)

1. Select group.
2. Click **M**odify .... Alt + M
3. Click **U**ngroup .... U

Start Edit Mode

1. Select group.
2. Click **E**dit .... Alt + E
3. Click **Edi**t Selected I
   OR
1. Click **Selection** tool V
2. Double-click group to edit.

Exit Edit Mode

1. Click **E**dit .... Alt + E
2. Click Edit **A**ll.

OR

1. Click **Selection** tool V
2. Double-click a blank area of the Stage.

Arrange the Stack Order

1. Select group.

   ✓ You can also rearrange symbols. You learn about symbols in Exercise 14.

2. Click **M**odify .... Alt + M
3. Click **A**rrange .... A
4. Click one of the following:
   - **Bring to Front** .... F to move object to top of stack.
   - **Bring Fo**r**ward** .... R to move object one position toward top of stack.
   - **Send Backward** .... E to move object one position toward bottom of stack.

- **Send to Back** .... B to move the object to bottom of stack.
- **Lock** .... L to lock object in its current position.

Use the Eraser

1. Click **Eraser** tool .... E
2. Click **Eraser mode** button.

   ✓ The Eraser mode button displays the most recently selected eraser option.

3. Click one of the following eraser options:
   - **Erase Normal** to erase all objects.
   - **Erase Fills** to erase fill objects only.
   - **Erase Lines** to erase stroke objects only.

- **Erase Selected Fills** 🔍 to erase selected fills only.
- **Erase Inside** 🔍 to erase fills inside closed shapes only.

4. Click **Eraser Shape** drop-down arrow.

5. Click desired shape.
6. Drag eraser on Stage.

Erase Everything on the Stage

- Double-click **Eraser** tool 🖉 ....E

Erase Stroke or Fill Segments

1. Click **Eraser** tool 🖉 ....E
2. Click **Faucet** option button 🚰.
3. Click stroke or fill to erase.

EXERCISE DIRECTIONS

Work with Segments and Overlaps

1. Start Flash.
2. Create a new document and save it as **07STAR**.
3. Set the ruler units to inches, if necessary, and then set the Stage dimensions to 8" by 8".
4. Display the rulers and the grid.
5. Hide the Timeline and collapse the Property Inspector, if necessary, and set the zoom to Show All.
6. Select the Oval tool. Set the stroke color to black and the fill color to red (#FF0000).
7. Position the mouse pointer at the upper-left corner of the Stage, press and hold Shift, and drag down and to the right to draw a circle 4.5" in diameter.
8. Change the fill color to blue (#0000FF), position the mouse pointer at the upper-right corner of the Stage, press and hold Shift, and drag down and to the left to draw another circle 4.5" in diameter.
9. Change the fill color to pink (#FF00FF), position the mouse pointer in the lower-left corner of the Stage, press and hold Shift, and drag up and to the right to draw a third circle 4.5" in diameter.
10. Change the fill color to purple (#6633FF), position the mouse pointer in the lower-right corner of the Stage, press and hold Shift, and drag up and to the right to draw a fourth circle 4.5" in diameter.
11. Select the stroke segments that surround the small rectangle in the middle of the overlapping circles and delete them.
12. Zoom in on the stroke between the red and blue circles.
13. Select the Eraser tool and then select the Erase Lines option. Select the second eraser shape from the top and then drag to erase the stroke between the red and blue circles.

   ✓ *Notice that although it appears as if you are erasing both strokes and fills, when you release the mouse button, only the strokes are erased.*

14. Erase the strokes between the pink and red circles, between the pink and purple circles, and between the purple and blue circles.
15. Set the zoom to Fit in Window. The drawing should look similar to the one in Illustration A on page 47.

Work with Grouped Objects

1. Select all objects on the stage and group them together.
2. Rotate the group 45 degrees.
3. Scale the group to 50% of its original size, both horizontally and vertically.
4. Move the group into the upper-left corner of the Stage. When positioned correctly, the X and Y coordinates for the transformation point should be 0 or very close to 0.
5. Display a horizontal guide and a vertical guide to locate the center of the grouped object.
6. Ungroup the objects and deselect them.

Complete the Drawing

1. Select the PolyStar tool and set options to draw a 5-pointed star with a .50 point size.
2. Set the stroke to black and the fill to pink (#FF00FF).
3. Position the mouse pointer at the intersection of the grid lines and drag up to draw a star, sized approximately 3" by 3".
4. Double-click the star fill to select the fill and the stroke, and then drag the object to the blank area to the lower right of the circles. When positioned correctly, the X and Y coordinates for the transformation point should be approximately 3.5.
5. Duplicate the star.
6. Change the fill color of the new star to purple (#6633FF).
7. Duplicate the star again, and change the fill color of the newest star to blue (#0000FF).

Illustration A

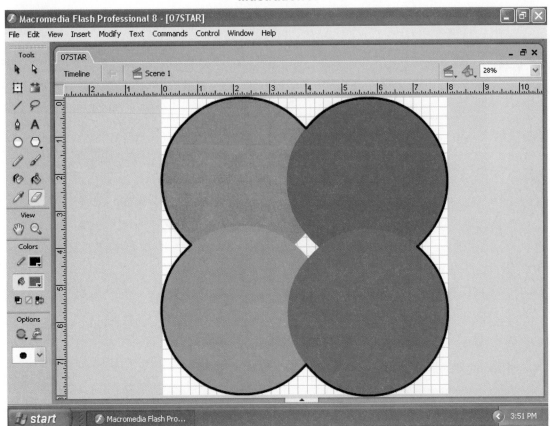

8. Duplicate one more star and fill it with red (#FF0000).

9. Use the Lasso tool to select the four stars and group them together.

10. Resize the star group to 4.5" by 4.5".

11. Move the group up and to the left so that the left point of the pink star aligns at the intersection of the guides. When positioned correctly, the X coordinate should be approximately 2.4 and the Y coordinate should be approximately 1.25.

12. Clear the guides. Collapse the Property Inspector, if necessary, and set the zoom to Fit in Window. The drawing should look similar to the one in Illustration B on page 48.

13. Display the Property Inspector and the Timeline. Close open panels.

14. Hide the grid.

15. Print the drawing and then close the file, saving all changes.

16. Exit Flash.

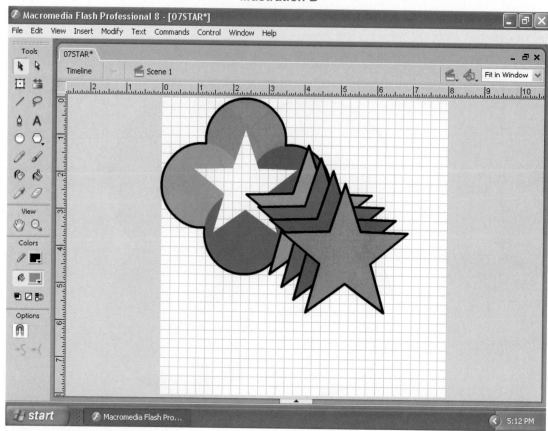

ON YOUR OWN

1. Start Flash and create a new document.

2. Save the document as **07MYPIC**.

3. Use the knowledge you have learned about drawing and modifying objects to create an abstract drawing of a sunrise. The sun may be rising over mountains, water, or over a flat horizon.

   - Use as many shapes and colors as you can.

   - Incorporate at least one cutout shape.

   - Practice working with grouped objects.

   - Try rearranging the stack order of groups.

   - Combine Merge Drawing objects with Object Drawing objects on the same Stage.

   - Use the transformation tools to enhance the objects.

4. When you are satisfied with your drawing, print it, and then save the changes.

5. Exit Flash.

End of Lesson Projects

- Summary Exercise
- Application Exercise
- Curriculum Integration Exercise
- Critical Thinking Exercise

Exercise | 8

Summary Exercise

Software Skills In this exercise, you will begin work on a drawing to use on the Web site for Castle Gate Productions, a music company. You will create a new document and prepare the Stage, and then use the Flash drawing tools to draw a castle.

DIRECTIONS

Prepare the Flash Document

1. Start Flash and create a new blank document.
2. Save the document as **08CASTLE**.
3. In the Document Properties dialog box, change the Ruler Units to inches and change the Stage size to 8" by 8".
4. Hide the Timeline.
5. Display the rulers and the grid.
6. Set Flash so objects snap to the grid.
7. Set the zoom to Fit in Window.
8. Collapse the Property Inspector.

Begin the Drawing

1. Select the Rectangle tool.
2. Set the Fill color to dark brown (#660000) and the Stroke to No Color.
3. Using the Merge Drawing model, position the mouse pointer 2" from the left edge and 4" from the top of the Stage, and drag to draw a rectangle 4" wide by 3" high.
4. Duplicate the rectangle.
5. Scale the duplicate to 50% of its original size both horizontally and vertically, and then move it so its top edge aligns with 3.5" on the vertical ruler and between 3" and 5" on the horizontal ruler.

6. Deselect the object. Note that it merges with the larger rectangle to become a single object, which is the main area of the castle.

Enhance the Drawing

1. Select the Rectangle tool and change the Fill color to brick red (#CC0000).
2. Position the mouse pointer at the lower-left corner of the brown rectangle and drag up and to the left to draw a rectangle 4" high by .5" wide. Increase the zoom if it helps you to get a closer look at the Stage.
3. Select the Line tool and change the Stroke color to the same brick red as the fill.
4. Position the mouse pointer at the upper-left corner of the red rectangle, press and hold Shift, and drag up and to the right to draw a straight diagonal line to the intersection of the grid lines at 2.75" on the vertical ruler and 1.75" on the horizontal ruler.
5. Draw another line between the end of the first line and the upper-right corner of the red rectangle.
6. Select the Paint Bucket tool and fill the area between the lines and the rectangle. This draws a turret on the left side of the castle.
7. Double-click the red fill to select the rectangle and the lines and then duplicate the selection.

8. Move the duplicate over to the right side of the brown rectangle, to create a matching turret on the right side of the castle.

9. Duplicate the selection again, and change the Stroke and Fill colors to brown.

10. Resize the selection to 3.75" high, leaving the width unchanged.

11. Move the smaller, brown turret down and to the right of the red turret.

12. Duplicate the selection and then move the duplicate to the left side if the drawing, so that there are two turrets on each side of the castle.

13. Select all objects on the stage and group them together.

Complete the Drawing

1. Deselect the group, and then select the Oval tool.

2. Change the Fill color to dark gray (#666666) and the Stroke color to black. Set the Stroke height to 4.

3. Select the Object Drawing Model option, press and hold Shift, and then drag to draw a circle 2" in diameter.

4. Move the circle so it is centered horizontally in the castle (between 3" and 5" on the horizontal ruler), and its top is at about 6" on the vertical ruler. The lower half of the circle should be below the castle.

5. Select the Eraser tool and select the option to Erase Normal. Change the eraser shape to square, in a medium size.

6. Zoom in on the lower half of the circle, and carefully erase all parts of the circle below the castle. If necessary, change the Eraser to erase only lines in order to erase the stroke even with the bottom of the castle.

7. Change the zoom to Show All. The drawing should look similar to the one in Illustration A.

8. Select the group and ungroup it.

9. Select all objects on the Stage and group them.

10. Print the file, and then exit Flash, saving all changes.

Illustration A

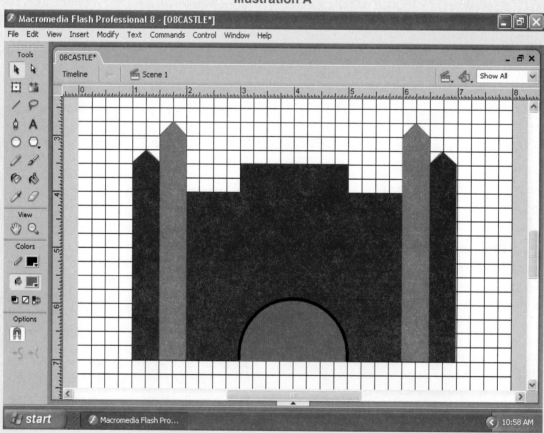

Application Exercise

Software Skills In this exercise, you will continue to work on the Castle Gate drawing. You will add shapes and use the transformation tools to enhance them.

DIRECTIONS

Enhance the Drawing

1. Open **09DATA** or **08CASTLE** and save the document as **09CASTLE**.

2. Hide the Timeline, if necessary.

3. Display the grid and the rulers, if necessary.

4. Display a vertical guide line down the middle of the Stage (along the 4" line) and a horizontal guide line across the middle of the Stage (also along the 4" line) so that the guides intersect at the center of the Stage.

5. Select the group and then select the Transform tool.

6. Position the group so its transformation point aligns with the center of the Stage—at the intersection of the vertical and horizontal guides.

7. Deselect the group.

8. Select the PolyStar tool and set options to draw a 9-pointed star with a .75 star point size.

9. Set the fill color to a warm yellow (#FFCC33) and the stroke color to black.

10. Set the stroke height to 4 and the stroke style to a dashed line.

11. Select the Object Drawing Model option, position the mouse pointer in the middle of the Stage, and drag up to draw a star approximately 6" wide by 6" high.

12. If necessary, rotate the star so that one point is directly vertical along the vertical guide line.

13. Arrange the star to send it back behind the grouped object to see how it looks.

14. Arrange the star to bring it forward so you can continue transforming it.

Apply Transformations

1. Resize the star to approximately 7.5" by 7.5".

2. Position the star so its transformation point is at the center of the stage.

3. Send the star to the back again, behind the castle group.

4. Select all objects on the Stage and group them.

5. Move the group to the lower-right corner of the Stage, so that the transformation handle in the lower-right corner of the bounding box is in the lower-right corner of the Stage.

6. Skew the selection approximately -15 degrees horizontally.

7. Position the selection so its transformation point is at the center of the Stage.

8. Deselect all objects and close all open panels, including the Property Inspector.

9. Hide the guides and set the zoom to Show All. The drawing should look similar to the one in Illustration A on page 52.

10. Print the file and then close it, saving all changes, and exit Flash.

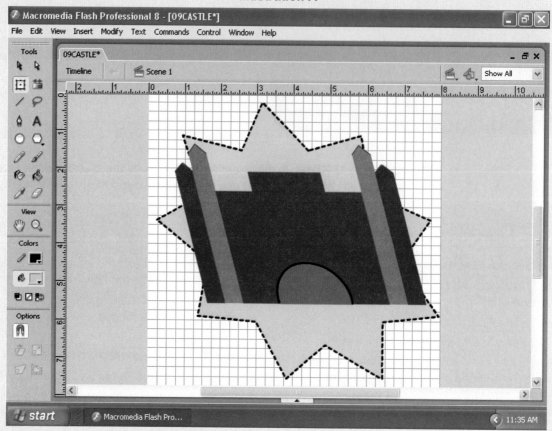

Curriculum Integration Exercise

Software Skills A tangram is an ancient Chinese puzzle made from a square divided into seven geometric shapes, called tans. The tans can be arranged into different pictures, such as the boat in the illustration below. In this exercise, you will use the Line tool to draw the tans as individual objects, and then arrange the tans into a picture. Before you begin this exercise, examine the drawing of the tangram below. You may also want to research tangrams on the Internet, or in your library.

DIRECTIONS

Start a new drawing and save it as **10TANS**.

Prepare the Stage by setting the ruler units to inches, and displaying visual tools you may find useful, such as the grid or guides.

Use the Line tool with no fill and a thin, black stroke to draw the shapes, using the tangram shown below as a pattern. Keep in mind that the shapes should all fit into a square. For example, the overall size of the square may be 6" or 7". Remember that if you hold down Shift while you drag, you will draw a straight line.

As each shape is complete, group the lines for that shape into one object so that you will be able to move and transform it. Keep in mind while drawing that you may overlap lines in order to draw shapes that fit into the tangram, and, if necessary, you may delete or erase extra lines once all of the tans are complete.

When the seven tans are complete, drag them off the Stage onto the surrounding Pasteboard.

Now, position and transform the tans into a picture such as the boat shown below, or the swan shown in Illustration A on page 54. You may be able to create your own picture from the tans. When the picture is complete, enhance it by modifying fills and strokes.

Save your changes, print, and close the document.

Tangram

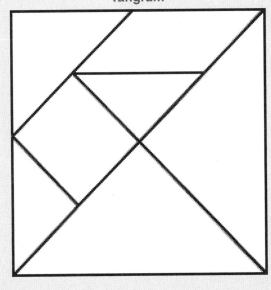

Tans Arranged into a Picture

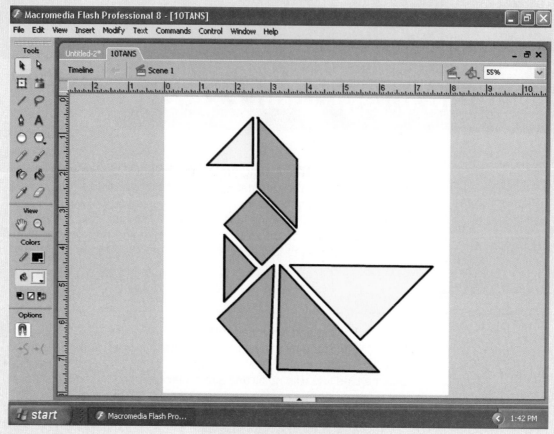

Critical Thinking Exercise

Software Skills Brighter Than Bright, a tooth-whitening franchise, has asked you to design an image it can use on its Web site and in promotional brochures and mailings. In this exercise, you will use the Flash drawing skills to draw a face that emphasizes bright, white teeth. See Illustration A for a sample.

DIRECTIONS

- Start a new document and save it as **11BRIGHT**.
- Set up the Stage to use inches, and display the rulers, grid, and guides, if you need them.
- Use the Oval tool to draw a shape for the head and eyes. Use a black stroke and no fill.
- Use the Oval tool to draw a large mouth, with a black fill and a red stroke. Reshape the curve of the stroke and the fill to make a smile.
- Use the Rectangle tool to fill the mouth with white teeth.
- Use the Line tool to draw a nose, if you want. You may also want to add details such as colored pupils in the eyes, eyelashes, or eyebrows.
- If you want, enhance the drawing by using transformations, or by changing colors or stroke modifiers.
- When you are satisfied with the drawing, print it. Close the document, saving all changes, and exit Flash.

Illustration A

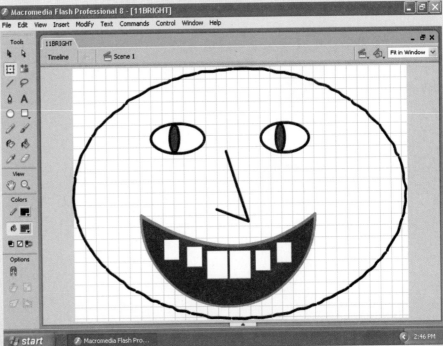

Lesson | 2

Creating an Animation

END OF LESSON
PROJECTS

Exercise 21

- Summary Exercise

Exercise 22

- Application Exercise

Exercise 23

- Curriculum Integration Exercise

Exercise 24

- Critical Thinking Exercise

Skills Covered

- **About Animation**
- **About Frames and Keyframes**
- **Work with Frames and Keyframes**

- **View Frames with the Timeline**
- **Preview an Animation**

Software Skills Once you have mastered the art of creating images with the Flash drawing tools, you are ready to start creating animated applications. Animations make a Web page or presentation exciting, and Flash makes it easy to create animations. You simply enter content on frames and keyframes, and then preview the animation right on the Flash Stage.

Application Skills The owner of Grace Notes, the small stationery boutique, has asked you to create an animated version of the envelope picture you created with the Flash drawing tools. In this exercise, you will open an existing file and use frame-by-frame animation to make the notes display one by one. You will preview the animation on the Stage, and use different frame rates to see how they affect the animation.

TERMS

Elapsed time The length of time it takes to reach the current frame when the animation plays.

Frame-by-frame animation Animation created by changing the content on each frame in a sequence.

Frame sequence A series of frames beginning with a keyframe and ending with the next keyframe.

Keyframe A frame in which you specify changes in an animation.

Tweened animation Animation in which you specify a starting point and an ending point and let Flash fill in the frames between.

NOTES

About Animation

- Flash provides the tools you need to animate the content you enter in a document so that it moves or changes on the computer screen.

- You create animation by changing the content of frames in a sequence. For example, you can make an object move across the Stage, change its size or color, or even its shape.

- There are two ways to create animation in a Flash document:
  - **Frame-by-frame animation**, in which you manually change content on each subsequent frame. This is best suited for complex animations in which an image changes in every frame instead of simply moving. Frame-by-frame

animation increases file size more rapidly than tweened animation.

  - **Tweened animation**, in which you specify the action on the first **keyframe** and the action on the last keyframe and let Flash fill in the frames between the two. Flash varies the object's attributes evenly between the starting and ending frames to create the appearance of movement. Tweened animation is useful for creating movement and changes over time.

    ✓ *Tweened animation is covered in Exercises 16–18.*

About Frames and Keyframes

- A frame is the basic unit used to create an animation in Flash.

- You enter content in each frame, and then display the frames in a sequence to play the animation.

- A frame in which you specify a change in animation, or in which you include frame actions, is called a *keyframe*.

- In frame-by-frame animation, every frame is a keyframe.

- In tweened animation, the first and last frames in a sequence are keyframes.

- Flash automatically inserts the contents of the previous keyframe into new frames inserted in a Timeline.

Work with Frames and Keyframes

- By default, Flash uses frame-based selection, in which you select individual frames in the Timeline.

- You can choose to use span-based selection, in which an entire **frame sequence**—from one keyframe to the next—is selected. The content of the selected frame displays on the Stage.

- You can select a series of frames in the Timeline, but only the first frame in the series displays on the Stage.

- You can insert a frame or keyframe at any location along the Timeline.

- Since Flash redraws the shapes in each keyframe, you should create keyframes only at those points in the artwork where something changes. Creating extra keyframes may result in unnecessarily large files.

- You can convert a keyframe to a frame, if you decide that a change is not going to take place at that location in the Timeline.

- Delete a frame or series of frames when you no longer need them.

- Copy or move a frame or frame series to a new location on the Timeline to rearrange or reorganize your animation, or to duplicate content from one frame to another.

View Frames with the Timeline

- You can select any frame in the Timeline to display it on the Stage. The location of the playhead indicates the current frame.

- The current frame number, frame rate, and **elapsed time** display on the Timeline status bar.

  ✓ *You can double-click the frame rate on the Timeline status bar to quickly open the Document Properties dialog box.*

- Flash uses visual codes to label frames and keyframes in the Timeline (see the illustration at the bottom of the page):

  - A solid circle indicates a keyframe with content.

  - A clear circle indicates a blank keyframe.

  - By default, frames containing content are tinted gray.

  - Tinted frames following a keyframe contain the same content as the keyframe.

  - A clear rectangle marks the last frame in a sequence.

- Using the Timeline options menu, you can modify the Timeline display. For example, you can increase or decrease the height of the entire Timeline. You can also remove the tint, display previews of the contents of frames, or change the width of frames in the Timeline.

Preview an Animation

- To see how an animation looks, you can play it on the Stage.

- Use the commands on the Control menu or the Controller toolbar to play the animation.

View Frames in the Timeline

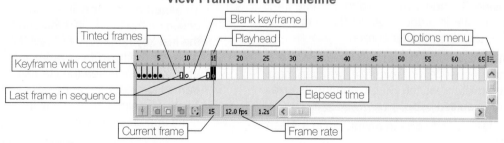

PROCEDURES

Select a Frame

- Click frame to select in Timeline.

Select a Frame Series

1. Click first frame in series.
2. Drag to last frame in series.

   OR

1. Click first frame in series.
2. Press and hold **Shift**........⟨⬆Shift⟩
3. Click last frame in series.

Select All Frames (Ctrl+Alt+A)

1. Click **Edit**...............⟨Alt⟩⟨+⟩⟨E⟩
2. Click **Timeline**...............⟨M⟩
3. Click **Select All Frames**...........⟨S⟩

Change to Span-Based Selection

1. Click **Edit**...............⟨Alt⟩⟨+⟩⟨E⟩
2. Click **Preferences**.
3. Click to select **Span-based selection** check box......⟨Alt⟩⟨+⟩⟨S⟩
4. Click **OK**...............⟨⏎Enter⟩

Change to Frame-Based Selection

1. Click **Edit**...............⟨Alt⟩⟨+⟩⟨E⟩
2. Click **Preferences**.
3. Click to deselect **Span-based selection** check box......⟨Alt⟩⟨+⟩⟨S⟩
4. Click **OK**...............⟨⏎Enter⟩

Insert a Frame in the Timeline (F5)

1. Click **Insert**...............⟨Alt⟩⟨+⟩⟨I⟩
2. Click **Timeline**...............⟨T⟩
3. Click **Frame**...............⟨F⟩

   OR

1. Right-click frame in Timeline.
2. Click **Insert Frame**.

   ✓ *The new frame displays to the right of the right-clicked frame.*

Create a Keyframe (F6)

1. Select a frame in Timeline.
2. Click **Insert**...............⟨Alt⟩⟨+⟩⟨I⟩
3. Click **Timeline**...............⟨T⟩
4. Click **Keyframe**...............⟨K⟩

   OR

1. Right-click frame in Timeline.
2. Click **Insert Keyframe**.

Create a Blank Keyframe (F7)

1. Select a frame in Timeline.
2. Click **Insert**...............⟨Alt⟩⟨+⟩⟨I⟩
3. Click **Timeline**...............⟨T⟩
4. Click **Blank Keyframe**...............⟨B⟩

   OR

1. Right-click frame in Timeline.
2. Click **Insert Blank Keyframe**.

Delete a Frame, Keyframe, or Frame Series (Shift+F5)

1. Select frame, keyframe, or frame series.
2. Click **Edit**...............⟨Alt⟩⟨+⟩⟨E⟩
3. Click **Timeline**...............⟨M⟩
4. Click **Remove Frames**...............⟨R⟩

   OR

1. Right-click frame, keyframe, or frame series.
2. Click **Remove Frames**.

Delete a Frame, Keyframe, or Frame Series (Shift+F5)

1. Select frame, keyframe, or frame series.
2. Click **Edit**...............⟨Alt⟩⟨+⟩⟨E⟩
3. Click **Timeline**...............⟨M⟩
4. Click **Remove Frames**...............⟨R⟩

   OR

1. Right-click frame, keyframe, or frame sequence.
2. Click **Remove Frames**.

Clear the Contents of a Frame or Keyframe (Alt+Backspace)

1. Select frame or keyframe.
2. Click **Edit**...............⟨Alt⟩⟨+⟩⟨E⟩
3. Click **Timeline**...............⟨M⟩
4. Click **Clear Frames**...............⟨L⟩

   OR

1. Right-click frame.
2. Click **Clear Frames**.

Convert a Keyframe to a Frame

1. Right-click keyframe.
2. Click **Clear Keyframe**.

Move a Frame or Frame Series

1. Select frame or series to move.
2. Drag to new location on Timeline.

   OR

1. Right-click frame or selected series to move.
2. Click **Cut Frames**.
3. Right-click new location on Timeline.
4. Click **Paste Frames**.

   OR

1. Select frame or series to move.
2. Click **Edit**...............⟨Alt⟩⟨+⟩⟨E⟩
3. Click **Timeline**...............⟨M⟩
4. Click **Cut Frames**...............⟨T⟩
5. Select new frame location in Timeline.
6. Click **Edit**...............⟨Alt⟩⟨+⟩⟨E⟩
7. Click **Timeline**...............⟨M⟩
8. Click **Paste Frames**...............⟨P⟩

   ✓ *Pasted frames replace existing frames in the new location.*

Copy a Frame or Frame Series

1. Select frame or series to copy.
2. Press and hold **Alt**...............⟨Alt⟩
3. Drag to new location on Timeline.

   OR

1. Right-click frame or selected series to copy.
2. Click **Copy Frames**.
3. Right-click new location on Timeline.
4. Click **Paste Frames**.

   OR

1. Select frame or series to copy.
2. Click **Edit**...............⟨Alt⟩⟨+⟩⟨E⟩
3. Click **Timeline**...............⟨M⟩
4. Click **Copy Frames**...............⟨C⟩

5. Select new frame location in Timeline.
6. Click **E**dit .... Alt + E
7. Click **Ti**meline .... M
8. Click **P**aste Frames .... P

   ✓ *Pasted frames replace existing frames in the new location.*

Copy Content from a Frame

1. Select content to copy.
2. Click **E**dit .... Alt + E
3. Click **C**opy C
4. Select destination keyframe.

   ✓ *The destination frame must be a keyframe.*

5. Click **E**dit .... Alt + E
6. Click one of the following:
   - **P**aste in Center .... A
     to paste copied contents in center of destination keyframe.
   - **P**aste in Place .... P
     to paste copied contents in same position as on original frame.

     ✓ *Copied content replaces existing content on the destination keyframe.*

Move Content from a Frame

1. Select frame.
2. Click **E**dit .... Alt + E
3. Click **C**ut .... T
4. Select destination keyframe.

   ✓ *The destination frame must be a keyframe.*

5. Click **E**dit .... Alt + E
6. Click one of the following:
   - **P**aste in Center .... A
     to paste copied contents in

center of destination keyframe.
   - **P**aste in Place .... P
     to paste copied contents in same position as on original frame.

     ✓ *Copied content replaces existing content on the destination keyframe.*

Modify the Timeline Display

1. Click **Timeline options menu** 📇.
2. Click desired option:
   - **Tiny** to display vary narrow frames.
   - **Small** to display narrow frames.
   - **Normal** (the default) to display normal frames.
   - **Medium** to display wider frames.
   - **Large** to display very wide frames.
   - **Preview** to display previews of frames sized to fit the Timeline frames.
   - **Preview in Context** to display previews including all white space.
   - **Short** to decrease the height of frames.
   - **Tinted Frames** to turn on or off the gray tint (on by default).

     ✓ *A check mark indicates that the option is on.*

Resize Timeline

■ Drag border between Timeline and Stage up or down.

Create Frame-by-Frame Animation

1. Select or create starting keyframe.

2. Create content for first frame in animation.
3. Select next frame in sequence.
4. Create a keyframe.
5. Modify contents on Stage to create next increment of animation.
6. Repeat steps 3 through 5 to complete animation.

Preview an Animation on the Stage

1. Click first frame in the sequence.
   OR
   a. Click **C**ontrol .... Alt + O
   b. Click **R**ewind .... R
2. Click **C**ontrol .... Alt + O
3. Click **P**lay .... P

Use the Controller Toolbar

1. Click **W**indow .... Alt + W
2. Click **T**oolbars .... O
3. Click **C**ontroller .... O
4. Click buttons as follows:
   - **Play** ▶ to play animation.
   - **Stop** ■ to stop animation.
   - **Rewind** ◄◄ to rewind to first frame.
   - **Step Back** ◄◄ to go to previous frame.
   - **Step Forward** ►► to go to next frame.
   - **Go to End** ►►| to go to last frame.

EXERCISE DIRECTIONS

Set Up the Animation

1. Start Flash and open ⬤12DATA. Save the file as **12NOTES**.
2. If necessary, display the Timeline and hide the rulers and the grid.
3. Decrease the height of the Timeline by dragging the border between the Timeline and the Stage up as far as possible.
4. Set the zoom to Show All.
5. Select frame 2.
6. Insert a keyframe on frame 2.

   ✓ *Flash inserts the content displayed on frame 1 on the new keyframe.*

7. Insert a keyframe on frame 3.
8. Insert a keyframe on frame 4.
9. Insert a keyframe on frame 5.

   ✓ *All frames in the sequence display the same content.*

Begin the Animation

1. Select frame 1.
2. Deselect all objects, and then select and delete all four notes.

   ✓ *The first frame in the sequence now displays no notes.*

3. Select frame 2.
4. Deselect all objects, and then select and delete the three notes on the right, leaving the first note on the left.
5. Select frame 3.
6. Deselect all objects, and then select and delete the two notes on the right, leaving the two notes on the left.
7. Select frame 4 and delete the note on the right.

8. Select frame 1.
9. Play the animation.

Expand the Animation

1. Insert a keyframe on frame 6.
2. Deselect all objects and then select and delete the note on the right.
3. Insert a keyframe on frame 7, and then delete the note on the right.
4. Insert a keyframe on frame 8, and then delete the note on the right.
5. Insert a keyframe on frame 9, and then delete the last note.
6. Preview the animation.
7. In the Property Inspector or the Document Properties dialog box, change the frame rate from 12 fps to 6 fps. It should progress more slowly.

Complete the Animation

1. Select frames 1 through 9 and copy them.
2. Select frame 10 and paste the copied frames.

   ✓ *The sequence is pasted into frames 10 through 18.*

3. Select frame 15.
4. Change the Timeline display to show the Preview in Context. If necessary, adjust the height of the Timeline so you can see the preview, and adjust the zoom to Show All. Your screen should look similar to Illustration A on page 64.
5. Preview the animation.
6. Print frame 15. If requested by your instructor, print each frame in the sequence.
7. Change the Timeline display to Normal.
8. Close the file, saving all changes, and exit Flash.

ON YOUR OWN

1. Start Flash and create a new document.
2. Save the document as **12MYPIC**.
3. Create an animation of a shape moving across the Stage, using at least 10 frames. For example, you might make an oval or star move from one side of the Stage to the other. Remember to use the Flash tools for positioning, such as for the grid, ruler, and guides.
4. Modify the animation so that the shape also increases in size as it moves across the Stage.
5. Add any other enhancements or transformations that you want in the animation, such as change in fill or stroke color, or rotation.
6. Try copying or moving frames from one location in the sequence to another.
7. When you are satisfied with the animation, save it and then exit Flash.

   ✓ *If requested by your instructor, print each frame of the animation before saving and exiting.*

Illustration A

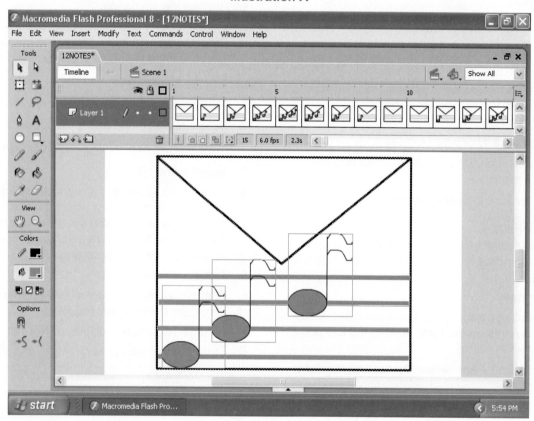

Exercise | 13

Skills Covered

- **About Layers**
- **View Layers in the Timeline**
- **Work with Layers**

Software Skills Use layers in an application to help keep your objects and animations separate and organized. Each Flash document can have as many layers as you want, limited only by the amount of memory on your PC. Layers help ensure the consistency in an application, and make it easy to find objects when you need them.

Application Skills You must create an animation for the Wish Upon a Star fundraiser. In this exercise, you will create a new document file that will have three layers. The first layer will contain a static background shape. The second layer will contain a star that increases in size, and the third layer will contain a star that rotates.

TERMS

Active layer The layer in which you are currently working.

Layer An invisible sheet used to separate objects on a frame.

Layer folder A folder in which you store layers and other layer folders.

Mask layer A layer used to create spotlight effects and transitions.

Motion guide layer A layer on which you draw paths along which you create tweened animation.

NOTES

About Layers

- Use **layers** to organize the content of your Flash applications.

- Layers are like clear sheets of paper piled on top of each other—you can see through them, but you can draw, edit, and animate objects on one layer without affecting objects on another layer.

- Each new document contains a single layer, but you can add as many layers as you want. The number of layers you can create is limited only by the amount of memory installed on your computer.

- Layers do not affect the size of your published application.

- Planning your layers before you create an animation can help you keep your objects organized.

- For example, it's a good idea to have a background layer that contains static images that don't change throughout the application. Additional layers might contain one animated object each.

Keeping animated objects on separate layers ensures that they don't overlap or segment each other.

- Using separate layers for objects such as sound files and actions makes it easier to find those objects when you need them.

- Flash includes some special types of layers to help you create sophisticated animations.

  - Use **motion guide layers** to make it easy to create motion animations.

    ✓ *Using a motion guide layer is covered in Exercise 19.*

  - Use **mask layers** to create special effects.

    ✓ *Using a mask layer is covered in Exercise 50.*

- In addition, you can use **layer folders** to organize layers into a hierarchical—or tree—structure similar to the file storage structure on your computer. Layer folders are useful for complex applications that contain many layers.

View Layers in the Timeline

- Layers are listed in the left pane of the Timeline, called the Layer pane.

- The layer at the top of the list is in the front of the frame, while the layer at the bottom of the list is in the back.

- When you create a new layer, it is inserted above—or on top of—the current layer.

- By default, the first layer in a document is named Layer 1. Subsequent layers are named according to the order in which they are created.

- A pencil icon displays to the right of the name of the **active layer** in the Timeline. Only one layer can be active at a time.

- Icons listed in columns to the right of each layer name provide information about the layer (see the illustration below):

  - A red X in the Show/Hide Layers column 👁 means a layer is hidden. Hidden layers do not display on the Stage.

  - A lock in the Lock/Unlock column 🔒 means a layer is locked. You cannot edit a locked layer.

  - A colored rectangular outline in the Show Layers as Outlines column ⬜ indicates that all objects on the layer are outlined with the color shown.

View Layers in the Timeline

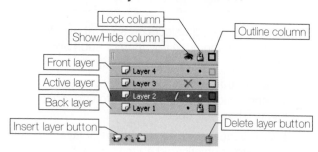

- Use the Layer Properties dialog box to modify aspects of a layer, such as its name, or outline color (see the following illustration).

Layer Properties Dialog Box

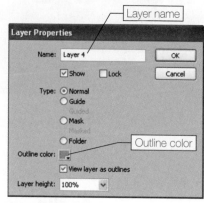

Work with Layers

- The contents of the active layer display on the Stage.

- You can insert a new layer at any time. By default, the new layer becomes the active layer.

- Move layers in the Timeline list to rearrange their stacking order. For example, move a layer up in the list to move it toward the front of the frame.

- It is a good idea to rename layers to reflect their contents. For example, you might name the layer containing static background objects *Background*.

- You can copy a layer to make an exact duplicate of it. All frames in the layer are copied.

- Delete a layer when you are certain you don't need it anymore.

- Hide layers when you want to work on one layer without being distracted by the content on other layers.

- Lock a layer when you do not want any changes made to it.

- You can also copy and move individual objects and frames from one layer to another.

PROCEDURES

Select a Layer

- Click layer name in Timeline.

Select Multiple Contiguous Layers

1. Click first layer name to select.
2. Press and hold **Shift**......⟨⬆Shift⟩
3. Click last layer name to select.

Select Multiple Noncontiguous Layers

1. Click first layer name to select.
2. Press and hold **Ctrl**............⟨Ctrl⟩
3. Click next layer name to select.
4. Repeat to select additional layers.

Insert a Layer

- Click **Insert Layer** button 🔲 on Timeline.

  OR

1. Click **Insert**................⟨Alt⟩⟨+⟩⟨I⟩
2. Click **Timeline**........................⟨T⟩
3. Click **Layer**...........................⟨L⟩

  OR

1. Right-click layer in Timeline.
2. Click **Insert Layer**.

  ✓ *The new layer displays above the active layer.*

Delete a Layer

- Click **Delete Layer** button 🗑 on Timeline.

  OR

1. Right-click layer in Timeline.
2. Click **Delete Layer**.

Show/Hide a Layer

- Click in **Show/Hide Layers** column to right of layer's name.

  ✓ *An X displays in the column when the layer is hidden.*

Show/Hide All Layers

- Click **Show/Hide All Layers** icon 👁.

Show/Hide Other Layers

1. Press and hold **Alt**............⟨Alt⟩
2. Click in **Show/Hide Layers** column to right of name of layer to show.

  OR

1. Right-click layer to show.

2. Click **Hide Others** to hide all other layers.

  OR

  Click **Show All** to display all layers.

Lock/Unlock a Layer

- Click in **Lock/Unlock Layers** column to right of layer's name.

  ✓ *A lock icon displays in the column when the layer is locked.*

Lock/Unlock All Layers

- Click **Lock/Unlock All Layers** icon 🔒.

Lock/Unlock Other Layers

1. Press and hold **Alt**............⟨Alt⟩
2. Click in **Lock/Unlock Layers** column to right of name of layer to keep unlocked.

  OR

1. Right-click layer to leave unlocked.
2. Click **Lock Others** to lock all other layers.

  OR

  Click **Show All** to unlock all layers.

Turn Outline Display On or Off

- Click colored rectangle in Show All Layers as Outlines column to right of layer's name.

  ✓ *The rectangle displays as an outline when the outline option is on.*

Show/Hide Outlines for All Layers

- Click **Show All Layers as Outlines** icon ⬜.

Show/Hide Outlines for Other Layers

1. Press and hold **Alt**............⟨Alt⟩
2. Click in **Show All Layers as Outlines** column to right of layer's name.

Display Layer Properties Dialog Box

1. Double-click **Layer Name** icon 🔲.

  OR

1. Right-click layer name.
2. Click **Properties**.

  OR

1. Select layer.
2. Click **Modify**...............⟨Alt⟩⟨+⟩⟨M⟩
3. Click **Timeline**........................⟨M⟩
4. Click **Layer Properties**.............⟨L⟩

Change Outline Color

1. Display Layer Properties dialog box.
2. Click **Outline color** palette.
3. Click desired color.
4. Click **OK**....................⟨⏎Enter⟩

Change Layer Row Height

1. Display Layer Properties dialog box.
2. Click **Layer height** drop-down arrow.
3. Click desired height as a percentage of original height.
4. Click **OK**....................⟨⏎Enter⟩

Rename a Layer

1. Double-click layer name.
2. Type new name.
3. Press **Enter**...................⟨⏎Enter⟩

  OR

1. Display Layer Properties dialog box.
2. Click **Name** box............⟨Alt⟩⟨+⟩⟨N⟩
3. Type new name.
4. Click **OK**....................⟨⏎Enter⟩

Copy a Layer

1. Insert new layer.
2. Select layer to copy.
3. Click **Edit**...................⟨Alt⟩⟨+⟩⟨E⟩
4. Click **Timeline**........................⟨M⟩
5. Click **Copy Frames**.................⟨C⟩
6. Select new layer.
7. Click **Edit**...................⟨Alt⟩⟨+⟩⟨E⟩
8. Click **Timeline**........................⟨M⟩
9. Click **Paste Frames**...............⟨P⟩

Rearrange Layers

- Drag layer name to new location in Timeline.

EXERCISE DIRECTIONS

Create the Background Layer

1. Start Flash and create a new document. Save the file as **13STARS**.

2. Set properties to display the ruler units as inches and change the Stage size to 8" by 8".

3. If necessary, display the Timeline, the rulers, and the grid. Set the zoom to Fit in Window.

4. Rename Layer 1 **Background**.

5. Select the Oval tool. Set the fill color to light gray (#CCCCCC) and the stroke color to black. Set the stroke height to 8.

6. Select frame 1 on the Background layer, and draw a circle with a diameter of 8 inches to fill the Stage.

7. Select frame 11 and insert a keyframe. Flash inserts the content from frame 1 on all frames in the sequence.

8. Lock the Background layer.

Create a New Layer

1. Select the Background layer and then insert a new layer.

2. Name the new layer **Yellow Star**.

3. Select the PolyStar tool and set options to draw a 5-pointed star.

4. Set the fill color to yellow (#FFFF00) and change the stroke to a black, dashed, 4-point line.

5. Click in the center of the circle (use guides, if necessary) and drag straight down to the bottom of the Stage to draw the star within the circle.

6. Hide the Background layer.

Animate the Yellow Star

1. On the Yellow Star layer, select frame 2 and insert a keyframe.

2. Scale the star object to approximately 80%.

3. Select frame 3 and insert a keyframe.

4. Scale the object to approximately 60%.

5. Insert a keyframe on frame 4 and scale the star to 40%.

6. Insert a keyframe on frame 5 and scale the star to 20%.

7. Insert a keyframe on frame 6 and scale the star to 0%.

8. Insert a keyframe on frame 7 and scale the star to 20%.

9. Insert a keyframe on frame 8 and scale the star to 40%.

10. Insert a keyframe on frame 9 and scale the star to 60%.

11. Insert a keyframe on frame 10 and scale the star to 80%.

12. Insert a keyframe on frame 11 and scale the star to 100%.

13. Lock the Yellow Star layer.

14. Show the Background layer and preview the animation.

Create Another Layer

1. Select the Yellow Star layer and insert a new layer.

2. Name the new layer **Blue Star**.

3. Select the PolyStar tool and set options to draw a 10-pointed star.

4. Set the fill color to blue (#0000FF) and change the stroke to a black, solid, 6-point line.

5. Click in the center of the circle (use guides, if necessary) and drag straight up to the top of the Stage to draw the star within the background circle.

6. Hide both the Background layer and the Yellow Star layer.

Animate the Blue Star

1. On the Blue Star layer, select frame 2 and insert a keyframe.

2. Rotate the object on frame 2 approximately 15 degrees to the right.

3. Select frame 3 and insert a keyframe.

4. Rotate the object on frame 3 approximately 30 degrees to the right.

5. Select frame 4 and insert a keyframe. Rotate the object approximately 45 degrees to the right.

6. Select frame 5 and insert a keyframe. Rotate the object approximately 60 degrees to the right.

7. Select frame 6 and insert a keyframe. Rotate the object approximately 75 degrees to the right.

8. Select frame 7 and insert a keyframe. Rotate the object approximately 90 degrees to the right.

9. Select frame 8 and insert a keyframe. Rotate the object approximately 105 degrees to the right.

10. Select frame 9 and insert a keyframe. Rotate the object approximately 120 degrees to the right.

11. Select frame 10 and insert a keyframe. Rotate the object approximately 135 degrees to the right.

12. Select frame 11 and insert a keyframe. Rotate the object approximately 150 degrees to the right.

13. Lock the Blue Star layer.

Arrange the Layers

1. Display all layers and preview the animation. Notice that the Blue Star is in front of the Yellow Star.

2. Move the Blue Star layer down one place in the list so it is between the Background and the Yellow Star layers.

3. Preview the animation again.

4. Change the frame rate to 10 fps.

5. Hide the grid and the guides, if necessary, and collapse the Property Inspector.

6. Preview the animation again. When the animation stops, your screen should look similar to Illustration A.

7. Print the last frame (frame 11). Your instructor may ask you to print all frames in the sequence.

8. Close the document, saving all changes.

9. Exit Flash.

Illustration A

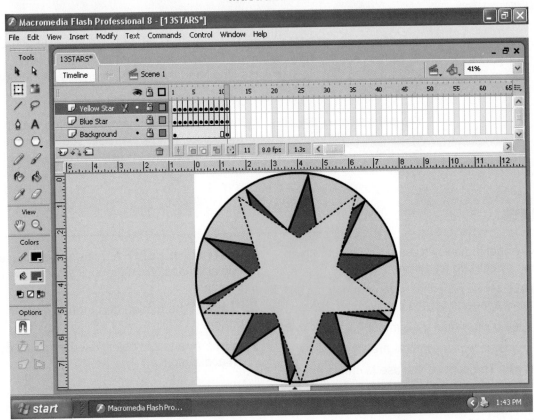

ON YOUR OWN

1. Start Flash and open ●13PIC or open 12MYPIC, the file you created in Exercise 12.

2. Save the document as 13MYPIC.

3. Add at least two more layers to the document. For example, you might want to add a static background layer behind the animation, and another layer of animation.

4. Name the layers appropriately. For example, name the background layer Background.

5. Arrange the layers appropriately. For example, the background layer should be at the bottom of the list of layers so it displayed behind all other layers.

6. While you work with layers, practice hiding and showing layers, or outlining objects.

7. When you have completed a layer, lock it to protect it from inadvertent edits.

8. Preview the animation.

9. Print at least the last frame of the animation.

10. Close the document, saving all changes, and exit Flash.

   ✓ If requested by your instructor, print each frame of the animation before saving and exiting.

Skills Covered

- Create Graphic Symbols
- Insert Instances
- Use the Library

- Align Objects on the Stage
- Edit a Registration Point

Software Skills Create symbols from your graphics objects when you need to insert multiple instances of the same object in an application. Using symbols ensures that file size stays small and that there is consistency throughout your application.

Application Skills You want to animate the multi-layered star that you created for the Wish Upon a Star fundraiser. In this exercise, you will create a symbol from the object and then you will insert instances to create an animation in which four copies of the instance move around the stage.

TERMS

Button A symbol that allows users to interact with an application by starting an action.

Components Movie clips that have parameters you set to control appearance and behavior.

Instance One occurrence of a symbol.

Library A folder in which symbols are stored.

Media assets The content you use to create an application.

Movie clip A symbol comprised of an animated sequence of frames.

Registration point A reference point used to position and transform a group, instance, text block, or bitmap.

Rollover The motion of a mouse pointer over a button.

Symbol A reusable object used to create content in an application.

NOTES

Create Graphic Symbols

- A **symbol** is a graphic object, **movie clip**, or **button** that you create once and can use many times.
- You can create a symbol by converting objects already entered on the Stage, or you can create an empty symbol.
- Any symbol that you create becomes part of the **library** for the current document; you can share symbols among documents.

- When you create a symbol, it has its own Timeline and Stage, which you can manage just as you manage the document's main Timeline and Stage. For example, you can add layers or keyframes to the symbol's Timeline.
- You specify the symbol type in either the Convert to Symbol or the New Symbol dialog box, which are virtually the same (see the illustration on page 71).

Convert to Symbol Dialog Box

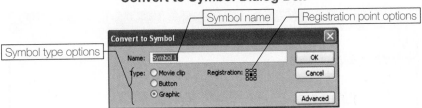

- Use graphic symbols for static images and to create reusable pieces of animation that are tied to the Timeline of the main application. Graphic symbols play in sync with the document's main Timeline, so interactive controls and sounds won't work in a graphic symbols animation sequence.

- Use button symbols to create interactive buttons in the application that respond to mouse clicks, **rollovers**, or other actions.

- Use movie clip symbols to create reusable pieces of animation. Movie clip symbols have a Timeline that is independent from the document's main Timeline. Movie clip symbols may contain interactive controls, sounds, and other movie clips.

  ✓ *You create button and movie clip symbols in Exercise 30.*

- When you convert an existing object into a symbol, you may also specify the location of its **registration point**. By default, the registration point is in the upper-left corner of the item, but you may prefer it in a different location, such as the center, for aligning and positioning the object.

  ✓ *When you create a new symbol, the registration point displays in the window so you may create the symbol around it.*

Insert Instances

- Each occurrence of a symbol in an application is called an **instance**.

- No matter how many instances of a symbol you have, the symbol is stored only once. This is one of the ways that Flash keeps the size of files small.

- For example, if you have a static graphic drawing that you use as a background on all frames in an animation, you can reduce the file size by converting the drawing to a symbol, and inserting instances on every frame.

- Using instances can also make applications play faster when viewed on a Web site because the symbol needs to be downloaded only once, no matter how many instances of the symbols are in the application.

- An existing object that is converted into a symbol automatically becomes an instance.

- Instances must be inserted on a keyframe.

- If a keyframe is not selected when you insert an instance, Flash automatically places the instance on the previous keyframe.

- If there are no keyframes on the current layer, Flash creates one on the first frame and places the instance there.

- When you insert a graphic instance, you must specify how many frames on which the instance should be displayed.

- By default, the instance is inserted from the current keyframe to the next keyframe. If there are no other keyframes, it is inserted until the last frame in the series.

- If there are no other frames in the series, you can insert one or more frames; the instance will be inserted on all of them.

- You cannot edit an instance directly on the Stage. Instead, use symbol-editing mode.

  ✓ *You learn about editing symbols in Exercise 15.*

Use the Library

- Symbols, **components**, and other **media assets** are automatically stored in the library for the current document.

- To view a library, display the Library panel (see the illustration at the top of page 72).

Library Panel

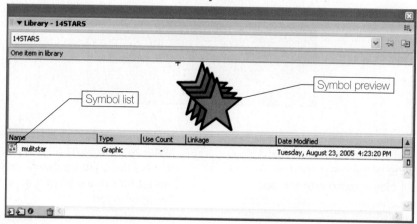

- From the Library panel, you can insert an instance into an application. You can also manage symbols and other items stored in the library.
- There is one library for each document, but you can easily share libraries among documents.
- In addition, Flash comes with three common libraries that contain built-in assets that you can use to create applications.

Align Objects on the Stage

- Aligning objects consistently is vital to ensure a smooth playing animation. If the objects are misaligned they will appear to jump irregularly around the Stage when you play the application.
- Use the commands on the Align menu or the options in the Align panel to position objects along the horizontal or vertical axis, in relation to other objects or to the Stage (see the following illustration).

Align Panel

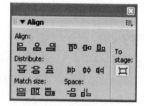

- Align objects horizontally along the top edge, center, or bottom edge of selected objects or the Stage.
- Align objects vertically along the right edge, center, or left edge of selected objects or the Stage.

✓ *Edges are set according to the bounding box around a selected object.*

- In addition, use the Align options to distribute objects so that they are evenly spaced based on their center points or edges, or to resize them to match the size of other objects on the Stage.

Edit a Registration Point

- Symbols and instances have registration points, which display as small crosshairs on the Stage (see the following illustration).

Registration Point in Upper-Left Corner

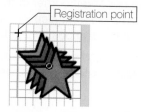

- Shapes and lines do not have registration points.
- You use a registration point to locate and position an object.
- When you create a symbol, you select the location of the registration point relative to its bounding box—either in the center, at any corner, or in the center of the top, bottom, left, or right side.
- You can move a registration point.

PROCEDURES

Open Library Panel (Ctrl+L)

1. Click **Window**............. Alt + W
2. Click **Library**.......... L , L , ↵Enter

   ✓ *A check mark next to the Library command indicates the Library panel is already displayed.*

Open a Common Library

1. Click **Window**............. Alt + W
2. Click **Common Libraries**........... B
3. Click desired library.

Resize Library Panel

■ Click **Wide Library View** button ▣ to increase panel size.

■ Click **Narrow Library View** button ▯ to decrease panel size.

Create a Graphic Symbol from Existing Objects (F8)

1. Select object(s) on Stage.
2. Click **Modify**............... Alt + M
3. Click **Convert to Symbol**.......... C

   ✓ *The Convert to Symbol dialog box displays.*

4. Type symbol name.
5. Click **Graphic** option button................. Alt + T , ↓
6. Click desired registration point location.
7. Click **OK**........................ ↵Enter

Create a New Graphic Symbol (Ctrl+F8)

1. Deselect all objects on Stage.
2. Click **Insert**................ Alt + I
3. Click **New Symbol**................ N

   OR

   a. Open Library panel.
   b. Click **New Symbol** button ⊡.

   ✓ *The Create New Symbol dialog box displays.*

4. Type symbol name.
5. Click **Graphic** option button................. Alt + T , ↓

6. Click **OK**........................ ↵Enter

   ✓ *Flash displays symbol-editing mode.*

7. Use the drawing tools to create the symbol.
8. Click **Edit**................... Alt + E
9. Click **Edit Document**........... E , E , ↵Enter

Insert an Instance

1. Select layer.
2. Select keyframe.
3. Open Library panel.
4. Double-click folder where symbol is stored, if necessary.
5. Drag symbol from preview area or symbol list onto Stage.

Display the Align Panel (Ctrl+K)

1. Click **Window**............. Alt + W
2. Click **Align**........................... G

   ✓ *A check mark next to the Align command indicates the panel is already displayed.*

Use the Align Panel

To Align Objects to the Stage

1. Select object(s) to align.
2. Display Align panel.
3. In Align panel, click to select **To Stage** button ⊐ .
4. Click one of the following horizontal alignments:
   • **Align left edge** ▤
   • **Align horizontal center** ▥
   • **Align right edge** ▦
5. Click one of the following vertical alignments:
   • **Align top edge** ▧
   • **Align vertical center** ▨
   • **Align bottom edge** ▩

To Align Objects to Other Objects

1. Select objects to align.
2. Display Align panel.

3. In Align panel, click to deselect **To Stage** button ⊐ .
4. Click one of the following horizontal alignments:
   • **Align left edge** ▤
   • **Align horizontal center** ▥
   • **Align right edge** ▦
5. Click one of the following vertical alignments:
   • **Align top edge** ▧
   • **Align vertical center** ▨
   • **Align bottom edge** ▩

To Distribute Objects Evenly

1. Select objects to align.
2. Display Align panel.
3. In Align panel, click to either select or deselect **To Stage** button ⊐ .

   ✓ *When To Stage button is selected, objects are distributed in relation to the Stage; when To Stage button is not selected, objects are distributed in relation to other selected objects.*

4. Click one of the following distribution alignments:
   • **Distribute top edge** ▤
   • **Distribute vertical center** ▥
   • **Distribute bottom edge** ▦
   • **Distribute left edge** ▥▥
   • **Distribute horizontal center** ◇◇
   • **Distribute right edge** ◁◁

To Match the Size of Objects

1. Select objects to match.
2. Display Align panel.
3. In Align panel, click one of the following match size options:
   • **Match width** ▤
   • **Match height** ▥
   • **Match width and height** ▦

To Space Objects Evenly

1. Select objects to space.
2. Display Align panel.

3. In Align panel, click to either select or deselect **To Stage** button ⊠.

   ✓ *When To Stage button is selected, objects are spaced in relation to the Stage; when To Stage button is not selected, objects are spaced in relation to other selected objects.*

4. Click one of the following spacing options:

   • **Space evenly vertically** 몹

   • **Space evenly horizontally** ᵈᵇ

Use the Align Menu

1. Select object(s) to align.
2. Click **Modify**...............(Alt)(+)(M)
3. Click **Align**...........................(N)
4. Click to select or deselect **To Stage**...............................(G)

   ✓ *A check mark indicates the command is selected.*

5. Click **Modify**...............(Alt)(+)(M)
6. Click **Align**...........................(N)
7. Click one of the following commands:

   • **Left**....................................(L)
   • **Horizontal Center**..................(C)
   • **Right**...............................(R)
   • **Top**.................................(T)
   • **Vertical Center**....................(V)
   • **Bottom**.............................(B)
   • **Distribute Widths**...............(D)
   • **Distribute Heights**...............(H)
   • **Make Same Width**..................(M)
   • **Make Same Height**...............(S)

EXERCISE DIRECTIONS

Create a Graphic Symbol

1. Start Flash and open **07STAR**, the file you created in Exercise 7, or open ⊚**14DATA**. Save the file as **14STARS**.
2. Select the group comprised of the four overlapping stars.
3. Resize the group to approximately 2" by 2".
4. Convert the object to a graphic symbol named **multistar**.
5. Delete everything from the Stage, including the group of stars.

   ✓ *To quickly delete everything on the Stage, double-click the Eraser tool.*

Work with Instances

1. If necessary, display the Timeline, the rulers, and the grid.
2. Rename Layer 1 **Star 1**.
3. Display the Library panel. The multistar symbol should be stored in the library.
4. Select the first frame of the Star 1 layer.
5. Insert an instance of the multistar symbol on the Stage.
6. Display the Align panel.
7. Align the instance to the Stage in the center horizontally and vertically.
8. Insert a new layer and name it **Star 2**.
9. Select the first frame of the Star 2 layer and insert an instance of the multistar symbol.

10. Align the instance to the Stage in the center horizontally and vertically, so that it covers the instance on the Star 1 layer.

    ✓ *You can hide the Star 1 layer so you see only the Star 2 layer, if desired.*

11. Insert a new layer and name it **Star 3**.
12. Select the first frame of the Star 3 layer, insert an instance of the multistar symbol, and align the instance to the Stage in the center horizontally and vertically.
13. Insert a new layer and name it **Star 4**.
14. Select the first frame of the Star 4 layer, insert an instance of the multistar symbol, and align the instance to the Stage in the center horizontally and vertically. Now there are four instances of the multistar symbol on the Stage, each in its own layer, aligned in the center of the Stage.
15. Close the library.
16. Save the changes to the document.

Create an Animation

1. Use the following steps to create an animation in which a single star appears to divide into four stars, which each move to a Stage corner and then rotate around the Stage edges. Once you complete a layer, lock it. While you work, hide the layers you are not using so that you are not distracted by the objects on those layers. Use the Controller toolbar to step through the frames, if necessary. Use the Align panel to be sure the instances are correctly aligned.

2. Animate the instance in the Star 1 layer in frames 1 through 9 so it moves in increments diagonally toward the upper-left corner of the Stage, reaching the upper-left corner in frame 9.

3. In frames 10 through 14, move the instance in increments halfway down the left side of the Stage.

4. In frame 15, center the instance horizontally along the left edge of the Stage.

5. Animate the instance in the Star 2 layer in frames 1 through 9 so it moves in increments diagonally toward the lower-right corner of the Stage, reaching the lower-right corner in frame 9.

6. In frames 10 through 14, move the instance halfway up the right side of the Stage.

7. In frame 15, center the instance horizontally along the right edge of the Stage.

8. Animate the instance in the Star 3 layer in frames 1 through 9 so it moves in increments diagonally toward the upper-right corner of the Stage, reaching the upper-right corner in frame 9.

9. In frames 10 through 14, move the instance halfway across the top of the Stage, right to left.

10. In frame 15, center the instance vertically along the top edge of the Stage.

11. Animate the instance in the Star 4 layer in frames 1 through 9 so it moves in increments diagonally toward the lower-left corner of the Stage, reaching the lower-left corner in frame 9.

12. In frames 10 through 14, move the instance left to right along the bottom edge of the Stage.

13. In frame 15, center the instance vertically along the bottom edge of the Stage.

14. Preview the animation. In frame 9, it should look similar to Illustration A.

15. Print frame 9. If requested by your instructor, print each frame in the sequence.

16. Close the file, saving all changes.

17. Exit Flash.

Illustration A

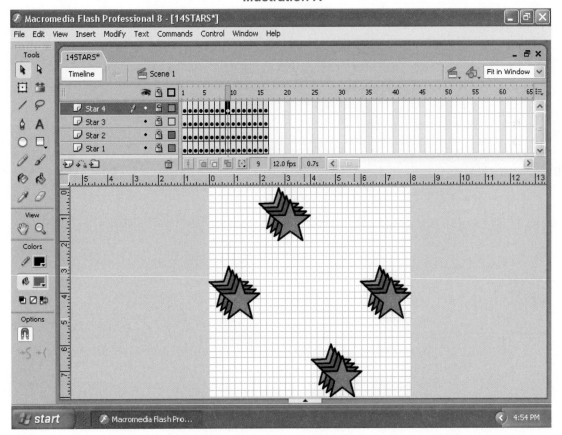

ON YOUR OWN

1. Start Flash and open ⊙14PIC or open 13MYPIC, the file you created in Exercise 13.

2. Save the document as 14MYPIC.

3. Convert at least one object in the application to a graphic symbol. Give the symbol an appropriate name, such as Blue Star.

4. Insert a new layer and give it an appropriate name, and then insert an instance of the graphic symbol.

5. Animate the instance, using alignment options to position it correctly on the Stage.

6. If necessary, edit the other layers so they align correctly as well.

7. When you have completed a layer, lock it to protect it from inadvertent edits.

8. Preview the animation.

9. If you want, insert additional instances of the symbol and animate them as well.

10. Print at least the last frame of the animation.

11. Close the document, saving all changes, and exit Flash.

   ✓ If requested by your instructor, print each frame of the animation before saving and exiting.

Skills Covered

- **Edit Symbols**
- **Modify Instances**

Software Skills Edit a symbol when you want to change every instance of that symbol in an application. Modify an instance when you want to change a single occurrence of the symbol.

Application Skills To make the moving star animation more exciting you decide to make some changes. First, you will edit the symbol to make it smaller and to rotate it, which will affect all instances of the symbol in the application. Next, you will modify the color and skew of selected instances to add variety to the animation.

TERMS

Alpha In Flash, a setting that controls the level of transparency of an instance.

Brightness The measurement of the amount of black or white added to a color. It controls the relative lightness or darkness of the image.

Symbol-editing mode The mode used to display only a symbol onscreen, so you can edit it without other objects on the Stage.

Tint The amount of a color other than black added to an image.

Transparency A measurement of how much you can see through a color, or, the level of opacity of a color.

NOTES

Edit Symbols

- You can edit a symbol to change its appearance or properties.
- When you edit a symbol, Flash updates all the instances of that symbol used in a document.
- There are three options for editing a symbol:
  - You can edit a symbol in place, which means you edit it on the Stage with other objects dimmed. The main Timeline is replaced by the symbol's Timeline, and the symbol's name displays in the edit bar at the top of the Stage.
  - You can edit a symbol in a new window so you are not distracted by other objects. You can minimize, restore, or resize the new window so that you can view the main window with the main Timeline. The new window displays the number 2 after the file name, and the symbol's name displays in the edit bar at the top of the Stage.
  - You can edit a symbol using **symbol-editing mode**. In symbol-editing mode, only the symbol

displays in the window, and the main Timeline is replaced by the symbol's Timeline. The symbol's name displays in the edit bar at the top of the Stage (see the illustration at the top of page 78).

- You can use all of Flash's drawing, modification, and transformation tools to edit a symbol just as you would edit any object.

Modify Instances

- You can edit or modify an instance without affecting the stored symbol.
- Changes made to an instance affect that instance only; other instances on other frames are not affected.
- You can skew, rotate, and scale an instance using the same commands you use to modify any object on the Stage.
- To modify the color and **transparency** of an instance you must use the options in the Property Inspector.

Symbol-Editing Mode

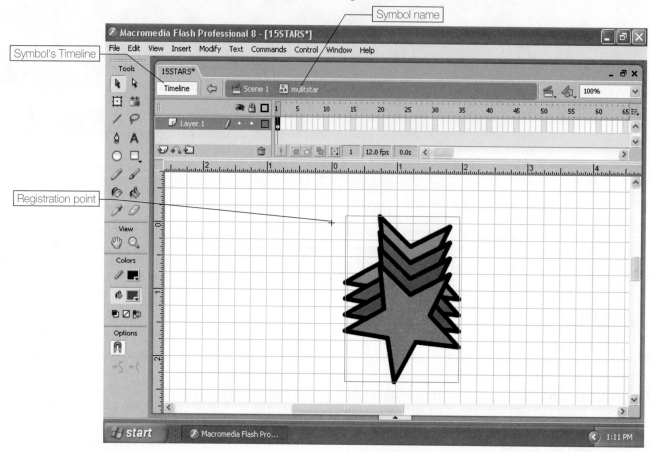

- In the Property Inspector, you may choose to modify one of the following for each instance:

  - **Brightness**, which controls the relative lightness or darkness of the instance. Set the scale on a range from 100%, which is white, to –100%, which is black.

  - **Tint**, which controls the amount of color applied to an instance (see the illustration below). You select the color, and then set the scale on a range from 0%, which is no tint, to 100%, which is completely saturated.

  - **Alpha**, which controls the transparency of an instance, without changing the color. Set the

    scale on a range from 0%, which is transparent, to 100%, which is opaque.

  - Advanced, which allows you to create customized colors and transparencies by setting the values independently. You can reduce the color or transparency values by a specified percentage, or you can modify the color or transparency values by a constant value.

- The properties that you set for an instance do not change, even if you edit the symbol on which the instance is based. For example, if you modify the tint of an instance, then change the color of the original symbol, the tint change remains in effect.

Setting Tint Options

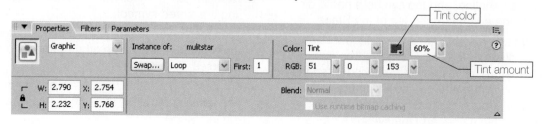

PROCEDURES

Edit a Symbol in Place

1. Double-click instance on Stage.

   OR

   a. Right-click instance on Stage.

   b. Click **Edit in Place**.

   OR

   a. Select instance.

   b. Click **Edit**.................Alt+E

   c. Click **Edit in Place**..........E, E, E, ↵Enter

2. Edit symbol as desired.

3. Double-click a blank area on Stage.

   OR

   a. Click **Edit**.................Alt+E

   b. Click **Edit Document**.............E

Edit a Symbol in a New Window

1. Right-click instance on Stage.

2. Click **Edit in New Window**.

3. Edit symbol as desired.

4. Click window **Close** button ✕.

Edit in Symbol-Editing Mode

1. Double-click symbol icon in Library panel.

   OR

   a. Right-click instance on Stage.

   b. Click **Edit**.

   OR

   a. Select instance.

   b. Click **Edit**.................Alt+E

   c. Click **Edit Symbols**............E, E, ↵Enter

2. Edit symbol as desired.

3. Click **Edit**....................Alt+E

4. Click **Edit Document**................E

Modify an Instance
To Transform the Instance

1. Select instance on Stage.

2. Use transformation tools to make changes.

To Set Brightness

1. Select instance on Stage.

2. Display Property Inspector.

3. Click **Color Styles** drop-down arrow.

4. Click **Brightness**.

   ✓ *Click None to remove color and transparency effects.*

5. Click **Brightness Amount** box.

6. Type brightness amount in a range from −100% to 100.

7. Press **Enter**....................↵Enter

   OR

   a. Click **Brightness Amount** drop-down arrow.

   b. Drag slider to set brightness in a range from −100% to 100%.

   c. Click outside slider to close it, if necessary.

To Set Tint

1. Select instance on Stage.

2. Display Property Inspector.

3. Click **Color Styles** drop-down arrow.

4. Click **Tint**.

   ✓ *Click None to remove color and transparency effects.*

5. Click color palette.

6. Click desired tint color.

   ✓ *You may also enter the specific amounts of red, green, and blue in the Red Color, Green Color, and Blue Color boxes to specify the tint color.*

7. Click **Tint Amount** box.

8. Type tint amount in a range from 0% to 100%.

9. Press **Enter**....................↵Enter

   OR

   a. Click **Tint Amount** drop-down arrow.

   b. Drag slider to set tint in a range from 0% to 100%.

   c. Click outside slider to close it, if necessary.

To Set Transparency

1. Select instance on Stage.

2. Display Property Inspector.

3. Click **Color Styles** drop-down arrow.

4. Click **Alpha**.

   ✓ *Click None to remove color and transparency effects.*

5. Click **Alpha Amount** box.

6. Type alpha amount in a range from 0% to 100%.

7. Press **Enter**....................↵Enter

   OR

   a. Click **Alpha Amount** drop-down arrow.

   b. Drag slider to set alpha amount in a range from 0% to 100%.

   c. Click outside slider to close it, if necessary.

To Customize Colors and Transparency

1. Select instance on Stage.

2. Display Property Inspector.

3. Click **Color Styles** drop-down arrow.

4. Click **Advanced**.

   ✓ *Click None to remove color and transparency effects.*

5. Click **Settings**.

   ✓ *The Advanced Effect dialog box displays.*

6. Use the controls on the left side to set the percentage of colors and transparency.

7. Use the controls on the right side to increase or decrease colors and transparency by a constant value.

8. Click **OK**........................↵Enter

EXERCISE DIRECTIONS

Edit a Symbol

1. Start Flash and open **14STARS**, the file you created in Exercise 14, or open **15DATA**. Save the file as **15STARS**.
2. Unlock all layers.
3. Open the mulitstar symbol in symbol-editing mode.
4. Rotate the symbol 45 degrees.
5. Resize the width of the symbol to approximately 1.75". The height should adjust automatically.
6. Close symbol-editing mode.
7. Select frame 15 on the Star 1 layer. Notice that all instances in the document have been modified.
8. Hide all but the Star 1 layer.

Modify Instances

1. Select frame 15 and then select the instance.
2. Display the Property Inspector.
3. Adjust the tint of the instance by selecting red #CC0066 from the color palette and setting the tint amount to 40%.

   ✓ Remember, you can type the code in the hexadecimal code box to select the color.

4. Skew the instance 25 degrees vertically.
5. Lock the Star 1 layer and hide it.
6. Display the Star 2 layer.
7. Select frame 15 and then select the instance. Adjust the tint using the same red (#CC0066) and setting the tint amount to 60%.
8. Skew the instance –25 degrees vertically.

9. Lock the Star 2 layer and hide it.
10. Display the Star 3 layer.
11. Select frame 15 and then select the instance. Adjust the tint by using blue #330049 and setting the tint amount to 40%.
12. Skew the instance 25 degrees horizontally.
13. Lock the Star 3 layer and hide it.
14. Display the Star 4 layer.
15. Select frame 15 and then select the instance. Adjust the tint using the same blue (#330049) and setting the tint amount to 60%.
16. Skew the instance –25 degrees horizontally.

Complete the Animation

1. In frames 8 through 15 on the Star 4 layer, make sure the instances align with the bottom edge of the Stage. If necessary, use the Align panel to adjust the alignment.
2. Lock the Star 4 layer.
3. Unlock the Star 2 layer and adjust the bottom edge alignment in frames 8 and 9 as necessary.
4. Lock the Star 2 layer.
5. Display all layers and preview the animation. Frame 15 should look similar to Illustration A. Note that the skew and color changes only affect the instances in frame 15.
6. Print frame 15. If requested by your instructor, print each frame in the sequence.
7. Close the file, saving all changes.
8. Exit Flash.

Illustration A

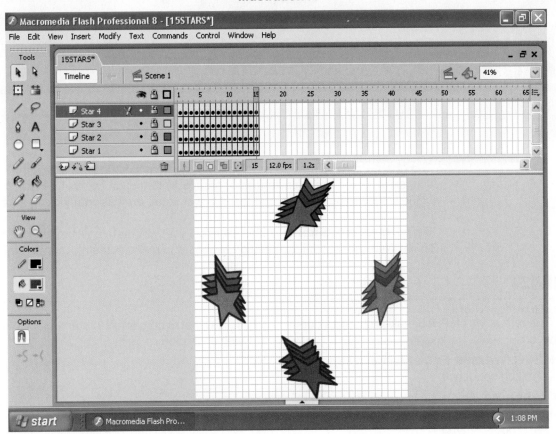

ON YOUR OWN

1. Start Flash and open ☺15PIC or open 14MYPIC, the file you created in Exercise 14.

2. Save the document as 15MYPIC.

3. Edit the symbol stored in the library. If there are multiple symbols, edit as many as you want.

4. Modify at least three instances in the animation. Scale, skew, or rotate the instances, and modify the color and transparency. You might want to try modifying the instances on more than one frame to extend the changes throughout the animation.

5. Preview the animation. Make adjustments to alignment as necessary.

6. If you want, insert additional instances of the symbol and animate them as well.

7. Print at least the one frame of the animation.

8. Close the document, saving all changes, and exit Flash.

   ✓ *If requested by your instructor, print each frame of the animation before saving and exiting.*

Skills Covered

- Motion Tweening
- Motion Tween Settings

Software Skills Use motion tweening to automatically animate the size, position, skew, or rotation of instances or groups. With motion tweening, Flash does most of the work for you, and the end result is a smooth, professional-looking animation.

Application Skills In this exercise, you will create an animation for the Grace Notes Web site. You will use motion tweening to make notes move and rotate.

TERMS

Easing The rate at which Flash makes changes during a tween.

Intermediate frames Frames between keyframes in an animation sequence.

Motion tweening Animation in which changes are made to position, size, rotation, and skew of instances, groups, or type.

Type Text that is converted into an object for use in a Flash animation.

NOTES

Motion Tweening

- In a Flash animation, the easiest way to create movement over time is to use **motion tweening**.

- With motion tweening, you can animate the size, position, rotation, and skew of instances, groups, or **type**.

  ✓ *Working with type is covered in Exercise 27.*

- To create motion tweened animation, you specify the starting properties of an object on the first keyframe and the ending properties of the object on the last keyframe.

- Flash fills in the frames between the two by evenly adjusting the properties to create the appearance of movement.

- If you change the number of frames between the two keyframes, or move the object in either keyframe, Flash automatically updates the animation.

- The easiest way to create a motion tween is by specifying tween properties in the Property Inspector.

- Alternatively, use the Create Motion Tween command.

- On the Timeline, **intermediate frames** in a motion tweened sequence are light blue, with a black arrow across them (see the following illustration).

Motion Tweened Frames in the Timeline

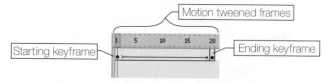

- You can also tween color or transparency.

  ✓ *Color tweening is covered in Exercise 17.*

- If you want to tween drawing objects, you must use shape tweening.

  ✓ *Shape tweening is covered in Exercise 18.*

Motion Tween Settings

- Set motion tween options in the Property Inspector.

- Motion tween options include the following (see illustration at the top of page 83):

- Scale. Select this check box if you are animating a change in size. There must be a change in size between the starting keyframe and the ending keyframe.
- Ease. Enter an **easing** value to control the rate of change between tweened frames. By default, the rate is constant.
  - Enter a negative value to begin the tween slowly and accelerate it toward the end of the sequence.
  - Enter a positive value to begin the tween rapidly and decelerate it toward the end of the sequence.
- Rotate. Select an option to control the direction of spin if you are animating rotation.

Motion Tween Options

- Orient to Path. Select this option to orient the baseline of the tweened object to a motion path.
- Sync. Select this option to synchronize the animation of graphic symbol instances with the main Timeline.
- Snap. Select this option to attach a tween object to a motion path by its registration point.

  ✓ *Motion paths are covered in Exercise 19.*

PROCEDURES

Create a Motion Tween

1. Select layer in Timeline.
2. Select keyframe where you want tween to begin.
3. Insert or create instance or group to tween.
4. Select frame where you want tween to end.
5. Insert a keyframe.
6. In ending keyframe, modify object so it appears as you want it at end of tween.
7. Select any frame between keyframes.

   ✓ *Tween becomes available in the Property Inspector.*

8. In Property Inspector, click **Tween Type** drop-down arrow.
9. Click **Motion**.

   ✓ *The Motion tween options become available.*

   OR

   a. Right-click any frame between keyframes
   b. Click **Create Motion Tween**

10. Set options as follows:
    - Select **Scale** check box to change the size of an object during a tween.
    - Enter a value in the **Ease** box to adjust the rate of change between tweened frames.
    - Select **Rotation options** to animate rotation clockwise, counterclockwise, automatically, or none.
    - Enter a value in the **Rotation count** box to specify how many times you want an item to rotate.

Use the Create Motion Tween Command

1. Select layer in the Timeline.
2. Select keyframe where you want tween to begin.
3. Insert or create instance or group to tween.
4. Click **Insert** .... Alt + I
5. Click **Timeline** .... T
6. Click **Create Motion Tween** C

7. Select frame where you want tween to end.
8. Insert a keyframe.

   ✓ *The Motion tween options become available in the Property Inspector.*

9. In ending keyframe, modify object so it appears as you want it at end of tween.
10. Select any frame between keyframes.
11. Set options as follows in the Property Inspector:
    - Select **Scale** check box to change the size of an object during a tween.
    - Enter a value in the **Ease** box to adjust the rate of change between tweened frames.
    - Select **Rotation options** to animate rotation clockwise, counterclockwise, automatically, or none.
    - Enter a value in the **Rotation count** box to specify how many times you want an item to rotate.

EXERCISE DIRECTIONS

Create a Motion Tween

1. Start Flash and open ⬤16DATA. Save the file as **16NOTES**.
2. Convert the grouped object to a graphic symbol named **Note 1**, with the registration point in the lower-left corner.
3. Change the zoom to Fit in Window.
4. Align the note in the upper-left corner of the Stage.
5. Insert a keyframe in frame 20.
6. Align the note in the lower-right corner of the Stage.
7. Select frame 10.
8. In the Property Inspector, select Motion from the Tween drop-down list.
9. In the Property Inspector, deselect the Scale check box.
10. Select CW from the Rotation options drop-down list and type **3** in the Rotation count box.
11. In the Timeline, select frame 1.
12. Preview the animation. The note should move diagonally from the upper left of the Stage to the lower right, while rotating three times clockwise.
13. Lock and hide layer 1.

Add a Second Motion Tween

1. Create a new layer and select frame 1.
2. Insert an instance of the Note 1 symbol and align it in the lower-left corner of the Stage.
3. Insert a keyframe in frame 20 and align the instance in the upper-right corner of the Stage.
4. Select frame 10 and then select Motion from the Tween drop-down list in the Property Inspector.

5. Insert a keyframe on frame 10. Notice that Flash automatically divides the motion tween into two parts.
6. Align the instance on frame 10 in the center of the Stage, horizontally and vertically.
7. Scale the instance on frame 10 to 300% of its original size.
8. Select frame 1 and preview the animation.
9. Lock layer 2 and show both layers.

Modify the Motion Tween Options

1. On layer 1, select frame 10.
2. In the Property Inspector, in the Ease box, enter the value 100.
3. On layer 2, select frame 5 and set the Ease value to -100.
4. On layer 2, select frame 15. Notice that there is no Ease value entered because frames 10 through 20 are a separate tween.
5. Set the Ease value to 100.
6. Select frame 1 and preview the animation.
7. Select frame 9. It should look similar to Illustration A.
8. Select frame 1 and print it.

   ✓ *Because no actual content is entered on the intermediate frames in the tween, there is no need to print any other frames.*

9. Close the file, saving all changes.
10. Exit Flash.

Illustration A

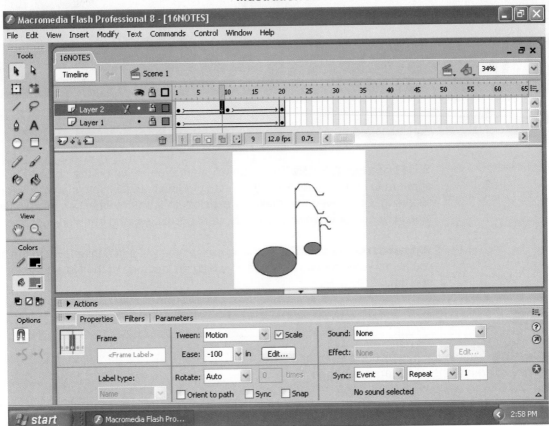

ON YOUR OWN

1. Start Flash and create a new document.
2. Save the document as **16MYPIC**.
3. Set the Stage Properties so that the ruler units are inches and the Stage size is 6" by 6".
4. Create a motion tween animation that you could use on a Web site or in a presentation for a club, organization, or sports team. For example, you could animate a bouncing ball for soccer or basketball, or animate a flower for a garden club.
5. Start by creating the drawing object you want to animate, and then convert it to a graphic symbol. You may work with more than one symbol, if desired.

6. Insert instances and create motion tweens to create the animation. Remember, you can use multiple layers to create multiple tweens. You can also create a Background layer to hold static images.
7. Use the motion tween options to optimize the tween, including easing, scaling, and rotations.
8. Preview the animation. Make adjustments as necessary or modify instances to enhance the animation.
9. Print frame 1 of the tween.
10. Close the document, saving all changes, and exit Flash.

Skills Covered

- **Tween the Color of an Instance**

Software Skills To create an animation in which the color of an instance appears to change over time, you use color tweening, which is a variation of motion tweening. Color tweening makes it possible to create animations in which instances fade in or out, or in which color tints, transparencies, and brightness change.

Application Skills In this exercise, you will add a third layer to the animation you just created for Grace Notes, in which an instance of the Note 1 symbol fades in and out.

TERMS

Color tweening Animation in which the color or transparency of an instance appears to change over time.

NOTES

Tween the Color of an Instance

- To make gradual color changes in an animation sequence, or to make an instance fade in or out, you can tween the color settings.

- **Color tweening** can only be used on instances. To change the color of a shape over time, use shape tweening.

  ✓ Shape tweening is covered in Exercise 18.

- To create a color tween, set the color or transparency in the starting keyframe and in the ending keyframe, and then use a motion tween to have Flash automatically fill in the frames between.

  ✓ Setting color and transparency options is covered in Exercise 15.

- As with a standard motion tween, you can create the tween by setting motion tween options in the Property Inspector by using the Create Motion Tween command.

- You can tween the position, scale, rotation, or skew of the instance as well.

  ✓ Refer to Exercise 16 for more on motion tweening.

PROCEDURES

Tween the Color of an Instance
Use the Property Inspector

1. Select layer in Timeline.
2. Select keyframe where you want tween to begin.
3. Insert or create instance to tween.
4. Select instance.
5. In Property Inspector, set the starting color and/or transparency properties.
6. Position or transform instance as desired.
7. Select frame where you want tween to end.
8. Insert a keyframe.
9. In ending keyframe, select instance and then set ending color and/or transparency properties.
10. Position or transform instance as desired.
11. Select any frame between keyframes.

    ✓ *Tween becomes available in the Property Inspector.*

12. In Property Inspector, click the **Tween Type** drop-down arrow.
13. Click **Motion**.

    ✓ *The Motion tween options become available.*

14. Set motion tween options.

Use the Create Motion Tween Command

1. Select layer in Timeline.
2. Select keyframe where you want tween to begin.
3. Insert or create instance to tween, setting color and transparency settings as desired.
4. Click **Insert**................Alt + I
5. Click **Timeline**.....................T
6. Click **Create Motion Tween**........C
7. Select frame where you want tween to end.
8. Insert a keyframe.

    ✓ *The Motion tween options become available in the Property Inspector.*

9. In ending keyframe, modify color and transparency so it appears as you want it at the end of the tween.
10. Select any frame between keyframes.
11. In Property Inspector, set motion tween options as follows:

    - Select **Scale** check box to change the size of an object during a tween.
    - Enter a value in the **Ease** box to adjust the rate of change between tweened frames.
    - Select **Rotation options** to animate rotation clockwise, counterclockwise, automatically, or none.
    - Enter a value in the **Rotation count** box to specify how many times you want an item to rotate.

EXERCISE DIRECTIONS

Create a Color Tween to Fade In

1. Start Flash and open **16NOTES**, the file you created in Exercise 16, or open ●**17DATA**. Save the file as **17NOTES**.
2. Insert a new layer in the Timeline and name it **Fade**.
3. Hide the other two layers.
4. Insert an instance of the Note 1 symbol on frame 1 of the Fade layer.
5. Resize the instance to approximately 3.5" high. The width should adjust automatically.
6. Align the instance so it is horizontally centered and vertically aligned with the top edge of the Stage. It should look similar to Illustration A on page 88.
7. Make sure the instance is selected, and then, in the Property Inspector, set the Alpha amount to 0%, making the instance completely transparent.
8. Insert a keyframe on frame 10 of the Fade layer.
9. Select the instance on frame 10 and change the Alpha amount to 100%, making it completely opaque.

    ✓ *Even though the instance is completely transparent, you can still select it. Simply click near the center top of the Stage and the bounding box displays.*

10. Select frame 5.
11. In the Property Inspector, select to create a motion tween.
12. Deselect the Scale check box.

Create a Color Tween to Fade Out

1. Insert a keyframe on frame 20, select the instance, and change the Alpha amount of the instance to 0%, making it transparent again.
2. Select frame 15 and create a motion tween.

3. Preview the animation with just the Fade layer displayed.

4. Display all layers, and then preview the animation again.

5. Move the Fade layer to the back of the Stage and preview the animation again. Now, the other animated notes display in front of the fading note.

✓ *There is nothing to print in this exercise. Frame 1 appears the same as in Exercise 16. Because the note is transparent, and because the animation is tweened, the other frames print the same as Frame 1.*

6. Close the file, saving all changes.
7. Exit Flash.

Illustration A

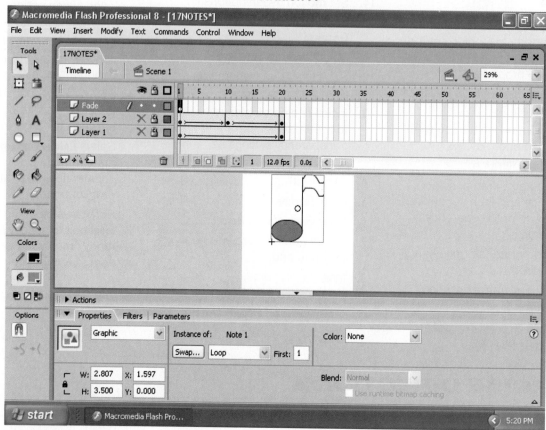

ON YOUR OWN

1. Start Flash and open **16MYPIC**, the file you created in Exercise 16, or open **17PIC**.

2. Save the document as **17MYPIC**.

3. Add a layer on which you can create a color tween to fade an instance in and out, or out and in. You may insert an instance from an existing symbol you created in Exercise 16, or create a new symbol so you can insert a different instance.

4. You may also add motion to the tween, such as a rotation, skew, or scale change.

5. Adjust alignment for the best effect.

6. Place the Fade layer in the appropriate position so other layers display in front of it, or behind it for the best effect.

7. Preview the animation. Make adjustments as necessary or modify instances to enhance the animation.

8. Close the document, saving all changes, and exit Flash.

Exercise | 18

Skills Covered

- Shape Tweening
- Use Shape Hints

Software Skills Use shape tweening in Flash to animate a change in a shape over time, in effect making one shape morph into a different shape. Use shape hints to control the way the shape changes.

Application Skills The Black Cat pet shop has asked you to design an animation for its Web site. In this exercise, you will use shape tweening to create a sequence in which a plain black rectangle morphs into a cat's head.

TERMS

Blend The way Flash changes lines and angles during a shape tween.

Shape hints Markers used to pinpoint corresponding locations in the starting keyframe and ending keyframe of a shape tween.

Shape tweening Animation in which a shape appears to change over time.

NOTES

Shape Tweening

- Use **shape tweening** to animate a change in a shape over time. For example, you can make a square tween into an oval.

- Shape tweening only works on shapes. You cannot use shape tweening to animate groups, instances, type, or bitmap graphics.

- You can use shape tweening to animate a change in location, size, and color of a shape.

- On the Timeline, the frames between keyframes in a shape tweened sequence are light green, with a black arrow across them (see the following illustration).

Shape Tweened Frames in the Timeline

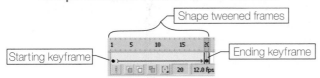

- You set properties for a shape tween in the Property Inspector.

- Shape tween properties include easing and **blend**.
  - Use Distributive blending when you are tweening shapes with curves and irregular lines.

  - Use Angular blending when you are tweening shapes with sharp corners and straight lines.

- To add elements to a shape during tweening you must insert the new elements on the last keyframe.

- Shape tweening creates a larger file than motion tweening. You should animate a sequence using a motion tween instead of a shape tween whenever possible.

Use Shape Hints

- Because of the way Flash fills in the frames between the starting keyframe and the ending keyframe, you might see blank areas or contorted lines during a complex shape tween sequence.

- Use **shape hints** to control the shape tween.

- Shape hints label a point in the starting keyframe and a corresponding point in the ending keyframe.

- Flash moves the starting point directly to the corresponding ending point, creating a smooth transition during the shape tween, resulting in a more realistic change.

- Shape hints are identified using the letters of the alphabet; you can have up to 26 shape hints in a tween (see the illustration on page 90).

Shape Hints

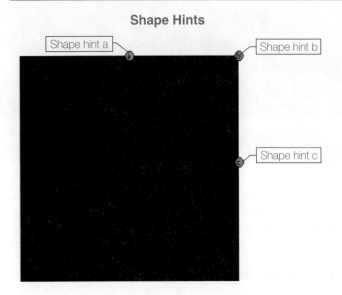

Shape hint a

Shape hint b

Shape hint c

- In order to keep track of shape hints, you should try to place them in order—either clockwise or counterclockwise around a shape.
- Shape hints are particularly useful in shape tweens involving more than one shape or color.
- Shape hints are usually not necessary to control a simple shape tween.

PROCEDURES

Tween a Shape

1. Select layer in Timeline.
2. Select keyframe where you want tween to begin.
3. Draw or paste starting shape.
4. Select frame where you want tween to end.
5. Insert a keyframe.
6. Modify shape on the ending keyframe.
7. Select any frame between keyframes.

   ✓ Tween becomes available in the Property Inspector.

8. In Property Inspector, click **Tween Type** drop-down arrow.
9. Click **Shape**.

   ✓ The Shape Tween options become available.

10. Click **Ease** box.
11. Enter an easing value.
12. Click **Blend** drop-down arrow.
13. Select one of the following:
    - **Distributive** to create an animation in which the intermediate shapes are smooth and regular.

    - **Angular** to create an animation that preserves the apparent corners and straight lines of the original object in the intermediate shapes.

Use Shape Hints

1. Create shape tween.
2. Select starting keyframe in shape tween.
3. Click **Modify**................[Alt]+[M]
4. Click **Shape**...........................[P]
5. Click **Add Shape Hint**.............[A]

   ✓ Flash inserts the first shape hint (a) on the frame.

6. Drag shape hint to the point you want to mark.
7. Select ending keyframe.
8. Drag shape hint to the point that corresponds to the point marked in step 6.
9. Repeat steps 3 through 8 to insert additional shape hints.

Show/Hide All Shape Hints (Ctrl+Alt+H)

1. Click **View**..................[Alt]+[V]
2. Click **Show All Shape Hints**.......[A]

OR

1. Right-click any shape hint.
2. Click **Show Hints**.

   ✓ A check mark beside the command indicates hints are displayed.

Delete a Shape Hint

1. Select starting keyframe.
2. Drag shape hint off Stage.

OR

1. Right-click shape hint to delete.
2. Click **Remove Hint**.

Delete All Shape Hints

1. Select starting keyframe.
2. Click **Modify**...............[Alt]+[M]
3. Click **Shape**.........................[P]
4. Click **Remove All Hints**............[M]

OR

1. Right-click any shape hint.
2. Click **Remove All Hints**.

EXERCISE DIRECTIONS

Create the Starting Shape

1. Start Flash and create a new document. Save the file as **18CAT**.
2. Set document properties to change the ruler units to inches.
3. Display the rulers and the grid, and set the zoom so you can see the Stage.
4. Select the Rectangle tool.
5. Set the fill color to black and the stroke color to no stroke.
6. On frame 1, draw a square approximately 3" by 3".
7. Align the square in the center of the Stage, horizontally and vertically.

Creating the Ending Shape

1. Select frame 20 and insert a keyframe.
2. Deselect the square, and then use the Selection tool to reshape it into an oval.

   ✓ *To reshape the square, position the mouse pointer along the middle of a side until the reshape curve pointer displays, then drag out to transform the edge of the square into a curve. Do not worry if the shape is not a perfect oval. Repeat on each side to draw an oval. For a refresher on reshaping, refer to Exercise 6.*

3. Select the Brush tool, and drag to draw two pointed ears at the top of the circle (refer to Illustration A on page 92).
4. Select the Oval tool and change the fill color to blue.
5. Drag to draw an oval cat's eye.
6. Duplicate the oval eye and then drag the duplicate into position as the second eye.
7. Change the fill color to pink and draw a small circle for the nose.

Create the Shape Tween

1. Select frame 10.
2. In the Property Inspector, select Shape from the Tween drop-down list.
3. Set the Easing to 100.
4. Set the Blend to Distributive.
5. Select frame 1.
6. Preview the animation. Although the square morphs into the cat's head, there are some uneven and awkward transformations in the intermediate frames of the sequence.

Add Shape Hints

1. Select frame 1.
2. Add a shape hint.
3. Drag the shape hint to the midpoint along the top edge of the square.
4. Select frame 20.
5. Drag the shape hint to the midpoint of the top of the circle. Frame 20 should look similar to Illustration A.
6. Print frame 20.
7. Select frame 1 and preview the animation. This time, it should morph more smoothly and realistically.
8. Close the file, saving all changes.
9. Exit Flash.

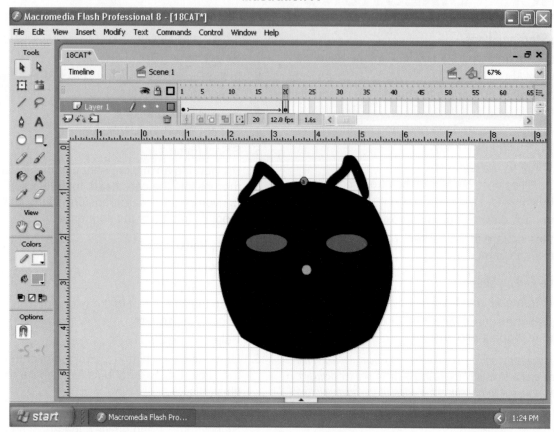

ON YOUR OWN

1. Start Flash and create a new document. Save the document as **18MYPIC.**

2. Create an animation using shape tweening to illustration a special event or holiday. For example, you might morph a circle into a heart for Valentine's day or a circle into a jack-o-lantern for Halloween.

3. Draw the shape in the starting keyframe, using the Flash drawing tools. Enhance and modify the shape as necessary using colors and other tools.

4. In the ending keyframe, modify the shape as you want it to appear at the end of the animation.

5. Use shape hints to control the tween.

6. If you want, create a background layer or even a motion tween layer to enhance the animation.

7. Preview the animation as often as necessary, and then tweak it until it creates a smooth, realistic morph.

8. When you are satisfied, print the ending keyframe.

9. Close the document, saving all changes, and exit Flash.

Skills Covered

■ **Tween Motion Along a Path**   ■ **Display Multiple Frames at Once**

Software Skills Use a motion guide layer to control the path along which an instance or group moves. You can link multiple layers to the same motion guide layer, ensuring consistency between animations. Display multiple frames at once on the Stage so you can check your animation for errors.

Application Skills The owner of Grace Notes has asked you to create another animation with multiple notes moving around the screen. In this exercise, you will use a motion guide layer to make sure all instances follow the same motion path. You will also use onion skinning to check the progress of each frame.

TERMS

Motion guide A layer in which you draw a path that can be linked to the motion of instances and groups in other layers.

Onion skins A Flash feature used to display multiple frames of a sequence on the Stage at the same time.

Path A line or shape that is used to define the linear motion of an instance or group.

NOTES

Tween Motion Along a Path

■ Use a **motion guide** when you want to animate motion along a set **path**.

■ You draw the path on the motion guide, and then link it to the layer(s) containing the motion tweened object.

■ You position the object along the path using its registration point or its snap ring.

■ Use the Pen, Pencil, Line, Circle, Rectangle, or Brush tool in Merge Drawing Model to draw the path.

■ If you draw the path in Object Drawing Model, it will not work correctly.

■ There should not be any breaks, gaps, or intersections along the path.

■ You can link multiple layers to a single motion guide in order to make multiple objects follow the same path.

■ Multiple objects can follow the path at the same time, or consecutively.

■ In the layer list, layers linked to a motion guide are displayed below the motion guide layer, with their names indented (see the following illustration).

Motion Guide Layer in the Timeline

■ Hide the motion guide layer if you don't want the path to show in the animation.

Display Multiple Frames at Once

■ By default, Flash displays one frame of an animation sequence at a time on the Stage.

■ Use **onion skins** to display multiple frames on Stage at once.

■ Onion skin markers in the Timeline header indicate which frames are displayed.

■ When the Onion Skin option is on, the current frame displays on the Stage in full color, while surrounding frames are dimmed (see the illustration below).

■ By default, only the current frame is active so that you cannot edit the frames that are dimmed.

■ You can set Flash to enable editing of multiple frames. In this mode, no objects are dimmed.

■ You can select the number of frames to display at once, and you can anchor the onion skin markers so that the display on Stage does not change when the playhead moves.

■ Hidden layers do not display when the Onion Skin option is on.

■ If a layer is locked, only the active frame displays.

Onion Skinning

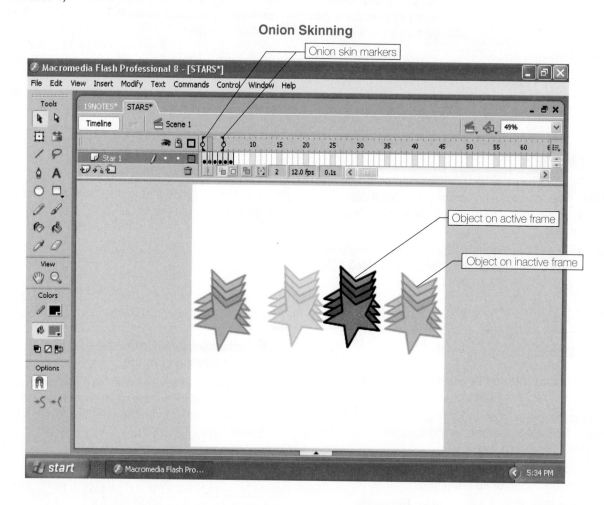

PROCEDURES

Tween Motion Along a Path

1. Create motion tween animation.

   ✓ Refer to Exercise 16.

2. Select starting keyframe.
3. In Property Inspector, select one of the following options:
   - **Orient to path** to set the baseline of the object to follow the path.
   - **Snap** to set the object to snap to the path at the snap ring location.
4. Select layer containing motion tween.
5. Click **Add Motion Guide** button under Layer list on Timeline.

   OR

   a. Click **Insert**...............[Alt]+[I]
   b. Click **Timeline**.......................[T]
   c. Click **Motion Guide**..............[M]

6. Make sure Object Drawing is off.
7. Draw the path.

   ✓ You may use the Oval, Rectangle, Pencil, Pen, or Brush tool.

8. Select frame 1 on motion tween layer.
9. Drag instance to start of path.

   ✓ When the instance is correctly positioned, the snap ring or the baseline should align with the path. It may take some practice to position the instance correctly.

10. Select ending keyframe.
11. Drag instance by its registration point to end of path.

   ✓ When the instance is correctly positioned, the snap ring or the baseline should align with the path. It may take some practice to position the instance correctly.

Link Layers to an Existing Motion Guide Layer

■ In Layer list, move layer containing animation to a spot directly below motion guide layer.

   OR

   Insert new layer directly below motion guide layer.

   OR

   a. Select a layer directly below the motion guide and its linked layers.
   b. Click **Modify**.............[Alt]+[M]
   c. Click **Timeline**.....................[M]
   d. Click **Layer Properties**..........[L]
   e. Click **Guided**.
   f. Click **OK**....................[↵Enter]

Unlink Layers from a Motion Guide Layer

■ In Layer list, move layer to a spot above motion guide layer.

   OR

   a. Select layer.
   b. Click **Modify**.............[Alt]+[M]
   c. Click **Timeline**.....................[M]
   d. Click **Layer Properties**..........[L]
   e. Click **Normal**.
   f. Click **OK**....................[↵Enter]

Delete a Motion Guide Layer

1. Right-click layer.
2. Click **Delete Layer**.

   OR

1. Select layer.
2. Click **Delete Layer** button.

Display Multiple Frames on Stage at Once

■ Click **Onion Skin** button.

   ✓ Click button again to return to normal display.

Show Inactive Frames as Outlines

■ Click **Onion Skin Outlines** button.

Change Onion Skin Display

■ Drag onion skin markers on Timeline header to new position.

   OR

1. Click **Modify Onion Markers** button.
2. Click one of the following options:
   - **Always Show Markers** to show onion skin markers on Timeline even when onion skinning is off.
   - **Anchor Onion** to keep onion skinning from moving with the playhead.
   - **Onion 2** to show two frames on either side of the current frame (default).
   - **Onion 5** to show five frames on either side of the current frame.
   - **Onion All** to show all frames.

Enable Editing of Multiple Frames

■ Click **Edit Multiple Frames** button.

EXERCISE DIRECTIONS

Create a Motion Tween

1. Start Flash and open the file ⊛19DATA. Save the file as **19NOTES**.

2. Display the rulers and the grid, and set the zoom so you can see the Stage.

3. Rename Layer 1 **Blue Note** and select frame 1.

4. Display the Library panel and insert an instance of the Note 1 symbol on frame 1 of the Blue Note layer.

5. Select frame 20 and insert a keyframe.

6. Move the instance to anywhere else on the Stage or the Pasteboard.

7. Select frame 1 and then, in the Property Inspector, select Motion from the Tween type drop-down list.

8. Deselect the Scale check box.

9. Select the Snap check box.

10. Save the changes to the document.

Create a Motion Guide

1. Select and hide the Blue Note layer and then insert a motion guide.

2. Select the Oval tool and set the fill color to no fill and the stroke color to black. Make sure that Object Drawing is off.

3. In frame 1 of the motion guide layer, draw an oval approximately 6" wide by 2.5" high.

4. Center the oval horizontally and vertically on the Stage.

5. Deselect the oval, and then select the Eraser tool.

6. Erase approximately 1.5" of the oval stroke, starting at the right end of the oval and moving up and to the left (refer to Illustration A).

7. Display the Blue Note layer and select frame 1.

8. Drag the instance by its center so that its center snap ring snaps to the end point of the path nearest to the top of the Stage (the upper end of the path).

   ✓ *Remember, it may take a few tries to get the instance to snap to the path.*

9. Select frame 20.

10. Drag the instance by its center so that its center snap ring snaps to the end point of the path nearest to the right edge of the Stage (the lower end of the path).

11. Preview the animation. The note should move smoothly counterclockwise around the path.

12. Save the changes to the file.

Illustration A

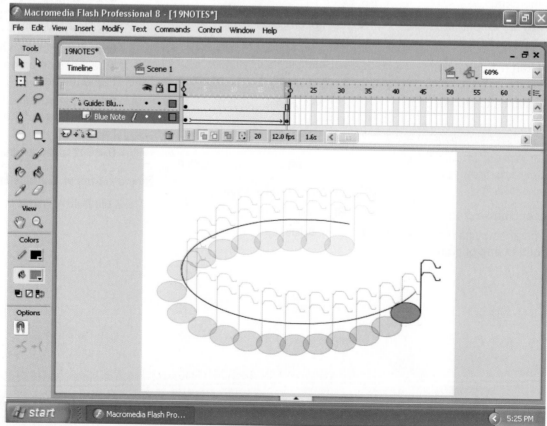

Display Multiple Frames at Once

1. Display onion skins.
2. Change the Onion Skin options to show all frames. The Stage should look similar to Illustration A.
3. Turn off onion skinning so that only one frame is displayed on the Stage.

Link Additional Layers to the Motion Guide

1. Select the Blue Note layer and lock it, and then insert a new layer.

   ✓ *The layer displays between the Blue Note layer and the guide layer, by default linked to the guide layer.*

2. Name the new layer **Green Note**.
3. Insert an instance of the Note 1 symbol on frame 1 of the Green Note layer, and position it so that it is exactly overlapping the note on the Blue Note layer.

   ✓ *When correctly positioned, it will appear as if there is only one note on the Stage.*

4. Select frame 20 of the Green Note layer and insert a keyframe.
5. Move the instance to a location along the path approximately 3" to the left of the Blue Note.

6. Select the note in frame 20 on the Green Note layer and modify the color tint to 60% green (#009966).
7. Select frame 1 and create a motion tween.
8. Deselect the Scale check box and select the Snap check box.
9. If necessary, adjust the position of the note in frame 1 and frame 20 to be sure it snaps to the path.
10. Preview the animation. Both notes should follow the path, with one note stopping sooner and changing to green.
11. Save the changes.
12. Repeat steps 1 through 10 to add a third note to the animation on a layer named **Violet Note**. Change its tint to 60% violet (#CC0099) and set it to stop about 3" to the left of the Green Note.
13. Preview the animation with all three notes and make adjustments as necessary. Frame 20 should look similar to Illustration B. Print frame 20.
14. Hide the guide layer and preview the animation again.
15. Display the guide layer and lock all layers.
16. Close the file, saving all changes.
17. Exit Flash.

Illustration B

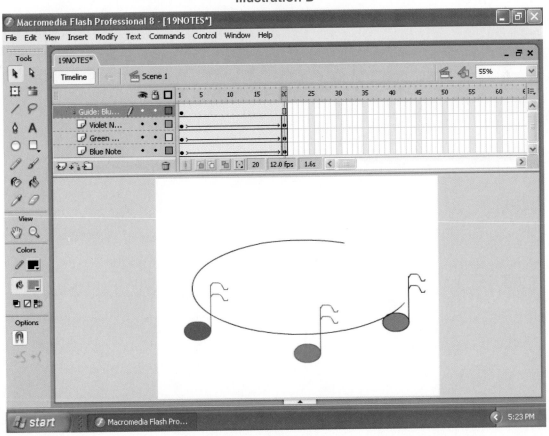

ON YOUR OWN

1. Start Flash and create a new document. Save the document at **19MYPIC**.

2. Create an animation using a motion guide layer to illustrate another special event or holiday. For example, you might animate presents to illustrate a birthday.

3. Start by drawing the shape you want to animate, and then converting it into a symbol. If you have a symbol from an earlier exercise that you want to use, copy and paste it from its current library into the library for the **19MYPIC** document.

4. Insert the instance you want to animate and create a motion tween.

5. Insert a motion guide and draw a path.

6. Align the instance along the path in the starting and ending keyframes to create the animation.

7. Link at least one more layer to the guide and animate another instance of the same symbol or of a different symbol.

8. Use onion skinning to view multiple frames at the same time so you can see how the motion tween progresses.

9. When you are satisfied, print the ending keyframe.

10. Close the document, saving all changes, and exit Flash.

Exercise | 20

Skills Covered

Software Skills Print the frames of your Flash animations so you can see them on paper and share them with others. You can set options to control the way frames print on a page, including printing storyboards that you can use to track the flow and development of an application.

Application Skills In this exercise you will print the animation you created for Grace Notes in Exercise 19.

TERMS

Frame margin The black space between printed frames in a storyboard.

Landscape orientation Content is printed horizontally across the wider side of the page.

Portrait orientation Content is printed horizontally across the narrower side of the page.

Scene A segment of an application.

Storyboard A pictorial depiction of an entire application, showing frame content and flow.

Thumbnail A miniature picture.

NOTES

Set Up Pages for Printing

■ Use the Page Setup dialog box to select page settings to control how frames will display on the printed page (see the following illustration).

Page Setup Dialog Box

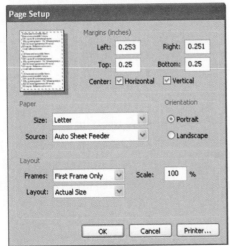

■ You can set page margins, specify centering options, and select whether to use **portrait** or **landscape orientation**.

■ In addition, use the Page Setup dialog box to select frame layout options.

■ For example, you can choose the size of the printed frames, how many frames to print per page, whether or not to label frames with the **scene** and frame numbers, and whether or not to use a **storyboard** format.

   ✓ *You learn about scenes in Exercise 29.*

■ If you decide to use a storyboard format, you can also select whether to include borders around each **thumbnail**, how many thumbnails to print across each page, and how wide a **frame margin** to leave.

Print an Animation

■ Print frames from your Flash files while you work.

■ Seeing the frames printed on paper can help you plan, organize, and revise your animations.

■ Use the Print dialog box to select the frames to print and the number of copies (see the illustration on page 100).

99

Print Dialog Box

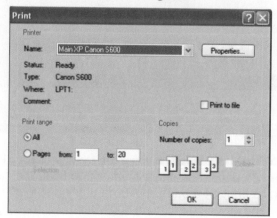

PROCEDURES

Set Up Pages for Printing

To Set Margins

1. Click **File**.....................`Alt`+`F`
2. Click **Page Setup**...................`U`
3. Click a margin box:
   - **Left**..........................`Alt`+`L`
   - **Right**.........................`Alt`+`R`
   - **Top**..........................`Alt`+`T`
   - **Bottom**.....................`Alt`+`B`
4. Type width of margin.
5. Click **OK**.........................`↵Enter`

To Set Centering

1. Click **File**.....................`Alt`+`F`
2. Click **Page Setup**...................`U`
3. Select one or both centering check boxes:
   - **Horizontal** to center content horizontally.
   - **Vertical** to center content vertically.
4. Click **OK**.........................`↵Enter`

To Set Orientation

1. Click **File**.....................`Alt`+`F`
2. Click **Page Setup**...................`U`
3. Select one of the following :
   - **Portrait**.....................`Alt`+`O` to print across the narrow side of page.
   - **Landscape**.....................`Alt`+`A` to print across the wide side of page.
4. Click **OK**.........................`↵Enter`

To Set Layout Options

1. Click **File**.....................`Alt`+`F`
2. Click **Page Setup**...................`U`
3. Click **Frames** drop-down arrow.....................`Alt`+`F`
4. Select one of the following:
   - **First Frame only** to print only the first frame of the animation.
   - **All Frames** to print all frames in the animation.
5. Click **Layout** drop-down arrow.....................`Alt`+`Y`
6. Select Layout options as follows:
   a. Click **Actual Size**.
   b. Enter scaling value, if necessary.

   OR

   a. Click **Fit on One Page**.

   OR

   a. Click a Storyboard option:
   - **Storyboard – Boxes** to print the storyboard with borders around each frame.
   - **Storyboard – Grid** to print the storyboard with grid-lines between frames.
   - **Storyboard – Blank** to print the storyboard without borders or gridlines.
   b. Click **Frames** box......`Alt`+`M`
   c. Enter number of frames to print across the page.

   d. Click **Frame margin** box..........................`Alt`+`G`
   e. Enter width of frame margin.
   f. Click to select or clear **Label** frames box.............`Alt`+`E` to include or remove frame number labels.
7. Click **OK**.........................`↵Enter`

To Set Paper Options

1. Click **File**.....................`Alt`+`F`
2. Click **Page Setup**...................`U`
3. If necessary, click **Size** drop-down arrow...............`Alt`+`Z` to select paper size.
4. If necessary, click **Source** drop-down arrow...............`Alt`+`S` to select paper source.
5. Click **OK**.........................`↵Enter`

Print an Animation

1. Click **File**.....................`Alt`+`F`
2. Click **Print**...........................`P`
3. Click **All**.....................`Alt`+`A` to print all pages.

   OR

   a. Click **Pages**..............`Alt`+`G`
   b. Click **from** box..........`Alt`+`F`
   c. Type first page to print.
   d. Click **to** box.............`Alt`+`T`
   e. Type last page to print.
4. Click **Number of copies** box..........................`Alt`+`C`
5. Enter number of copies to print.
6. Click **OK**.........................`↵Enter`

EXERCISE DIRECTIONS

1. Start Flash and open the file **⊙20DATA**. Save the file as **20NOTES**.
2. Open the Page Setup dialog box.
3. Select options as follows:
   - Leave the default page margins and centering.
   - Select landscape orientation.
   - Select to print all frames.
   - Select to print a storyboard with boxes.
   - Select to print five frames across the page with the frame margin set to .2.
   - Select to print frame labels.
4. Click OK to store the settings and close the dialog box.
5. Print all pages in the animation. The result should look similar to Illustration A.

6. Open the Page Setup dialog box and change back to the default options as follows:
   - Margins should be .25" on all sides.
   - Both Horizontal and Vertical centering should be selected.
   - Orientation should be Portrait.
   - Flash should be set to print All frames in their actual size, at 100% scale.
7. Click OK to store the settings and close the dialog box.
8. Close the file, saving all changes.
9. Exit Flash.

Illustration A

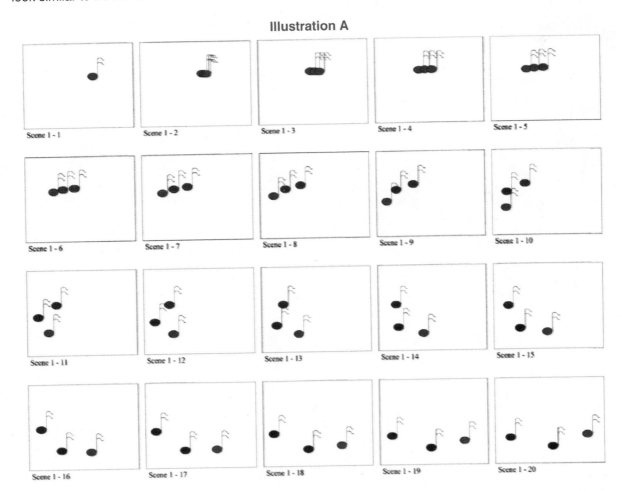

ON YOUR OWN

1. Start Flash and open **19MYPIC**, the file you worked with in Exercise 19, or open **20PIC**. Save the document as **20MYPIC**.

2. Select page setup options and print the animation.

3. Try different page setup options and print the animation again.

4. Change the page setup options back to the defaults.

5. Close the document, saving all changes, and exit Flash.

End of Lesson Projects

- Summary Exercise
- Application Exercise
- Curriculum Integration Exercise
- Critical Thinking Exercise

Exercise | 21

Summary Exercise

Software Skills In this exercise, you will begin work on an animation to use on the Web site for Castle Gate Productions, a music company. You will create a symbol from the castle drawing you created in Exercise 8 and you will use step-by-step animation to move an instance of the symbol onto the Stage. You will then add a layer and use a motion tween to move an instance into position.

DIRECTIONS

Convert a Drawing to a Symbol

1. Start Flash and open ⏺**21DATA**. Save the file as **21CASTLE**.
2. Display the rulers and the grid and adjust the height of the Timeline, if desired.
3. Change the zoom to Fit in Window.
4. Select the group of drawing objects and convert it to a graphic symbol with the name **Castle 1**.
5. Move the instance into the Pasteboard area to the left of the Stage, so that its right edge abuts the left edge of the Stage.
6. Use the Align panel or the Align menu to align the instance with the top of the Stage.

Create a Step-by-Step Animation

1. Rename Layer 1 **Step-by-Step**.
2. Select frame 2 of the layer and insert a keyframe.
3. Move the instance .5" (two grid lines) to the right, using the Align Top command to keep it aligned with the top of the Stage.
4. Select frame 3 and insert a keyframe.
5. Again, move the instance .5" to the right, aligned with the top of the Stage.

6. Repeat the process until the instance is centered vertically at the top of the Stage. This should take to frame 15.
7. Preview the animation.
8. Lock the Step-by-Step layer and save the changes to the file.

Add a Motion Tween on a New Layer

1. Select the Step-by-Step layer and insert a new layer.
2. Name the new layer **Castle Drop**.
3. Select frame 15 on the Castle Drop layer and insert a keyframe.
4. On frame 15, insert an instance of the Castle 1 symbol and align it in the vertical center with the top of the Stage, exactly over the instance on the Step-by-Step layer.
5. Select frame 30 and insert a keyframe.
6. Move the instance so it is aligned in the vertical center with the bottom of the Stage.
7. Select frame 20.
8. In the Property Inspector, click the Tween type drop-down arrow and select Motion.

9. Deselect the Scale check box.

10. Select the Ease box and enter the value 100.

11. Preview the animation. In frame 30, your screen should look similar to Illustration A.

12. Lock the Castle Drop layer.

13. Print the current frame.

14. Close the document and exit Flash, saving all changes.

Illustration A

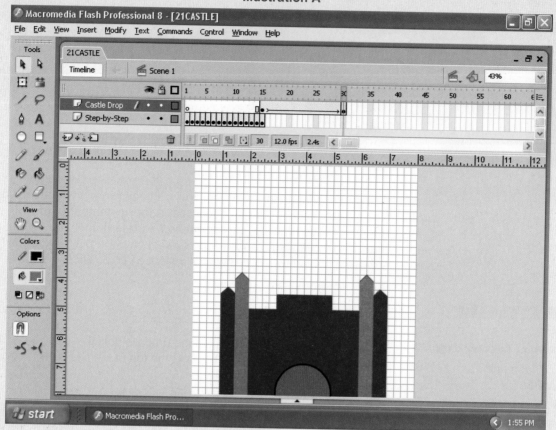

Application Exercise

Software Skills In this exercise, you will continue to work on the Castle Gate animation. You will add a motion tween that uses color tweening and a motion guide to cause a sun to move across the sky, and you will add a shape tween of a black polygon morphing into a golden crown. Finally, you will print the animation.

DIRECTIONS

Add a Motion Tween with Color Tweening

1. Open **22DATA** or **21CASTLE** and save the document as **22CASTLE**.
2. Adjust the display so that you have access to the tools you need but also have room to work on the Stage.
3. Select the Castle Drop layer and insert a new layer. Name the new layer **Sun**.
4. Select frame 15 of the Sun layer and insert a keyframe.
5. Select the Oval tool with the fill color set to a dark orange (#CC6600) and draw a circle about 1" in diameter in the upper-left corner of the Stage.
6. Convert the circle to a graphic symbol named **Sun**.
7. Select frame 30 of the Sun layer and insert a keyframe.
8. Move the sun instance to the upper-right corner of the Stage.
9. Modify the color of the instance in frame 30 to apply an 80% bright yellow tint (#FFFF00).
10. Select frame 20 and create a motion tween.
11. Deselect the Scale check box and enter 100 in the Ease box.
12. Preview the animation.
13. Save the changes.

Add a Motion Guide

1. Select the Sun layer and add a motion guide.
2. Use the Oval, Brush, or Pencil tool the in Merge Drawing model to draw a semicircle—or arc—path above the castle, starting on the left side of the Stage about 2" from the top and ending on the right side of the Stage about 2" from top.

3. Leave at least 1" between the top of the arc and the top of the Stage so that the Sun instance can display without moving outside the edges of the Stage.

   ✓ Be sure that Object Drawing is turned off before you draw the guide.

   ✓ If you use the Oval tool, erase the bottom half of the oval to create the semicircle.

4. Select frame 15 of the Sun layer.
5. In the Property Inspector, select the Snap check box in the Tween options area.
6. Drag the Sun instance in frame 15 so that its Snap ring snaps to the left end of the semicircle.
7. Select frame 30 of the Sun layer and drag the instance so that its Snap ring snaps to the motion guide, about 1" from the edge of the Stage (so that it does not extend off the Stage).
8. Lock all layers and then preview the animation.
9. Save the changes.

Add a Shape Tween

1. Select the Guide layer and insert a new layer. Name the new layer **Crown**.
2. Select frame 15 of the Crown layer and insert a keyframe.
3. Select the PolyStar tool and set options to draw a 5-sided polygon.
4. Set the fill color to black, with no stroke.
5. On frame 15 of the Crown layer, draw the polygon approximately 2.3" wide and 2.1" high, with a flat side down and an angle straight up.

6. Center the shape horizontally on the Stage, and position it vertically so that its base is sitting on the gridline at 4.5" on the vertical ruler.

7. Select frame 30 of the Crown layer and insert a keyframe.

8. Change the fill color of the shape to golden yellow (#FFCC00).

9. Deselect the shape.

10. Use the Selection tool to reshape the polygon into a crown as follows:

   - Position the mouse pointer along the side about halfway between the angle pointing straight up and the first angle to the left.

   - When the mouse pointer displays the Reshape Curve pointer, drag the side diagonally down and to the right approximately .5".

   - Position the mouse pointer along the side about halfway between the angle pointing straight up and the first angle to the right.

   - Use the Reshape Curve pointer to drag the side diagonally down and to the left approximately .5".

11. Select frame 20 of the Crown layer and create a shape tween.

12. Lock all layers and preview the animation. Frame 30 should look similar to the last frame in page 2 of Illustration A. Make adjustments as necessary.

13. Save the changes.

Print the Animation

1. Open the Page Setup dialog box.
2. Leave the default margins.
3. Select Landscape orientation.
4. Select to print all frames in the Storyboard – Grid layout.
5. Print 4 slides across the page, with the default frame margin.
6. Print frame labels.
7. Click OK to the close the Page Setup dialog box.
8. Print all pages in the animation. It should look similar to Illustration A.
9. Open the Page Setup dialog box.
10. Select Portrait orientation and change the Layout options to First Frame Only in its Actual Size.
11. Close the document and exit Flash, saving all changes.

Illustration A, page 1

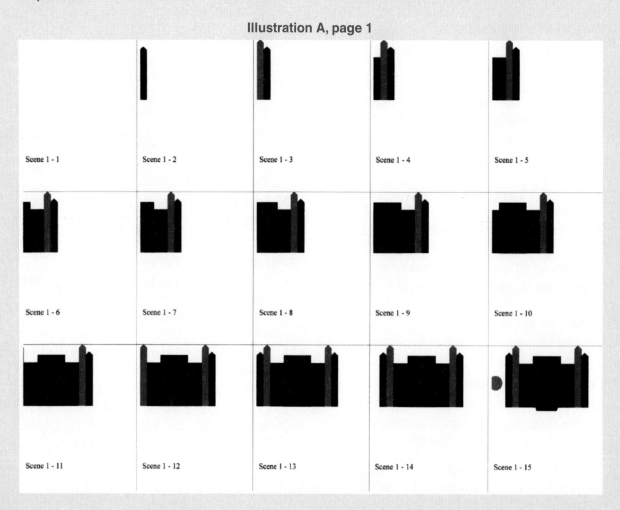

Illustration A, page 2

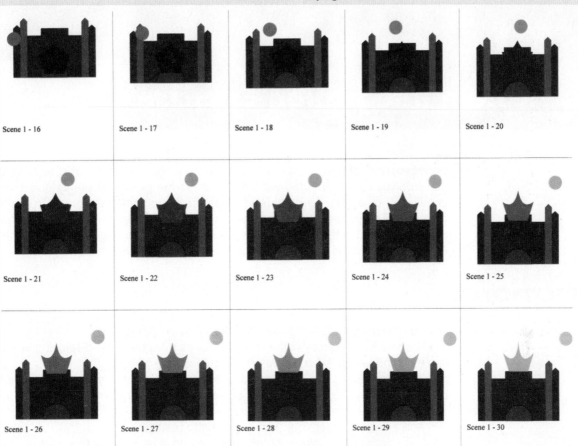

Exercise | 23

Curriculum Integration Exercise

Software Skills Use animation to illustrate the results of a science project that involves either change over time, such as the growth of plants under different conditions, or a variable motion, such as the bounce of balls made from different materials. The project should involve at least three trials and a constant. Create an animation to show the comparison (see Illustration A on page 109 for an example). Before beginning this project, you must complete your research for the science project.

DIRECTIONS

Start a new document and save it as **23RESULTS**.

Prepare the Stage by setting the ruler units to inches, and displaying visual tools you may find useful, such as the grid or guides.

Use the drawing tools to draw a picture representing the test object, such as a ball or a plant, and then convert the object into a graphic symbol.

On one layer, animate the object to show the results of the trial for the constant.

Add a layer for each trial, and animate the results.

You may want to include a static background layer to show the scale.

When you play the animation, it should display a comparison of all trials in the project.

Print the completed animation and print a single page image of the final frame.

You may want to write on the printed page of the final frame to add labels to each trial and to the scale.

Save your changes and close the document.

Illustration A

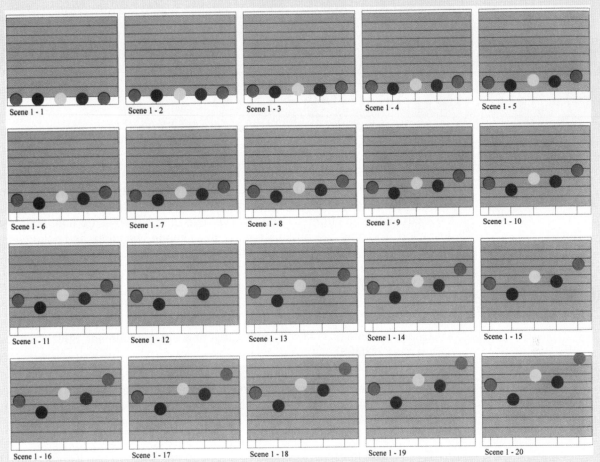

Exercise | 24

Critical Thinking Exercise

Software Skills In this exercise, you will create an animation for the Brighter Than Bright tooth-whitening franchise in which teeth move into an open mouth. You may use the teeth you drew in Exercise 11, or start with a new document and draw the teeth and mouth from scratch. You will use both step-by-step and motion tween animation. You may use a motion guide layer, shape tweening, and color tweening. When you are finished, you will print the animation.

DIRECTIONS

- Open ⊘**24DATA** or **11BRIGHT**, or create a new Flash document. Save the document as **24BRIGHT**.

- If you chose to use an existing document, convert the mouth and at least one of the tooth shapes into graphic symbols so you can insert them as instances in the document. Delete unnecessary shapes or groups. Remember that you can insert many instances of a single symbol, modifying each instance any way you want.

- If you chose to use a new document, set up the Stage to use inches, and display the rulers, grid, and guides if needed. Then, draw a mouth and at least one tooth and convert them into graphic symbols.

- Create a motion tween to cause the mouth to grow from very small to large enough to fill the Stage.

- Add a layer and create a step-by-step animation to move teeth into position in the mouth. Refer to Illustration A on page 111 to see an example.

  ✓ *To be sure the content in one layer displays through the entire animation, simply click the frame corresponding to the end of the animation and insert a frame.*

- Create a color tween to change the color of the teeth from yellow to white.

- If you want, add additional layers and move more teeth into the mouth along a motion guide.

- Preview the animation and make adjustments as necessary.

- Print the animation.

- Close the document, saving all changes and exit Flash.

Illustration A

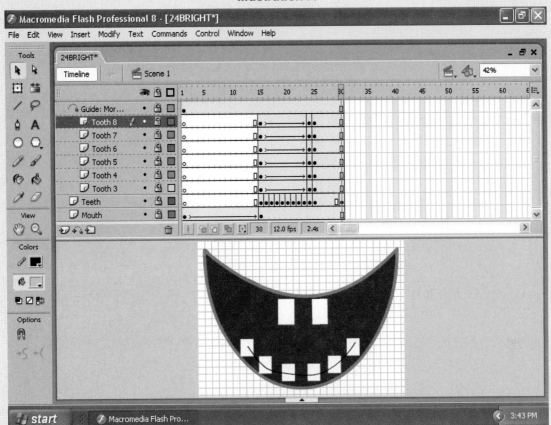

Lesson | 3

Enhancing an Animation

END OF LESSON
PROJECTS

Exercise 33

- Summary Exercise

Exercise 34

- Application Exercise

Exercise 35

- Curriculum Integration Exercise

Exercise 36

- Critical Thinking Exercise

Exercise | 25

Skills Covered

■ Import Graphics

Software Skills Import graphics into Flash to use as backgrounds, or to insert as instances that you can animate or enhance. Importing graphics can save you time and improve the quality of your applications. You can import many types of graphics, including drawings created with other programs, photographs, or images you have purchased or downloaded from the Internet.

Application Skills An environmental protection group has asked you to design an animation for its Web site. It has provided you with pictures it would like you to include. In this exercise, you will import two graphics images: one to use as a background for the animation, and one to use as an instance in the animation. After importing the graphics, you will create an animation sequence.

TERMS

Import To make a non-Flash file available for use in a Flash document.

NOTES

Import Graphics

■ You can incorporate artwork created in other programs into your Flash applications.

■ To make the graphics available, you must **import** them into Flash.

■ You can import files to the library or the Stage using the Import command, or by copying and pasting the pictures from another program.

■ Some file formats will retain their original formatting during importing; others will not:

- You can import vector images created in Macromedia Freehand directly into a Flash document. Freehand images are the most compatible with Flash, and retain most of their formatting and features.

- PNG images created in Macromedia Fireworks can also be imported directly into a Flash document. However, if you use the Cut or Copy and Paste commands to transfer the graphic, Flash converts the file to a bitmap.

- Vector images from Shockwave, Adobe Illustrator, and Windows Metafile Format are imported as a group into the current Flash layer.

- Bitmaps, including all .bmp files and scanned photographs, are imported as single objects into the current Flash layer.

- A sequence of images, such as an animated GIF file, is imported as successive frames into the current Flash layer.

■ You can edit imported vector graphics as if they were created with the Flash drawing tools, including grouping them, applying transformations, and changing fill and stroke properties.

■ You can rotate, skew, flip, and scale imported bitmaps, or break them apart so that you can edit the individual objects.

  ✓ *Working with bitmaps is covered in Exercise 49.*

■ Keep in mind that importing bitmaps into a Flash document will likely increase the file size.

■ Copyright laws protect the rights of artists. Be sure to obtain permission to use copyrighted artwork and to cite the source of the work.

- You can import the following graphics file formats into Flash:

File type	Extension
Adobe Illustrator	.eps, .ai, .pdf
AutoDesk's AutoCAD DXF	.dxf
Bitmap	.bmp
Enhanced Windows Metafile	.emf
Macromedia FreeHand	.fh7, .fh8, .fh9, .fh10, .fh11
FutureSplash Player	.spl
GIF and animated GIF	.gif
JPEG	.jpg
PNG	.png
Flash Player 6/7	.swf
Windows Metafile	.wmf

- If you have Apple Computer Corp.'s QuickTime 4 installed, you can import the following bitmap file formats into Flash:

File type	Extension
Apple MacPaint	.pntg
Adobe Photoshop	.psd
PICT	.pct, .pic
Apple QuickTime Image	.qtif
Silicon Graphics Image	.sgi
TGA	.tga
TIFF	.tif

PROCEDURES

Import a Graphics File to the Stage (Ctrl+R)

1. Select keyframe.
2. Click **File**.................... Alt + F
3. Click **Import**.......................... I
4. Click **Import to Stage**.............. I

   ✓ Flash displays the Import dialog box.

5. Click **Look in** drop-down arrow...................... Alt + I
6. Select location where file is stored.
7. Click **Files of type** drop-down arrow.......................... Alt + T
8. Click format of file to import.
9. Click file to import.
10. Click **Open**.................. Alt + O

   ✓ Depending on the type of file, Flash may display an Import Settings dialog box. Select options as desired and then click OK.

   ✓ If the name of the file to import ends with a number, and there are multiple sequentially numbered files in the same folder, Flash asks whether to import the sequence of files. Click Yes to import all of the sequential files. Click No to import only the selected file.

Import a Graphics File to the Library

1. Click **File**.................... Alt + F
2. Click **Import**.......................... I
3. Click **Import to Library**............ L

   ✓ Flash displays the Import to Library dialog box.

4. Click **Look in** drop-down arrow...................... Alt + I
5. Select location where file is stored.
6. Click **Files of type** drop-down arrow....................... Alt + T
7. Click format of file to import.
8. Click file to import.
9. Click **Open**.................. Alt + O

   ✓ Depending on the type of file, Flash may display an Import Settings dialog box. Select options as desired and then click OK.

   ✓ If the name of the file to import ends with a number, and there are multiple sequentially numbered files in the same folder, Flash asks whether to import the sequence of files. Click Yes to import all of the sequential files. Click No to import only the selected file.

Copy and Paste an Image to the Stage

1. Select image.
2. Click **Copy** button.
   OR
   a. Click **Edit**.............. Alt + E
   b. Click **Copy**...................... C
3. Switch to Flash.
4. Select keyframe where you want to insert image.
5. Right-click Stage.
6. Click **Paste**.

EXERCISE DIRECTIONS

Import a Vector Graphic

1. Start Flash and create a new document. Save the file as **25BIRD**.
2. Set document properties to change the ruler units to inches and the Stage size to 7" wide by 5.5" high. Display the rulers.
3. Set the zoom to Fit in Window.
4. Rename Layer 1 **Background**.
5. Import to the Stage the file ●**25PARK.wmf** supplied with this book.

   ✓ The file is in Windows Metafile format and is imported as multiple vector objects.

6. Make sure all objects on the Stage are selected, and then group them together.

7. Scale the group to fill the Stage (7" by 5.5").

8. Select frame 26 and insert a frame. This extends the background through the animation.

9. Save the changes to the document.

10. Lock the Background layer.

Import a Bitmap Graphic

1. Insert a new layer and name it **Bird**.

2. Import to the Stage the file ⊙**25DOVE.gif** supplied with this book.

   ✓ *The file is in .gif format and is imported as a bitmap.*

3. Flip the image horizontally so the bird is facing to the left.

4. Resize the image to approximately .5" by .5" (very small), and align it to the upper right of the Stage.

5. Select frame 25 of the Bird layer and insert a keyframe.

6. On frame 25, resize the image to approximately 1.5" by 1.5" and move it to the lower left of the Stage.

7. Select frame 15 and create a motion tween.

8. Keep the Scale check box selected, and verify that the Snap check box is selected.

9. Save the changes.

Add a Motion Guide

1. Select the Bird layer and add a motion guide.

2. Use the Pencil tool with Object Drawing turned off to draw a motion guide path that starts near the upper-right corner of the Stage, follows the path of the river toward the lower-left corner of the Stage, then curves up to the top of the trunk of the tree on the left (refer to Illustration A).

3. Select frame 1 of the Bird layer and snap the image to the start of the path.

4. Select frame 25 of the Bird layer and snap the image to the end of the path.

5. Select frame 26 of the Bird layer and insert a keyframe.

6. In frame 26, flip the image horizontally so that the bird is facing to the right. Your screen should look similar to Illustration A.

7. Preview the animation and make adjustments as necessary.

8. Print Frame 26. If requested by your instructor, print the animation.

9. Lock all layers.

10. Close the file, saving all changes, and exit Flash.

Illustration A

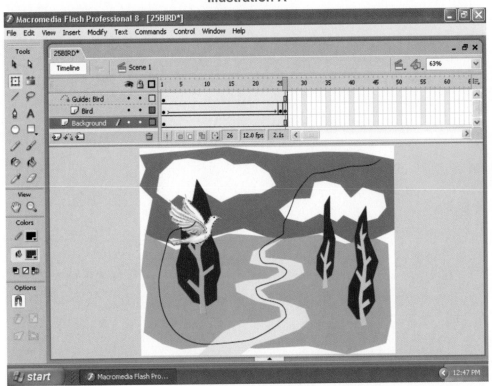

ON YOUR OWN

1. Start Flash and create a new document.
2. Save the document as **25MYPIC**.
3. Create an animation incorporating at least two imported graphics. You may locate and import any graphics files, or use the files provided with this book (⊙**25BUG.wmf**—a ladybug, ⊙**25FLY.wmf**—a butterfly, and ⊙**25FLOWERS.jpg**—flowers).
4. Create a background layer to display a static graphic image. Create another layer to animate a graphic image. Keep in mind that you may have to convert an imported object into a symbol in order to use certain animations, such as a motion guide.
5. When you are satisfied with the animation, print the final frame.
6. Save the file and close it, and then exit Flash.

Exercise | 26

Skills Covered

- **About Sounds**
- **Insert Sounds**

Software Skills Insert sounds in an application to create a soundtrack, accent an animation, or call attention to an object. You can set sound files to play in sync with the Timeline, independently, or to start and stop on a specified keyframe.

Application Skills In this exercise, you will add sound to the environmental group's animation that you created in Exercise 25.

TERMS

Amplitude A measure of loudness.

Event sound A sound file that plays independently from the Timeline.

Loop To start over from the beginning.

Sound card A hardware device that enables the computer to manipulate and output sound.

Sound fade A change in volume over time.

Streaming sound A sound file that is synchronized with frames on the Timeline.

Waveform A visual representation, or graph, of a sound, showing amplitude over time.

NOTES

About Sounds

- Insert a sound on a layer in any Flash document to add instant audio.

- There are two basic types of sound in Flash applications: **event sounds** and **streaming sounds**.

- Event sounds play independently of the Timeline. They start to play when the starting keyframe is first displayed, and they play in their entirety, even if the animation stops.

- Event sounds are often used to indicate interaction between a viewer and the animation, such as clicking a button, or to highlight an action.

- Event sounds must download completely before playing, which may cause a noticeable delay in the animation.

- Streaming sounds play only for the frames specified on the Timeline.

- Flash synchronizes the sound by forcing the animation to keep pace with it.

- Streaming sounds are often used to coordinate sounds with action in an animation, such as to play a song to accompany an animation.

- Streaming sounds can start playing after only a small amount of data has been downloaded.

- You can insert different sounds on different layers. Each layer acts like a separate sound channel, so the sounds on all layers combine when you play the animation.

- In the Timeline, the **amplitude** of the sound is visually represented by a **waveform** display (see the following illustration).

Waveform in Timeline

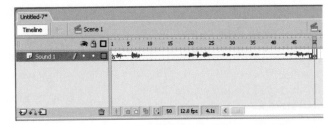

- In order to successfully play sounds your PC must be equipped with speakers and a **sound card**.

Preview a Sound in the Library

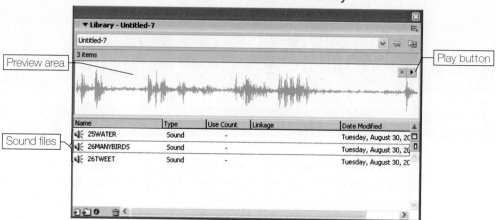

Preview area · Play button · Sound files

Insert Sounds

- To make a sound available for use in a Flash document, import it into the document's library.

- From the library, you insert the file on a keyframe to add it to an application. The sound displays in the Timeline.

- You may import .wav or .mp3 sound files. If you have Apple's QuickTime, you can also import .aiff, Sound Only QuickTime movies, or Sun AU files.

- You need only one copy of a sound file stored in the library to insert that sound multiple times in an application.

- You can preview a sound in the library by clicking the Play button in the Preview area (see the illustration above).

- You set options in the Property Inspector to control the way a sound plays, including the effect, which determines the **sound fade**, the sync, which determines when the sound stops and starts, and whether the sound should **loop** in the Property Inspector (see the following illustration).

  ✓ *Streaming sounds should not be looped.*

Set Sound Options in the Property Inspector

PROCEDURES

Import a Sound File to the Library

1. Click **File**.................... Alt+F
2. Click **Import**.......................... I
3. Click **Import to Library**............ L

   ✓ *Flash displays the Import to Library dialog box.*

4. Click **Look in** drop-down arrow...................... Alt+I
5. Select location where file is stored.
6. Click **Files of type** drop-down arrow...................... Alt+T
7. Click format of file to import.
8. Click file to import.
9. Click **Open**................. Alt+O

Preview a Sound

1. Display Library panel.
2. Click sound to preview.
3. Click **Play** button ▸ in Preview area.

Insert a Sound

1. Insert new layer.
2. Select keyframe.
3. Display Library panel.
4. Drag sound file from Library panel to Stage.

Set Sound Options

1. Select keyframe where sound was inserted.

2. Display Property Inspector.
3. Click **Effect** drop-down arrow.
4. Click one of the following:
   - **None** to apply no sound effects or to remove existing effects.
   - **Left channel** to play the sound in the left channel only.
   - **Right channel** to play the sound in the right channel only.
   - **Fade left to right** to shift the sound from the left channel to the right channel.
   - **Fade right to left** to shift the sound from the right channel to the left channel.

- **Fade in** to gradually increase the amplitude of the sound.

- **Fade out** to gradually decrease the amplitude of the sound.

- **Custom** to create your own In and Out points.

  ✓ *Click the Edit button to display the Edit Envelope dialog box to proceed.*

5. Click the **Sync** drop-down arrow.

6. Select one of the following synchronization options:

   - **Event** to synchronize the sound to the occurrence of an event.

   - **Start** to start an event sound at the current keyframe.

   - **Stop** to stop a sound at the current keyframe.

   - **Stream** to synchronize the sound with the Timeline.

7. Click the **Sound Loop** drop-down arrow.

8. Select one of the following:

   - **Repeat** to play the sound one or more times.

   - **Loop** to loop the sound from beginning to end until the end continuously.

EXERCISE DIRECTIONS

Insert a Sound

1. Start Flash and open the file ●**26DATA**, or open **25BIRD**. Save the file as **26BIRD**.

2. Select the Guide:Bird layer and insert a new layer.

3. Name the new layer **Flapping wings**.

4. Import the file ●**26WINGS.wav** supplied with this book into the library.

   ✓ *If prompted to update QuickTime files, click Do it now to continue.*

5. Preview the **26WINGS** file in the library.

6. Select frame 1 of the Flapping wings layer.

7. Insert the **26WINGS** file.

   ✓ *It does not matter where you drop the sound file on the Stage, as it is not visible.*

8. With frame 1 of the Flapping wings layer selected, in the Property Inspector, set the Sync to Event, if necessary.

9. Rewind and play the animation. Because the sound is set to Event, it continues playing after the animation ends.

10. Select frame 1 of the Flapping wings layer again. In the Property Inspector, set the Sync to Stream, and then preview the animation again. The sound should stop playing at the end of the animation.

11. Select frame 1 and then, in the Property Inspector, set the Effect to Fade in.

12. Preview the animation again.

13. Save the changes.

Extend the Animation

1. Select frame 50 on the Background layer and insert a frame. This extends the background image through frame 50.

2. Insert a frame on frame 50 of the Bird layer.

3. Select the Flapping wings layer and insert a new layer.

4. Name the layer **Birdsong**.

5. Select frame 26 of the Birdsong layer and insert a keyframe.

6. Import the file ●**26TWEET.wav** supplied with this book into the library.

7. Preview the **26TWEET** file in the library.

8. Insert the **26TWEET** file on frame 26 of the Birdsong layer.

9. With frame 26 selected, in the Property Inspector, set the Sync to Stream, if necessary.

10. Hide the motion guide layer and preview the animation. When the bird alights on the tree, the sound of flapping wings should stop, and the bird should start singing.

11. Make adjustments as necessary. The Timeline should look similar to Illustration A on page 122.

12. If requested by your instructor, print the last frame in the animation, or print the animation.

13. Lock all layers.

14. Close the file, saving all changes.

15. Exit Flash.

Illustration A

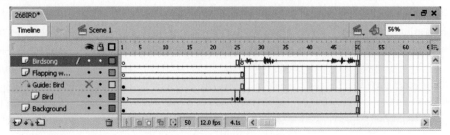

ON YOUR OWN

1. Start Flash and open **25MYPIC**, the file you worked with in Exercise 25, or open **26PIC**. Save the document as **26MYPIC**.

2. Add at least one sound file to the animation. You may locate sound files on your computer system, on the Internet, or you may use **26BUGS1.wav**, **26BUGS2.wav**, and **26BUGS3.wav**, the sound files provided with this book.

3. Remember to insert the sound on a new layer. If you use more than one sound, insert each one on a different layer.

4. Try using different events and syncs until you achieve the result you want. If you use a short sound, try repeating it more than once, or setting it to loop.

5. Preview the animation frequently so you can hear how the sounds fit with the images.

6. When you are satisfied with the results, save the changes and lock the layers.

7. If requested by your instructor, print the last frame, or print the animation.

8. Close the document, saving all changes, and exit Flash.

Skills Covered

- **Create Text Blocks**
- **Enter and Edit Text**
- **Format Text**
- **About Text Rendering**

- **About Device Fonts**
- **Transform Text**
- **Check Spelling**

Software Skills Add static text to your Flash applications as part of an image, part of an animation, or to provide information. You can edit and format text like you do in a word processing file, and also transform a block of text the way you do objects and instances. For example, you can rotate, scale, and skew text blocks.

Application Skills In this exercise, you will use text to enhance the animation you created for the environmental group. First, you will add the group's name and address to the Background layer. Next, you will add the group's slogan to a new layer. You will edit, format, and transform the text, and you will check the spelling.

TERMS

Anti-aliasing Techniques used to eliminate jagged outlines and interference patterns to improve readability onscreen.

Device fonts Fonts that specify to use fonts stored on the local computer to display text onscreen.

Editing mode The mode in which you can enter and edit text in a text block.

Font A set of characters in a particular typeface.

Font rendering The way fonts are displayed onscreen.

Font size The height of an uppercase letter in a font set, measured in points.

Font style The slant and weight of a character in a font set, such as italics or bold.

Insertion point A blinking vertical line that indicates where typed characters will be entered. Characters are inserted to the left of the insertion point.

Kern To adjust the space between specific pairs of characters.

Static text Text that does not change based on updating information or user input.

Text block An object drawn with the Text tool in which you type alphanumeric characters such as numbers, letters, and symbols.

Text orientation The directional flow of text within a text block.

Wrap A feature that causes text to automatically move from the end of one line to the beginning of the next.

NOTES

Create Text Blocks

- Use the Text tool **A** to draw a **text block** on the Stage when you want to add **static text** to a Flash document.

  ✓ You can also add dynamic—or updating—text to a Flash document.

- You can create either a one-line extendable text block or a multi-line fixed-size text block.

- In a fixed block, text automatically **wraps** from the end of one line to the beginning of the next. You can also force a new line by pressing Enter.

- In an extendable text block the text displays on a continuous line without wrapping.

- The **text orientation** determines the orientation of the text block:
  - Horizontal flows text left to right and wraps from top to bottom.
  - Vertical, left to right flows text vertically, top to bottom, with subsequent lines extending to the right.
  - Vertical, right to left flows text vertically, top to bottom, with subsequent lines extending to the left.
- You can identify the type of text block and the orientation by looking at the text block handle (see the illustrations below):
  - A round handle displays in the upper-right corner of horizontal, extendable text blocks.
- A square handle displays in the upper-right corner of horizontal, fixed-width blocks.
- A round handle displays in the lower-right corner of vertical, left to right extendable blocks.
- A round handle displays in the lower-left corner of vertical, right to left extendable blocks.
- A square handle displays in the lower-right corner of vertical, left to right fixed-height blocks.
- A square handle displays in the lower-left corner of vertical, right to left fixed-height blocks.
- You can easily convert from one block style to the other.

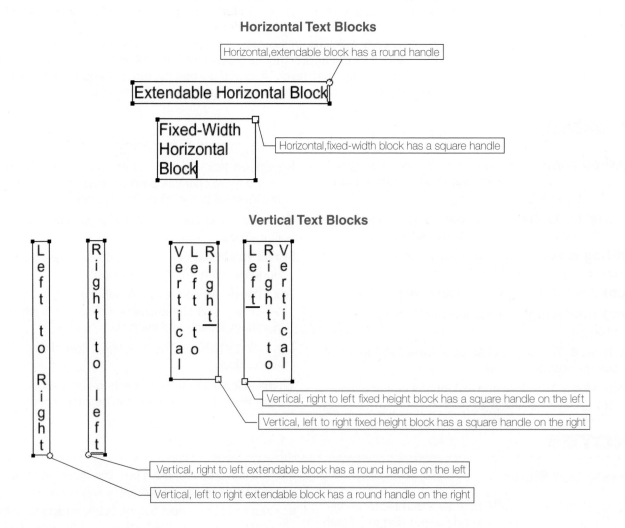

Horizontal Text Blocks

Horizontal, extendable block has a round handle

Extendable Horizontal Block

Fixed-Width Horizontal Block

Horizontal, fixed-width block has a square handle

Vertical Text Blocks

Left to Right

Right to left

Vertical Left to Right

Left Right Vertical to

Vertical, right to left fixed height block has a square handle on the left

Vertical, left to right fixed height block has a square handle on the right

Vertical, right to left extendable block has a round handle on the left

Vertical, left to right extendable block has a round handle on the right

Enter and Edit Text

- When you draw a new text block, Flash displays an **insertion point** in it so you can enter and edit text.
- New text is displayed in the current fill color.
- Use typical word processing techniques to enter and edit text within a text block.
- For example, drag across text to select it, use the arrow keys to move the insertion point, use the Delete key to delete the character to the right of the insertion point, and use the Backspace key to delete the character to the left. You can also use the Cut, Copy, and Paste commands to copy and move selected text.
- To edit text in an existing text block you must switch to text **editing mode**.

Format Text

- Text formatting options in a Flash text block are similar to those in word processing and desktop publishing programs.
- Use the options in the Property Inspector or the commands on the Text menu to format text (see the illustration below):
  - Apply **font** formatting such as selecting a font, **font size**, and **font style**.
  - Apply paragraph formatting such as alignment, indentation, margins, and line spacing.
  - Set letter spacing, character position, **font rendering**, and text orientation options.
  - Turn the Auto **kern** feature off or on.

About Text Rendering

- Text—or font—rendering is a process that controls the readability of text onscreen by using **anti-aliasing** techniques.
- Text rendering settings may impact file size, because fonts are usually embedded in the published Flash file.
- Font rendering settings include the following:
  - Use **device fonts**, which substitutes a device font for the current font in order to improve readability and minimize file size.
  - Bitmap text (no anti-aliasing), which turns off anti-aliasing and provides no text smoothing. The text may display sharp and clear at the published size, but when scaled it loses readability.
  - Anti-alias for animation, which creates a smoother animated sequence by ignoring text alignment and kerning. This option works best on font sizes of 10 points or larger. Select this option when animating the text block.
  - Anti-alias for readability (the default), which uses FlashType, a new text rendering feature designed to improve the display and readability of text in Flash 8 documents and applications published for Flash Player 8. All font sizes are improved using this option, but there may be animation performance problems. This option is available only for files published for Flash Player 8.
  - Custom anti-alias (available for Flash 8 Professional only), which lets you set sharpness to control the smoothness of the transition between text edges and the background, and thickness to control how thick the font anti-aliasing transition appears.

Text Formatting Options in the Property Inspector

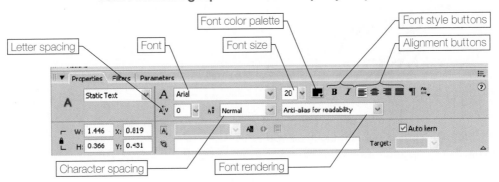

- FlashType anti-aliasing for readability cannot be used on a text block that has been skewed or flipped.
- Using FlashType anti-aliasing for readability may cause a delay when playing published Flash applications, particularly if you use more than three fonts in an opening sequence.
- FlashType anti-aliasing for readability can also increase an application's memory usage.

About Device Fonts

- For static, horizontal text, you may select to use device fonts.
- With device fonts, Flash Player uses fonts on the local computer that most resemble the selected device font.
- Because the device fonts are not embedded in the application file, the file may be a little smaller than if you use embedded fonts.
- Flash comes with three device fonts:
  - _sans, which is a sans serif font similar to the commonly used Helvetica or Arial.
  - _serif, which is a serif font similar to the commonly used Times New Roman.
  - _typewriter, which is a similar to Courier.
- To use device fonts, simply format the text with one of the three available device fonts.

Transform Text

- You can transform a selected text block the way you transform a drawn object.
- For example, you can rotate, scale, skew, and flip it (see the following illustration).

Skewed Text Block

- You can also align and position a text block as you would any object.

- When you scale a text block as an object, the font size settings are no longer applied.
- Although you may edit text after the text block is transformed, the changes may make the text difficult to read.
- Also, anti-aliasing may be disabled once a text block is transformed.

Check Spelling

- Use the Check Spelling feature to check the spelling of text in text blocks as well as other text in a Flash document, such as layer names.
- During the check, Flash identifies words not in its dictionary. You have the option of adding the word to the dictionary, ignoring the word, or changing the spelling. You can also delete the word from the document (see the following illustration).

Check Spelling Dialog Box

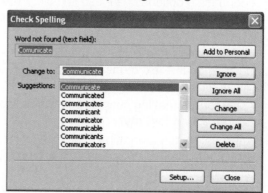

- Before using the Check Spelling feature, set Spelling Setup options in the Spelling Setup dialog box.
- For example, you can select which elements to check and which dictionary to use.

PROCEDURES

Create an Extendable Text Block

1. Click **Text** tool A ....T
2. Click the **Text type** drop-down arrow in Property Inspector.
3. Click **Static Text**.
4. Click **Change Orientation of Text** button in Property Inspector.
5. Click one of the following:
   - **Horizontal**
   - **Vertical, left to right**
   - **Vertical, right to left**
6. Click anywhere on Stage.
7. Type text.

Create a Fixed-Width or Fixed-Height Text Block

1. Click **Text** tool A ....T
2. Click the **Text type** drop-down arrow in Property Inspector.
3. Click **Static Text**.
4. Click **Change Orientation of Text** button in Property Inspector.
5. Click one of the following:
   - **Horizontal**
   - **Vertical, left to right**
   - **Vertical, right to left**
6. Click and drag on Stage to draw rectangular text block.
7. Type text.

Change Text Block Type

- Double-click text block handle.

Resize Fixed-Size Text Block

- Drag text block handle.

Select a Text Block

1. Click **Selection** tool V
2. Click text block to select.
3. Press and hold **Shift** ......⇧Shift
4. Click additional text block(s) to select.

Change to Editing Mode

1. Click **Selection** tool V
2. Double-click text box.

OR

1. Click **Text** tool A ....T
2. Click within text block.

OR

1. Select text block.
2. Click **Edit**...............Alt+E
3. Click **Edit Selected**..............I

Select Text

1. Click **Selection** tool V
2. Do one of the following:
   - Drag across text to select.
   - Double-click word to select.

Select a Font

1. Select text or text block.
2. Click **Font** drop-down arrow in Property Inspector.
3. Click desired font.

OR

1. Click **Text**...................Alt+T
2. Click **Font**...........................F
3. Click desired font.

Select Font Size

1. Select text or text block.
2. Click **Font size** drop-down arrow in Property Inspector.
3. Click desired font size.

OR

1. Select text or text block.
2. Click in **Font size** box in Property Inspector.
3. Type desired font size.
4. Press **Enter**...................↵Enter

OR

1. Click **Text**...................Alt+T
2. Click **Size**..........................S
3. Click desired font size.

Select Font Style

1. Select text or text block.
2. Click one of the following in Property Inspector:
   - **Bold** button B
   - **Italic** button I
3. Click **Character Position** drop-down arrow.

4. Click one of the following:
   - **Superscript** to position text above the baseline.
   - **Subscript** to position text below the baseline.
   - **Normal** to position text on the baseline.

OR

1. Click **Text**...................Alt+T
2. Click **Style**...........................Y
3. Click desired style:
   - **Plain**......................P
   - **Bold**.......................B
   - **Italic**......................I
   - **Subscript**..................S
   - **Superscript**.................U

   ✓ *A check mark next to a style indicates it is selected.*

Select a Text Color

- Select fill color.

OR

1. Select text or text block.
2. Click **Text Color** palette.
3. Click desired color.

Set Letter Spacing

1. Select text or text block.
2. Click **Letter Spacing** drop-down arrow in Property Inspector.
3. Drag slider to set spacing as follows:
   - Drag up to enter a positive value and increase spacing.
   - Drag down to enter a negative value and decrease spacing.

OR

1. Click **Text**...................Alt+T
2. Click **Letter Spacing**...............L
3. Click one of the following:
   - **Increase**...........................I
   - **Decrease**...........................D
   - **Reset**..............................R

Turn Kerning On or Off

1. Select text or text block.
2. Click to select or clear **Auto Kern** check box in Property Inspector.

   ✓ *When Auto Kern is selected, Flash automatically uses built-in font kerning.*

Set Paragraph Alignment

1. Select text or text block.
2. Click one of the following buttons in Property Inspector:
   - **Align Left** ≡
   - **Align Center** ≡
   - **Align Right** ≡
   - **Justify** ≡

   OR

1. Click **Text**...................... Alt + T
2. Click **Align**........................... A
3. Click one of the following:
   - **Align Left**........................ L
   - **Align Center**.................... C
   - **Align Right**...................... R
   - **Justify**............................. J

Set Paragraph Format Options

1. Select text or text block.
2. Click **Edit Format Options** button ¶ in Property Inspector.

   ✓ *The Format Options dialog box displays.*

3. Click **Indent** box drop-down arrow.
4. Drag slider to set indent.

5. Click **Line spacing** drop-down arrow.
6. Drag slider to set line spacing.
7. Click **Left margin** drop-down arrow.
8. Drag slider to set left margin.
9. Click **Right margin** drop-down arrow.
10. Drag slider to set right margin.
11. Click **OK**...................... ↵Enter

    ✓ *Values in the Format Options dialog box are in current ruler units. Line spacing may be measured in points.*

Set Font Rendering

1. Select text or text block.
2. Click **Font rendering method** drop-down arrow in Property Inspector.
3. Click one of the following:
   - **Use device fonts**
   - **Bitmap text (no anti-alias)**
   - **Anti-alias for animation**
   - **Anti-alias for readability**
   - **Custom anti-alias**

   ✓ *If you select Custom anti-alias, enter values for font thickness and sharpness and then click OK.*

Set Spelling Setup Options

1. Click **Text**.................. Alt + T
2. Click **Spelling Setup**.............. P

3. Select or deselect options as desired.
4. Click **OK**...................... ↵Enter

Check Spelling

1. Click **Text**.................. Alt + T
2. Click **Check Spelling**.............. C
3. If Flash finds an error, click one of the following:
   - **Add to Personal**.......... Alt + A to add word to personal dictionary.
   - **Ignore**...................... Alt + I to leave the word as is and move on.
   - **Ignore All**.................. Alt + G to ignore all occurrences of the word.
   - **Change**...................... Alt + C to change the word to the one in the Change to box.
   - *You may click a word in the Suggestions list to enter it in the Change to box, or type a word in the Change to box.*
   - **Change All**.................. Alt + L to change all occurrences of the word to the one in the Change to box.
   - **Delete**...................... Alt + D to delete the word.
4. When the spell check is complete, click **OK**.............. ↵Enter

EXERCISE DIRECTIONS

Create a Fixed-Width Text Block

1. Start Flash and open the file ⊚**27DATA**, or open **26BIRD**. Save the file as **27BIRD**.
2. Unlock the Background layer.
3. Select the Text tool, and then, in the Property Inspector, select a serif font, such as Times New Roman or Garamond.
4. Set the font size to 20 points.
5. Set the text color to black, and the font style to Bold.

6. Select frame 1 of the Background layer and create a static horizontal fixed width text block approximately 3" wide.
7. In the text box, type the following: **Green Space Partnership 523 North Maple Street Skaneateles, NY 13152**.

   ✓ *The address should wrap to three lines automatically as you type.*

8. Select the text block and align it to the lower-left corner of the Stage.

9. Make sure the text rendering is set to Anti-alias for readability.

10. Save the changes.

Create an Extendable Text Block

1. With the Background layer selected, insert a new layer and name it **Slogan**.

2. Select the Text tool, and then select a sans serif font such as Arial.

3. Set the font size to 32 points, the font style to Bold and Italic, and the text color to the same green as the grass in the background (#9CB366).

   ✓ You can type the color's number in the palette, or use the palette's eye dropper pointer to pick it up: Click the color palette, then click the pointer on the grass-colored area of the Stage.

4. Select frame 1 of the Slogan layer and create a static, horizontal, extendable text block.

5. In the text box, type **Protecting Open Space**.

6. Align the text block so its top is approximately .25" from the top of the Stage and center it horizontally.

7. Set the text rendering to Anti-alias for animation.

8. Check the spelling in the document and make corrections, if necessary.

9. Save the changes.

Edit and Transform the Text Blocks

1. Select the fixed-width block and remove the bold.

2. Center-align all three lines within the text box.

3. Select the extendable text box and edit the text to read Protect Our Open Space.

4. Rotate the extendable text box -20 degrees.

5. Position the extendable text box so that its top corner is approximately .5" from the top of the Stage and center it vertically.

6. Change the text color of the word *Protect* to white and the text color of the words *Our Open Space* to the same green as the trees (#173A00).

   ✓ Again, you can type the number into the palette or use the palette's eye dropper pointer to pick it up from a tree on the Stage.

7. Select the text in the extendable text box and change the font size to 44 points

8. Make sure the Guide layer is hidden and then preview the animation. In the last frame, the Stage should look similar to Illustration A.

9. If requested by your instructor, print the last frame in the animation, or print the animation.

10. Lock all layers.

11. Close the file, saving all changes.

12. Exit Flash.

Illustration A

ON YOUR OWN

1. Start Flash and open **26MYPIC**, the file you worked with in Exercise 26, or open **27PIC**. Save the document as **27MYPIC**.

2. Add at least one extendable text block and one fixed text block to the application. You may want to put the text on an existing layer, or insert new layers.

3. Experiment with different text orientations. For example, try using vertical, left to right orientation for a name.

4. Try different font colors, sizes, and styles.

5. Transform one of the text blocks by either skewing, scaling, or rotating.

6. Check the spelling and make corrections if necessary.

7. Preview the animation when you are finished and make adjustments, if necessary.

8. When you are satisfied with the results, save the changes and lock the layers.

9. If requested by your instructor, print the last frame, or print the animation.

10. Close the document, saving all changes, and exit Flash.

Skills Covered

- **Break Text Apart**
- **Distribute to Layers**
- **Animate Text**

Software Skills Use animated text to create exciting and interesting effects in your applications, such as flying characters that come together to form a word. Use text blocks in motion tweens and text shapes in shape tweens. Convert text to shapes so you can transform them like drawing objects.

Application Skills In this exercise, you will use text to enhance an animation for the Grace Notes stationery boutique. You will animate text blocks using motion tweens, then convert text characters to shapes so you can skew and fill them.

TERMS

There is no new vocabulary in this exercise.

NOTES

Break Text Apart

- Use the Break Apart command on a text block containing multiple characters to place each character into its own text block.
- Use the Break Apart command on a text block containing a single character to convert the character to a shape comprised of lines and fills.
- You can modify the shape as you would any drawing object. For example, you can change the fill and stroke, and apply transformations such as rotation, scaling, skewing, and reshaping (see the following illustration).

Character Shapes Can Be Filled and Transformed

- You can also group the shapes, convert them to symbols, and animate them.
- You cannot edit the shapes as text.

Distribute to Layers

- Use the Distribute to Layers command to quickly move selected objects from a single layer to individual layers.
- The objects are moved to new layers, leaving the original layer blank.
- The new layers are inserted below the original layer.
- You can distribute graphic objects, instances, bitmaps, video clips, and text blocks.
- Distributing objects to layers makes it easier to apply motion tweens to the individual objects.
- For example, break apart a text block and then use the Distribute to Layers command to place each character on a separate layer so you can animate the characters individually.

Animate Text

- Use frame-by-frame or motion tween animation to animate text blocks.
- Convert a text block into a graphic symbol if you want to insert multiple instances of it in an animation, or group text blocks with other objects in order to animate the entire group.

- To create color tweens, you must convert the text block to a graphic symbol.
- Use shape tweening to animate text shapes you create when you break apart a text block.
- If you want to use motion tweening on a shape, you must convert it to a graphic symbol, or create a group.

PROCEDURES

Break Apart a Text Block (Ctrl+B)

1. Select text block containing multiple characters.
2. Click **Modify** .... Alt + M
3. Click **Brea̲k Apart** .... K

Convert a Text Character to a Shape (Ctrl+B)

1. Select text block containing a single character.
2. Click **Modify** .... Alt + M
3. Click **Brea̲k Apart** .... K

Distribute Objects to Layers (Ctrl+Shift+D)

1. Select objects to distribute.
2. Click **Modify** .... Alt + M
3. Click **Timeline** .... M
4. Click **Distribute to Layers** .... D
5. Set other shape tween options as necessary.

EXERCISE DIRECTIONS

Animate a Text Block

1. Start Flash and open the file 📀**28DATA**. Save the file as **28NOTES**.
2. Play the animation. The document is similar to one you created in Exercise 20, with a background layer added.
3. Select the Background layer and insert a new layer. Name the new layer **Address**.
4. Select the Text tool and then select a sans serif font such as Arial. Set the font size to 18 points, the text color to black, and the alignment to center.
5. Select frame 1 of the Address layer and create a static, horizontal, fixed-width text block approximately 2.5" wide.
6. In the text box, type **512 Bayberry Lane Omaha, NE 68183**.

   ✓ The address should wrap to two lines automatically as you type.

7. Select frame 20 on the Address layer and insert a keyframe.
8. Position the text block so its bottom is about 2" from the top of the Stage and center it horizontally.
9. Select frame 1 of the Address layer and drag the text box into the Pasteboard area on the left side of the Stage.
10. Scale the text block to 30% and align it with the top of the Stage.
11. Select frame 10 of the Address layer and insert a motion tween.
12. Keep the Scale check box selected, set the easing to 100, and set the object to rotate clockwise two times.
13. Preview the animation.
14. Lock the Address layer and save the changes.

Break Apart and Distribute Text

1. Select the Address layer and insert a new layer named **Name**.
2. Select the Text tool and then select a handwriting or script font such as Bradley Hand ITC. Set the font size to 48, the text color to black, and the font style to bold, no italics.
3. On frame 1 of the Name layer, create a horizontal, extendable text block and type the text **Grace Notes**.
4. Break the text apart.
5. Distribute the selected text blocks to layers.
6. Save the changes.

Animate Multiple Text Blocks

1. Select frame 20 in the G layer and insert a keyframe.
2. Select frame 1 in the G layer and move the G text block into the Pasteboard to the right of the Stage, aligned near the bottom.
3. Select frame 10 in the G layer and create a motion tween. Deselect the Scale check box.
4. Select frame 20 in the r layer and insert a keyframe.
5. Select frame 1 in the r layer and move the r text block into the Pasteboard to the right of the Stage, somewhere between the top of the Stage and the G text block.

6. Select frame 10 in the r layer and create a motion tween. Deselect the Scale check box.

7. Repeat steps 4 through 6 to animate the a, c, and e text blocks.

8. Repeat the steps to animate the N, o, t, e, and s text blocks, positioning them in the Pasteboard along the left side of the Stage in each frame 1.

9. Preview the animation. The individual characters in the word Grace should appear to fly in from off the right side of the Stage into position, and the individual characters in the word Notes should appear to fly in from the left side of the Stage.

10. Lock the layers and save the changes.

Convert Text to Shapes

1. Select frame 1 of the Name layer.

2. Select the Text tool and then select a sans serif font such as Arial. Set the font size to 48, and the text color to black, no bold.

3. Unlock the Name layer and then on frame 1 create a horizontal, extendable text block and type a lowercase **g**.

4. Break the text apart.

5. Resize the shape to approximately 1" wide. The height should adjust automatically.

6. On frame 1 of the Name layer, create a horizontal, extendable text block and type a lowercase **n**.

7. Break the text apart.

8. Resize the shape to approximately 1" wide.

Format the Shapes

1. Select the g shape.

2. Change the fill color to the same color as the blue note (#0099FF).

3. Skew the shape 20 degrees horizontally.

4. Use the Paint Bucket tool to fill the closed center of the shape with the same color as the purple note (#7A3CC1).

   ✓ Select the Paint Bucket, select the fill color, and then click the area you want to fill.

5. Position the shape so it appears to be sitting on the top horizontal line, with its right-most point (the upper-right corner) about 3" from the left edge of the Stage.

6. Select the n shape.

7. Change the fill color to the same color as the purple note (#7A3CC1).

8. Skew the shape 20 degrees horizontally.

9. Position the shape so it appears to be sitting on the top horizontal line, with its left-most point (the lower-left corner) about 3" from the right edge of the Stage.

10. Use the Paint Bucket tool to fill the white space between the shape and the horizontal line with blue (#0099FF).

11. Select frame 20 of the Name layer and insert a keyframe.

12. Preview the animation. The Timeline should look similar to Illustration A, and the final frame should look similar to Illustration B on page 134.

13. If requested by your instructor, print the last frame in the animation, or print the animation.

14. Lock all layers.

15. Close the file, saving all changes.

16. Exit Flash.

Illustration A

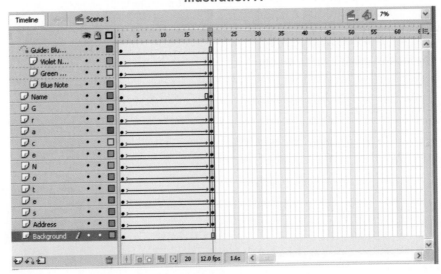

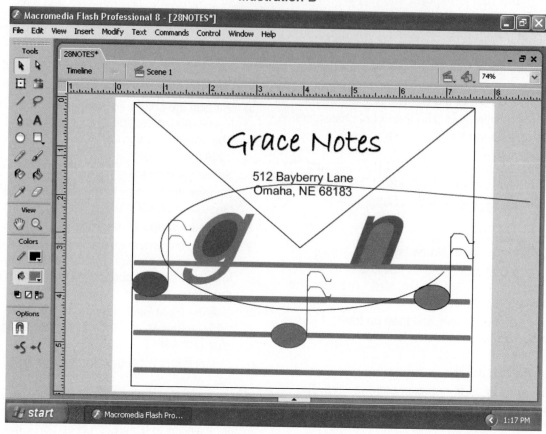

ON YOUR OWN

1. Start Flash and open **27MYPIC**, the file you worked with in Exercise 27, or open ⊕**28PIC**. Save the document as **28MYPIC**.

2. Animate at least one text block. You may break apart a text box first, in order to animate the individual characters. You may want to distribute the text blocks to layers.

3. Convert at least one text character to a shape and then transform it. Animate it using a shape tween, or convert it to a graphic symbol and animate it with a motion tween. For example, you can make the text fade in using a color tween.

4. Preview the animation when you are finished and make adjustments, if necessary.

5. When you are satisfied with the results, save the changes and lock the layers.

6. If requested by your instructor, print the last frame, or print the animation.

7. Close the document, saving all changes, and exit Flash.

Exercise | 29

Skills Covered

- **Work with Scenes**
- **Edit Animated Sequences**

Software Skills Create multiple scenes to help keep a large, complex application organized. Each scene can contain a section of the application, so you can work with a smaller animation. Edit an animated sequence to change a single frame, multiple frames, or to rearrange the flow of an animation. For example, you can move a sequence to another scene, change the duration of a tween, or even reverse an entire sequence.

Application Skills The Green Space Partnership has asked your fund-raising consulting company to help promote a charity golf tournament. In this exercise, you will start with an existing document that contains one scene. You will add two new scenes, copy frames from the existing scene to the new scenes, and then add and animate text in the new scenes. Finally, you will preview all three scenes consecutively.

TERMS

There is no new vocabulary in this exercise.

NOTES

Work with Scenes

- Use scenes to help keep a large, complex Flash document organized.
- Scenes may also be useful for animations that have clearly defined segments, or themes.
- For example, you can create separate scenes for an introduction, a loading message, the body of the animation, and the closing sequence.
- Each scene has its own Timeline; when the playhead reaches the last frame in a scene, it moves to the first frame in the next scene.
- When you publish the application, Flash combines the Timelines from each scene into one Timeline.
- In a multi-scene application, the scenes play back in the sequence in which they are listed in the Scene panel (see the following illustration).

Scene Panel

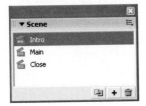

- You must select the Play All Scenes command in order to preview multiple scenes consecutively.
- Frames are numbered consecutively through the entire application; numbering does not restart with each scene.
- You can add, delete, duplicate, rename, and change the order of scenes.
- You generally should use scenes only when you are creating a very long, complex application, as they increase file size and can be cumbersome to work with. Scenes may be particularly difficult to work with in group or team projects.

Edit Animated Sequences

- You can edit the content on keyframes in an animation simply by selecting the frame and making changes.
- To edit tweened frames, you must modify the content in the beginning or ending keyframes.

- You can change the length of a tween by moving the starting or ending keyframe, or by inserting or removing intermediate frames.

- You can reverse an animation sequence. This may be useful for fading content in and then out.

- You can also cut, copy, and move frames or sequences to a new location, such as a new layer or a new scene.

✓ For a review of working with frames, see Exercise 12.

PROCEDURES

Work with Scenes

Display Scene Panel (Shift+F2)
1. Click **Window**............. Alt + W
2. Click **Other Panels**...... R, R, →
3. Click **Scene**.............. S, ↵Enter

Add a Scene
1. Display Scene panel.
2. Click **Add Scene** button + in Scene panel.
   OR
1. Click **Insert**.............. Alt + I
2. Click **Scene**.......................... S

Delete a Scene
1. Display Scene panel.
2. Click **Delete Scene** button 🗑 in Scene panel.

Rename a Scene
1. Display Scene panel.
2. Double-click scene name.
3. Type new name.
4. Press **Enter**.................... ↵Enter

Duplicate a Scene
1. Display Scene panel.
2. Click **Duplicate Scene** button 🗗 in Scene panel.

Change the Order of Scenes
1. Display Scene panel.
2. Drag scene up to make scene play earlier.
   OR
   Drag scene down to make scene play later.

Make a Scene Active
1. Display Scene panel.
2. Click desired scene.
   OR
1. Click **Edit Scene** button 🎬 on edit bar.
2. Click desired scene.

Preview All Scenes
1. Click **Control**.............. Alt + O
2. Click **Play All Scenes**.............. A

   ✓ A check mark next to Play All Scenes indicates the command is selected.

3. Click **Control**.............. Alt + O
4. Click **Rewind**........................ R
5. Click **Control**.............. Alt + O
6. Click **Play**........................... P

Edit an Animated Sequence

Reverse a Sequence
1. Select sequence to reverse.

   ✓ There must be a keyframe at the beginning and end of the selection.

2. Click **Modify**.............. Alt + M
3. Click **Timeline**........................ M
4. Click **Reverse Frames**.............. R

Select a Frame
- Click frame to select in Timeline.

Select a Frame Sequence
1. Click first frame.
2. Drag to last frame.
   OR
1. Click first frame.
2. Press and hold **Shift**........ ⇧Shift
3. Click last frame.

Move a Starting Keyframe
1. Select starting keyframe.
2. Drag left to start sequence earlier.
   OR
   Drag right to start sequence later.

Move an Ending Keyframe
1. Select ending keyframe.
2. Drag left to end sequence earlier.

   OR
   Drag right to end sequence later.

Extend the Length of a Tweened Sequence
1. Select one or more intermediate frames in the sequence.
2. Right-click selection.
3. Click **Insert Frame**.

   ✓ Flash inserts the selected number of frames.

Shorten the Length of a Tweened Sequence
1. Select one or more intermediate frames in the sequence.
2. Right-click selection.
3. Click **Remove Frames**.

   ✓ Flash removes the selected number of frames.

Move a Frame Sequence
1. Select sequence.
2. Drag to new location on Timeline.
   OR
1. Right-click selected sequence.
2. Click **Cut Frames**.
3. Right-click new starting keyframe on Timeline.
4. Click **Paste Frames**.
   OR
1. Select sequence.
2. Click **Edit**.................... Alt + E
3. Click **Timeline**........................ M
4. Click **Cut Frames**.................... T
5. Select new starting keyframe on Timeline.
6. Click **Edit**.................... Alt + E
7. Click **Timeline**........................ M

8. Click **Paste Frames**..............P

✓ *Pasted frames replace existing frames in new location.*

Copy a Frame Sequence
1. Select sequence to copy.
2. Press and hold **Alt**...........Alt
3. Drag to new location on Timeline.
   OR
1. Right-click selected sequence to copy.

2. Click **Copy Frames**.
3. Right-click new starting keyframe on Timeline.
4. Click **Paste Frames**.
   OR
1. Select sequence to copy.
2. Click **Edit**..............Alt+E
3. Click **Timeline**.................M
4. Click **Copy Frames**...........C
5. Select new starting keyframe on Timeline.

6. Click **Edit**..............Alt+E
7. Click **Timeline**.................M
8. Click **Paste Frames**...........P

✓ *Pasted frames replace existing frames in new location.*

EXERCISE DIRECTIONS

Add and Name Scenes
1. Start Flash and open the file ⊘**29DATA**. Save the file as **29GOLF**.
2. Look at the Timeline, and then play the animation. It uses a combination of a grouped background, a motion tweened rolling ball, a frame-by-frame dropping ball, and a sound file.
3. Display the Scene panel.
4. Rename Scene 1 **Putt**.
5. Insert a new scene and name it **Title**.
6. Drag the Title scene above the Putt scene so that it plays first.
7. Insert a third scene, and name it **Close**.
8. Drag the Close scene below the Putt scene, so that it plays last.
9. Save the changes.

Copy Frames to a New Location
1. Make the Putt scene active.
2. Select all frames—frames 1 through 27—on the Background layer.
3. Copy the frames.
4. Make the Title scene active and select frame 1 on Layer 1.
5. Paste the frames into the Timeline.

   ✓ *Notice that Flash automatically changes the name of the layer to Background.*
6. Make the Close scene active and select frame 1 on Layer 1.
7. Paste the frames into the Timeline.

   ✓ *The copied frames remain on the Clipboard and available for pasting until you cut or copy a different item.*

Animate a Text Block
1. Make the Title scene active and select the Background layer.
2. Insert a new layer and name it **Text 1**.

3. Select the Text tool, and insert a static, horizontal, fixed-width text block approximately 3.5" wide.
4. Select a serif font such as Times New Roman, 48 points, black, with centered alignment and then type **Charity Golf Tournament**.

   ✓ *The text should wrap to two lines.*
5. Convert the text block to a graphic symbol named **Text 1**.
6. Align the instance on frame 1 so it is aligned vertically with the top of the Stage and its left edge is about 3" from the left edge of the Stage.
7. On frame 1, select the text block and then, in the Property Inspector, set the Color to Alpha and the Alpha Amount to 100%.
8. Select frame 27 of the Text 1 layer and insert a keyframe.
9. Select the Text 1 instance on the Stage, and then, in the Property Inspector, select Alpha from the Color list and set the Alpha Amount to 0%.
10. Select frame 15 and create a motion tween, with the Scale check box deselected. Rewind and play the animation. The text block should fade out.
11. Lock the layer and save the changes.

Animate a Second Text Block in the Same Scene
1. Select the Text 1 layer and add a new layer, named **Text 2**.
2. Insert a static, horizontal, fixed-width text block approximately 3.5" wide.
3. Use the same font that you used in Text 1, set to 24 points, black, and centered, and type **Proceeds to Benefit Green Space Partnership**.

   ✓ *The text should wrap to two lines.*
4. Convert the text block to a graphic symbol named **Text 2**.

5. Align the instance on frame 1 so it is centered vertically on the Stage and its left edge is about 3" from the left edge of the Stage.

6. Select frame 13 of the Text 2 layer and insert a keyframe.

7. On frame 13, select the Text 2 instance and then, in the Property Inspector, set the Color to Alpha and the Alpha Amount to 100%.

8. Select frame 1, and then select the Text 2 instance and set the Alpha Amount to 0%.

9. Select frame 10 of the Text 2 layer and create a motion tween, deselecting the Scale check box. This should create a tween to fade in the text block.

Edit an Animated Sequence

1. Select frames 1 through 13 of the Text 2 layer and copy the frames.

2. Select frames 14 through 27 of the Text 2 layer and paste the frames.

3. Hide the Text 1 layer and preview the animation. The Text 2 instance fades in, and then fades in again.

4. Select frames 14 through 26 of the Text 2 layer and reverse the frames.

5. Preview the animation again. The instance now fades in and then fades out.

6. Insert a frame between frames 14 and 26 of the Text 2 layer in order to extend the tween through frame 27.

7. Show all layers and preview the animation. In frame 15 of the Title scene, the Stage and Timeline should look similar to Illustration A.

8. Lock all layers and save the changes.

Complete the Application

1. Make the Close scene active and insert a new layer named **Contact**.

2. Insert a static, horizontal, fixed-width text block approximately 3.5" wide.

3. Use the same font that you used in Text 1, set to 24 points, black, and centered, and type **For more information or to register a team, contact Jeannie at 555-6345**.

   ✓ The text should wrap to three lines.

4. Align the text block on frame 1 so it is centered vertically on the Stage and its left edge is about 3" from the left edge of the Stage.

5. Save the changes.

Illustration A

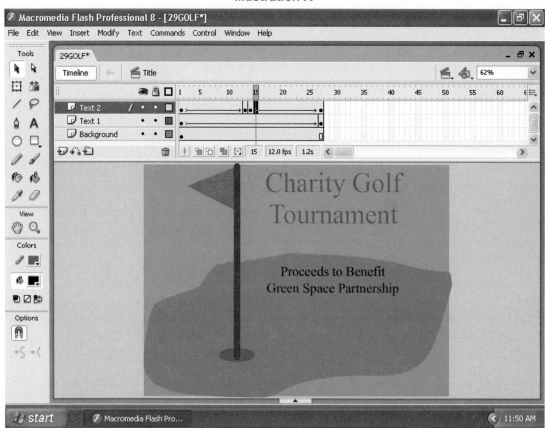

Illustration B

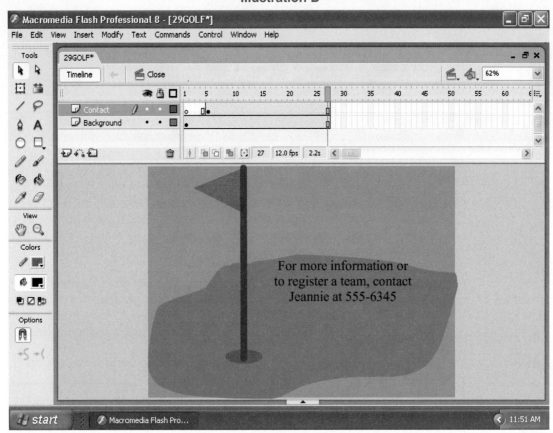

6. Select the Title scene, rewind the animation, and set Flash to play all scenes.

7. Preview the entire application.

   ✓ *Notice that the text block in the Close scene appears quite suddenly.*

8. Make the Close scene active and drag the keyframe on the Contact layer from frame 1 to frame 5. The Stage and Timeline should look similar to Illustration B.

9. Rewind and preview the application again.

10. If requested by your instructor, print the last frame in each scene, or print the entire animation.

11. Lock all layers.

12. Close the file, saving all changes.

13. Exit Flash.

ON YOUR OWN

1. Start Flash and open **28MYPIC**, the file you worked with in Exercise 28, or open **29PIC**. Save the document as **29MYPIC**.

2. Add at least two scenes to the document, and name all three scenes using descriptive names. Organize the scenes so that they play in the correct order.

3. Copy the background from the original scene to the two new scenes in order to maintain continuity.

4. Create content in the new scenes by inserting and animating new objects, or by copying content or animations from the original scene.

5. Preview all scenes in the animation when you are finished and make adjustments, if necessary.

6. When you are satisfied with the results, save the changes and lock the layers.

7. If requested by your instructor, print the last frame of each scene, or print the animation.

8. Close the document, saving all changes, and exit Flash.

Skills Covered

■ **Create a Movie Clip Symbol**   ■ **Create a Button Symbol**

Software Skills Use a movie clip symbol to store an animation that you need to use more than once in an application. This is very important for keeping file size small, because you store the animation once as a symbol and insert instances when you need them. Use button symbols to create interactive buttons that users can click to navigate in an application. For example, a user might click a button to go to a specific scene in an animation.

Application Skills In this exercise, you will enhance the animation for the Green Space Partnership. You will create a movie clip symbol from the Putt animation sequence and then insert instances on all three scenes. You will also create a button symbol that plays the sound of the ball dropping in the cup when clicked.

TERMS

There is no new vocabulary in this exercise.

NOTES

Create a Movie Clip Symbol

■ Use movie clip symbols to store animated sequences that you can reuse many times.

■ For example, if you create an animation of a logo, you might want to use it in different places throughout an animation.

■ You can convert an animation sequence you create on the Stage with the main Timeline into a movie clip symbol, or you can create a blank movie clip symbol and then create the sequence in symbol editing mode.

■ Once you create the movie clip symbol, you can insert an instance in any keyframe; you can even replace the original animated sequence with an instance.

■ Since an instance of a movie clip symbol takes up only a single keyframe in the main Timeline, it is an efficient way to minimize file size.

■ Movie clips can also help simplify the main Timeline because you can replace multiple layers and frames with a single keyframe.

■ The movie clip Timeline plays independently from the main Timeline.

■ To see the movie clip Timeline, you must change to symbol editing mode.

■ To play the entire animation including the movie clip, use the Test Movie command.

■ When you test the animation, Flash exports the animation to a Flash movie file and plays it in a separate Flash Player window in a continuous loop. The movie file is stored in the same location with the same name as the document file.

✓ *You learn more about testing animations in Exercise 37.*

Create a Button Symbol

■ Use button symbols to create interactive buttons that respond to mouse clicks, rollovers, or other actions.

■ You can convert an existing object on the Stage to a button symbol, or you can create a new button symbol and enter the content in symbol editing mode.

■ When you create a button symbol, Flash creates a Timeline with four frames, corresponding to four button states so you can define each state (see the illustration on page 141):

  ● The Up state is the default appearance of the button.

  ● The Over state is the way the button looks or reacts when the user rolls the mouse pointer over it, or rests the mouse pointer on it.

Button Symbol Timeline

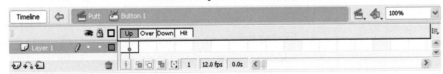

- The Down state is the way the button looks or reacts when the user clicks it with the mouse.
  - The Hit state defines the area around the button that will respond to the rollover or mouse click. The Hit state is invisible when the movie is played.
- You may incorporate drawing objects, graphic symbol instances, sounds, and movie clip symbol instances in any button state, but you cannot use a button symbol in another button symbol.
- Use a movie clip symbol if you want the button to appear animated.

- When you insert a sound in the button symbol Timeline it is stored with the button symbol so it applies to every instance of the symbol.
- The button symbol Timeline doesn't actually play; it simply reacts to the user's pointer.

  ✓ You can assign an action to a button to define what should happen when the user rolls over or clicks the button. Actions are covered in Exercise 31.

- By default, buttons are disabled in Flash. You must enable buttons in order to test them on the Stage.

PROCEDURES

Create a New Movie Clip Symbol

1. Deselect all objects on the Stage.
2. Click **Insert** .... Alt+I
3. Click **New Symbol** .... N
4. Type symbol name in Name box.
5. Click **Movie Clip** option button.
6. Click **OK** .... ↵Enter

   ✓ Flash displays symbol editing mode.

7. Create animation as you would in main movie Timeline.
8. Click **Edit** .... Alt+E
9. Click **Edit Document** .... E

Create a Movie Clip Symbol from an Existing Animation

1. Select every frame in every layer you want to include in movie clip.

   ✓ To select all frames in all layers, click Edit and then click Select All.

2. Right-click selection.
3. Click **Copy Frames**.
4. Deselect all objects on Stage.
5. Click **Insert** .... Alt+I
6. Click **New Symbol** .... N

7. Type symbol name in Name box.
8. Click **Movie Clip** option button.
9. Click **OK** .... ↵Enter

   ✓ Flash displays symbol editing mode.

10. Right-click keyframe in frame 1 of Layer 1.
11. Click **Paste Frames**.
12. Click **Edit** .... Alt+E
13. Click **Edit Document** .... E

Insert a Movie Clip Instance

1. Display Library panel.
2. Select keyframe in Timeline where you want to insert instance.
3. Drag movie clip symbol from Library panel to Stage.
4. If necessary, insert an ending frame to extend the sequence in the layer containing the movie clip instance.

   ✓ The movie clip layer should extend as far as the sequences in other layers.

Create a Button Symbol

1. Deselect all objects on Stage.
2. Click **Insert** .... Alt+I

3. Click **New Symbol** .... N
4. Type symbol name in Name box.
5. Click **Button** option button.
6. Click **OK** .... ↵Enter

   ✓ Flash displays the button Timeline in symbol editing mode.

7. Select **Up** keyframe.
8. Insert or create button as you want it to display when there is no user interaction.

   ✓ You can use the drawing tools; import files; or insert a graphic, sound, or movie clip instance.

9. Select **Over** frame.
10. Insert a keyframe.
11. Modify content to create the button as you want it to display when user rolls the mouse pointer over it.
12. Select **Down** frame.
13. Insert a keyframe.
14. Modify content to create the button as you want it to display when user clicks it.
15. Select **Hit** frame.
16. Insert a keyframe.

17. Use the Oval or Rectangle tool to define an area around the button that will react to a rollover or click.

✓ *The Hit area should be at least as large as the button object, and it may be larger. It is invisible on the Stage.*

18. Click **Edit** .... Alt + E

19. Click **Edit Document** .... E

Enable Buttons (Ctrl+Alt+B)

1. Click **Control** .... Alt + O

2. Click **Enable Simple Buttons** ...... T

✓ *A check mark next to the option indicates that it is already selected.*

Test a Button

1. Enable buttons.

2. Do the following:
- Move mouse pointer over button on Stage to view Over state.
- Click button on Stage to view Down state.

Select a Button Instance when Buttons are Enabled

1. Click **Selection** tool ↖ V

2. Drag selection rectangle around button to select.

Preview a Button or Movie Clip Symbol

1. Display Library panel.

2. Select symbol to preview.

3. Click **Play** button ▶ in Preview area.

OR

1. Click **Control** .... Alt + O

2. Click **Test Movie** .... M

✓ *Animation plays in new Flash Player window.*

3. Click **File** .... Alt + F

4. Click **Close** .... C to close the test window.

EXERCISE DIRECTIONS

Create a Movie Clip Symbol

1. Start Flash and open the file **29GOLF** that you worked with in Exercise 29, or open 🌐**30DATA**. Save the file as **30GOLF**.

2. Make the Putt scene active.

3. Select all frames on all four layers in the scene.

✓ *This is the content you want to convert to a movie clip symbol.*

4. Right-click the selection and click Copy Frames.

5. Deselect all objects.

6. Create a new movie clip symbol named **Ball Roll**.

7. Right-click frame 1 of Layer 1 in the movie clip symbol Timeline and click Paste Frames. Your screen should look similar to Illustration A.

8. Play the animation.

9. Close symbol editing mode and return to editing the main document.

10. Save all changes.

Insert Movie Clip Instances

1. In the Putt scene, delete the Sound, Drop, and Ball layers and remove all frames from the Background layer.

2. Rename the Background layer **Ball Roll Clip**.

3. In frame 1, insert a keyframe.

4. Display the Library panel and insert an instance of the Ball Roll movie clip.

5. Align the instance with the left and bottom edges of the Stage.

6. Select frame 27 of the Ball Roll Clip layer and insert a frame. This extends the sequence.

7. Make the Title scene active.

8. Remove all frames from the Background layer.

9. Rename the Background layer **Ball Roll Clip**.

10. In frame 1, insert a keyframe.

11. Display the Library panel and insert an instance of the Ball Roll movie clip.

12. Align the instance with the left and bottom edges of the Stage.

13. Select frame 27 of the Ball Roll Clip layer and insert a frame. This extends the sequence.

14. Make the Close scene active and repeat steps 8 through 13 to insert the movie clip instance.

15. Save the changes.

Preview the Animation

1. Make the Title scene active and rewind the animation.

2. Make sure the controls are set to play all scenes.

3. Use the Test Movie command to play the entire application.

✓ *It will play in a continuous loop.*

4. Close the test window.

Illustration A

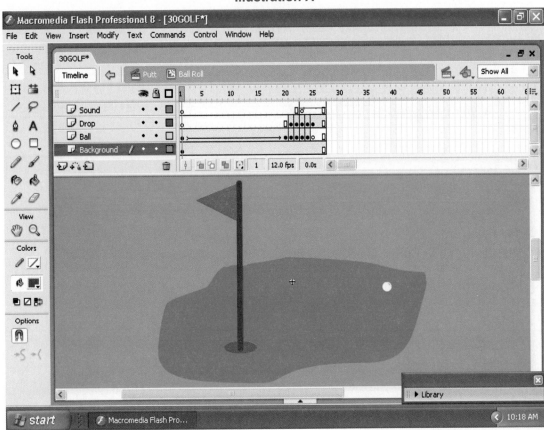

Create a Button Symbol

1. Make the Close scene active.

2. Deselect all objects and then insert a new button symbol named **Golf Button**.

3. Display the Library panel.

4. Select the Up keyframe and insert an instance of the Golf Ball graphic symbol.

5. Resize the instance on the Stage to .75" wide by .75" high.

6. Select the Over frame and insert a keyframe.

7. Select the instance on the Stage.

8. Modify the color of the instance by applying a 60% blue (#3300FF) tint.

9. Select the Down frame and insert a keyframe.

10. Modify the color of the instance by applying a 60% red (#FF0000) tint.

11. From the Library panel, insert an instance of the Putt sound onto the Stage.

12. Select the Hit frame and insert a keyframe.

13. Select the Oval tool and draw a circle about 1.25" in diameter around the golf ball, and then send the circle backward so you can see the golf ball. Center the golf ball within the circle. The Stage should look similar to Illustration B on page 144.

14. Return to editing the document.

Insert and Test a Button Symbol Instance

1. In the Close scene, select the Contact layer and insert a new layer, named **Golf Button**.

2. Select frame 1 of the Golf Button layer.

3. Display the Library panel and insert an instance of the Golf Button symbol.

4. Align the instance with the bottom right of the Stage.

5. Enable simple buttons.

6. Rest the mouse pointer on the button. The button should tint purple.

7. Click the button. The button should tint red and the sound of the ball falling in the cup should play.

8. Make the Putt scene active and insert a new layer, named **Golf Button**.

9. Repeat steps 2 through 4 to insert an instance of the button symbol.

10. Make the Title scene active and insert a new layer, named **Golf Button**.

11. Repeat steps 2 through 4 to insert an instance of the button symbol.

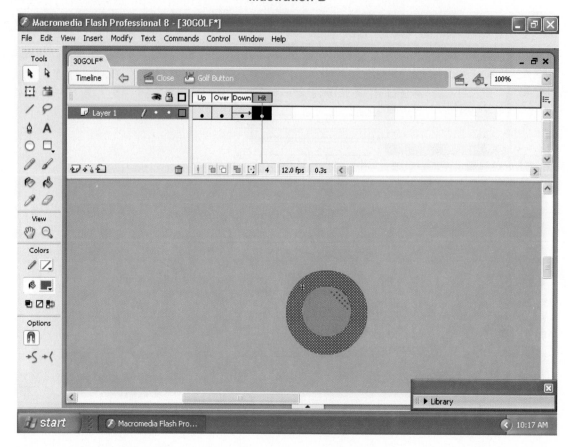

12. Test the movie. While it plays in the Flash Player window, you can see how the button reacts to a rollover and to a click.

13. Close the Flash Player window.

14. Save all changes to the document. If requested by your instructor, print the last frame in each scene, or print the entire animation.

15. Lock all layers in all scenes.

16. Close the file, saving all changes.

17. Exit Flash.

ON YOUR OWN

1. Start Flash and open **29MYPIC**, the file you worked with in Exercise 29, or open ●**30PIC**. Save the document as **30MYPIC**.

2. Create a movie clip symbol from an animation already in the document.

3. Replace the animation in the document with an instance of the movie clip. Insert at least one other instance of the movie clip. For example, insert an instance on one of the other scenes.

4. Test the animation.

5. Create a button symbol that transforms depending on the state. For example, the symbol may increase in size, rotate, or change color in the Over or Down state. You may want to include sound in one of the states.

6. Insert an instance of the button symbol in the application and then test it. Test the entire animation.

7. When you are satisfied with the results, save the changes and lock the layers.

8. If requested by your instructor, print the last frame of each scene, or print the animation.

9. Close the document, saving all changes, and exit Flash.

Skills Covered

- **About Actions**
- **Use Script Assist**

- **Assign an Action to a Frame, Movie Clip, or Button**

Software Skills Use actions in your Flash documents to add interactivity, playback control, and data display to Flash applications. The actions provide instructions for what Flash should do next, such as go to a specific frame or start a sound.

Application Skills In this exercise, you will add actions to the Golf Tournament animation for the Green Space Partnership to control the flow of the animation. First, you will insert a stop action at the end of each scene and the end of the movie clip. Next, you will insert a goto action on each button instance to direct Flash to play the next scene when the button is clicked.

TERMS

Action A set of instructions that cause an action to occur.

Parameters Variable values that define how an action will perform.

Script Assist A feature of Flash 8 that lets you build scripts by selecting items instead of by writing code.

Script statement The written, coded instructions for an action.

NOTES

About Actions

- Insert **actions** in your Flash documents to control the flow and to make an application interactive.

- Actions range from the simple, such as play or stop, to the complex, such as those built around mathematical functions and conditional statements.

- Flash comes with built-in actions, objects, and functions. If you are proficient with object-oriented programming and other scripting languages, such as JavaScript, you can use ActionScript in Flash to write your own statements.

- You access actions via the Actions panel, which by default displays between the Stage and the Property Inspector.

- In the Actions panel, the items you need to build an action—such as functions, statements, and operators—are organized into categories and subcategories. Click a category to display

subcategories, then click a subcategory to display the items. For example, you will find gotoAndPlay and the stopAllSounds items in the Timeline Control subcategory under the Global Functions category.

- In the Actions toolbox, unopened categories and subcategories have square icons; when you click them they open and the icons display as open books. Actions have round icons.

Use Script Assist

- Use **Script Assist** to build **script statements** for simple actions without having an in-depth knowledge of ActionScript or programming.

- With Script Assist, you select items from the Actions toolbox in the Actions panel (see the illustration at the top of page 146). If necessary, Flash prompts you to enter **parameters** in the Parameters pane, and then automatically builds the statement.

Actions Panel

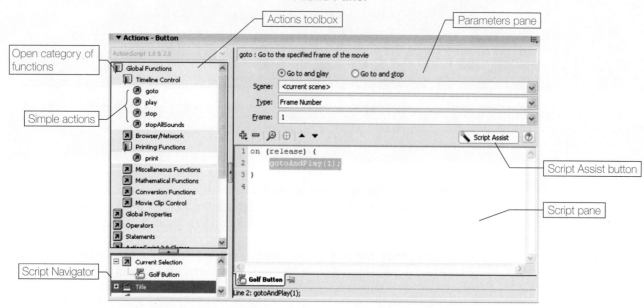

- When Script Assist is on, only simple actions are available in the Actions toolbox.
- You toggle Script Assist off and on using the Script Assist button 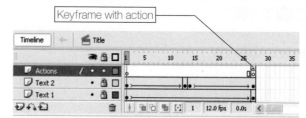 in the Actions panel.
- By default, you cannot preview actions on the Stage. In order to display basic actions on the Stage, you must select the Enable Simple Frame Actions command.

- If you assign an action to an instance of a movie clip or button, not to the symbol itself, only the specified instance triggers the action.
- You can create a separate layer for attaching actions to a keyframe in order to easily locate the action in the Timeline.
- When an action is assigned, a lowercase *a* displays in the Timeline (see the following illustration).

Assign an Action to a Frame, Movie Clip, or Button

- All actions in Flash must be attached to a button, a movie clip, or to a keyframe in the Timeline.
- The action is triggered by an event, such as when the playhead reaches the keyframe, when a movie clip loads, or when a user clicks a button.

A Lowercase *a* Indicates an Action in the Timeline

PROCEDURES

Display the Actions Panel (F9)

1. Click **Window**.............. Alt + W
2. Click **Actions**........................ A

Turn Script Assist On or Off (Ctrl+Shift+E)

1. Display Actions panel.
2. Click **Script Assist** button

   .

   ✓ When Script Assist is on, the button displays with a white background, and the Script pane is

reduced to half height so Flash can display parameters above it.

Insert a Simple Action Using Script Assist

1. Select keyframe, movie clip instance, or button instance.
2. Display Actions panel.
3. Turn on Script Assist.
4. Click category in Actions toolbox.
5. Click subcategory in Actions toolbox.

OR

Double-click action to insert.

6. Set parameters as necessary.

Insert the Go To Action

1. Select keyframe, movie clip instance, or button instance.
2. Display Actions panel.
3. Turn on Script Assist.
4. Click **Global Functions** in Actions toolbox.

5. Click **Timeline Control** in Actions toolbox.

6. Double-click **goto** action.

7. Do one of the following in the Parameters pane:
   - Click **Go to and play** option to set Flash to go to a frame and play the animation.
   - Click **Go to and stop** option to set Flash to go to a frame and stop the animation.

8. Click **Scene** drop-down arrow.

9. Click scene containing frame to go to.

10. Click **Type** drop-down arrow.

11. Select type of element to go to.

12. Click **Frame** box.

13. Type number of frame to go to.

Delete an Action

1. Select keyframe, movie clip instance, or button instance.

2. Display Actions panel.

3. Select action in Script pane.

4. Click **Delete the Selected Action** button ⊟.

Enable Simple Frame Actions (Ctrl+Alt+F)

1. Click **Control**.............Alt+O

2. Click **Enable Simple Frame Actions**.....................I

   ✓ A check mark indicates the command is enabled.

EXERCISE DIRECTIONS

Insert a Stop Action on Keyframes

1. Start Flash and open the file **30GOLF** or open 🔘**31DATA**. Save the file as **31GOLF**.

2. Make the Title scene active and insert a new layer at the top of the layer list named **Actions**.

3. Select frame 27 of the new layer and insert a keyframe.

4. With the keyframe in frame 27 selected, display the Actions panel.

5. In the Actions toolbox, click the Global Functions category and then click the Timeline Control category.

6. Double-click the stop action.

7. Collapse the Actions panel.

8. Enable simple frame actions, then rewind and play the animation. Even with the Play All Scenes command enabled, the animation should stop at the end of the Title scene. The Timeline should look similar to Illustration A.

9. Make the Putt scene active and insert a new layer at the top of the layer list named **Actions**.

10. Repeat steps 3 through 7 to insert a stop action at the end of the scene.

11. Make the Close scene active and insert a new layer at the top of the layer list named **Actions**.

12. Repeat steps 3 through 7 to insert a stop action at the end of the scene.

13. Save the changes.

Insert a Stop Action on a Movie Clip

1. Display the Library panel.

2. Right-click the Ball Roll movie clip symbol and click Edit.

3. Insert a new layer at the top of the layer list named **Actions**.

4. Select frame 27 of the new layer and insert a keyframe.

5. With the keyframe in frame 27 selected, display the Actions panel.

6. In the Actions toolbox, click the Global Functions category if necessary and then click the Timeline Control category.

7. Double-click the stop action.

8. Collapse the Actions panel.

9. Return to editing the document.

Insert a GoTo Action on Buttons

1. Make the Title scene active and unlock all layers.

2. Select the button instance on the lower-right corner of the Stage.

   ✓ If simple buttons are enabled, use the Selection tool to drag around the instance to select it.

3. Display the Actions panel.

4. In the Actions toolbox, click the Global Functions category if necessary and then click the Timeline Control category.

5. Double-click the goto action.

6. In the Parameters pane, make sure that *Go to and play* is selected.

7. Click the Scene drop-down list and click Putt.

   ✓ Alternatively, click <next scene>.

8. Verify that the Type parameter is Frame Number and that the Frame parameter is 1. The Actions panel should look similar to Illustration B on page 148.

Illustration A

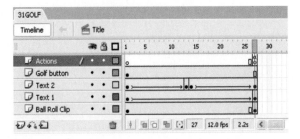

9. Collapse the Actions panel.

10. Enable simple buttons, if necessary, and then click the button on the Stage. The animation should go to frame 1 of the Putt scene and play.

11. Make the Putt scene active and unlock all layers.

12. Select the button instance on the Stage.

13. Display the Actions panel and double-click the goto action.

14. In the Parameters pane, make sure that *Go to and play* is selected.

15. Click the Scene drop-down list and click Close or <next scene>, then verify that the Type parameter is Frame Number and that the Frame parameter is 1.

16. Collapse the Actions panel, enable simple buttons, and then click the button on the Stage. The animation should go to frame 1 of the Close scene and play.

17. Repeat the steps to insert a goto action on the button in the Close scene so that it goes to frame 1 of the Title scene and plays.

18. Save all changes.

Preview and Test the Animation

1. Make the Title scene active and rewind it to the beginning.

2. Enable simple frame actions and simple buttons.

3. Play the animation. It should stop at the end of the scene.

   ✓ *Remember, the movie clip instance won't play on the Stage.*

4. Click the Golf Ball button. The animation should play the Putt scene, and stop at the end.

5. Click the Golf Ball button. The animation should play the Close scene, and stop at the end.

6. Click the Golf Ball button. The animation should play the Title scene, and stop at the end.

7. If requested by your instructor, print the last frame in each scene, or print the entire animation.

8. Lock all layers.

9. Close the file, saving all changes.

10. Exit Flash.

Illustration B

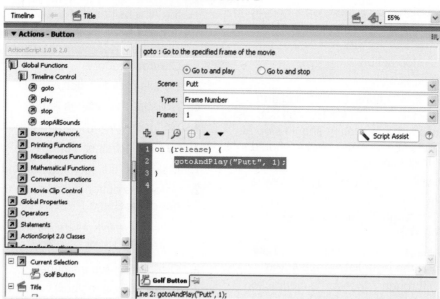

ON YOUR OWN

1. Start Flash and open **30MYPIC**, the file you worked with in Exercise 30, or open **31PIC**. Save the document as **31MYPIC**.

2. Insert actions to control the flow of the animation so that at the end of the first scene the user has a choice of skipping the middle scene or playing the middle scene.

    -   Add a stop action to the ending keyframe of the first scene and to the ending keyframe of the last scene.

    -   Add a goto action to the button in the first scene to skip the middle scene and play the last scene.

    -   Create a new button on the first scene and add a goto action to it to play the middle scene.

    -   Add a goto action to the button in the last scene to go to the first frame of the first scene and play.

    -   Add a goto action in a keyframe at the end of the middle scene to go to and play the last scene.

3. Add a stop action to the ending keyframe of the movie clip symbol so that the movie clip does not play in a continuous loop.

4. Preview all scenes in the animation when you are finished, or test the movie. Make adjustments, if necessary.

5. When you are satisfied with the results, save the changes and lock the layers.

6. If requested by your instructor, print the last frame of each scene, or print the animation.

7. Close the document and exit Flash.

Skills Covered

- **Import Video**

Software Skills Insert video in a Flash document to add live action to your animations. You can integrate video with other elements on the Stage, such as text and graphics, or size the video to fill the Stage and let it stand on its own.

Application Skills With municipal funds tight, the town of Marion, Ohio, has asked your fund-raising consulting company to help it raise private funds for its annual Fourth of July celebration. In this exercise, you will import video of last year's parade into Flash and create a movie clip that you will insert in an existing Flash document. You will use buttons and actions to provide controls so users can stop, play, and rewind the video.

TERMS

Codec A compression/decompression algorithm.

NOTES

Import Video

- Import digital video files into Flash documents in order to include video in your Web-based presentations.

- The most basic method of incorporating video is to embed the video file in the Flash document.

- When you import a video for embedding, you select options on the pages of the Import Video Wizard dialog box (see the illustration in the opposite column). The options vary depending on the type of video you are importing, and the options you select.

- For example, you have the option of embedding the video directly into the Timeline, or as a movie clip or graphic symbol, and you have the option of importing the video to the Stage and library, or just to the library.

  ✓ *If you import the video directly into the Timeline, you can later convert it to a movie clip symbol if desired.*

- You may be able to import the audio as a separate object or as part of the video, depending on the type of video you are using.

- If you embed the video in the Timeline you can preview the video on the Stage. If you embed it as a movie clip, you must use the Test Movie command to preview it.

Embedding Page of the Import Video Wizard

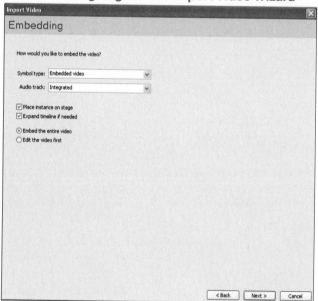

- Flash extends the Timeline to accommodate the full length of the video, which may be quite long.

- You can calculate the number of frames you will require by multiplying the frame rate by the length of the video. For example, if the video is 10 seconds long and the frame rate is 12 fps, you will need 120 frames.

▨ To ensure a smooth playback, the video frame rate and the Flash document frame rate should be the same.

▨ If you embed the video in a movie clip, you extend the Timeline in the movie clip symbol, not in the main document.

▨ You may incorporate graphics and other elements with the video by using multiple layers, either in a movie clip or the main Timeline.

▨ For example, you can use drawing objects to call out segments of a video, or insert buttons with actions so users can control the flow of the video.

▨ Embedded video in Flash should be kept short because of synchronization issues.

▨ When you preview a video on the Stage the audio does not play; use the Test Movie command to hear the audio.

▨ Once a video file is imported into Flash, you cannot edit it in Flash.

▨ However, during the import procedure, you may select to edit the video in order to reduce its length.

▨ The quality of the video in Flash depends on the quality of the recording and the file format.

▨ If you have Apple QuickTime 7 installed on your computer, supported video file types include:
  • QuickTime video .mov
  • Audio-Video Interleave .avi
  • Moving Picture Experts Group .mpeg
  • Digital video .dv

▨ If you have DirectX 9 or later installed, supported video file types include:
  • Audio-Video Interleave .avi
  • Moving Picture Experts Group .mpeg
  • Windows Media File .wmf, .asf

▨ By default, Flash uses the On2 VP 6 **codec** to import and export video, but support for other codecs is available in the Import Video Wizard.

▨ Alternative methods of incorporating video into a Flash application include:
  • Linking Apple QuickTime video formatted files to your Flash application.
  • Importing Flash formatted video files into the library.
  • Progressively downloading video from a Web server.
  • Using the Flash Communication Server to host streaming video content.

PROCEDURES

Embed Video

1. Click **File** .... Alt + F
2. Click **Import** I
3. Click **Import Video**.

   ✓ The Import Video Wizard displays.

4. Click **On your computer**.
5. Enter path to stored video file.

   OR

   a. Click **Browse**.

   b. Locate and select video file.

   c. Click **Open** .... ↵Enter

6. Click **Next**.
7. Click **Embed video in SWF and play in timeline**.
8. Click **Next**.

9. Click **Symbol type** drop-down arrow.
10. Click one of the following:
    • **Embedded video**
    • **Movie clip**
    • **Graphic**
11. Click **Audio track** drop-down arrow.
12. Click one of the following:
    • **Integrated**
    • **Separate**
13. Select or clear the following check boxes:
    • **Place instance on stage**
    • **Expand timeline if needed**

14. Select one of the following:
    • **Embed the entire video**
    • **Edit the video first**

      ✓ Use the controls to edit the video clip as desired.

15. Click **Next**.
16. Set encoding options as desired.
17. Click **Next**.
18. Click **Finish**.

EXERCISE DIRECTIONS

Import a Video to a Movie Clip

1. Start Flash and open the file ●**32DATA**. Save the file as **32MARCH**.
2. Click File > Import > Import Video to start the Import Video Wizard.
3. Select the On Your Computer option button, and then browse to select and open the video file ●**32BAND.mpg** provided with this book.
4. Click Next in the Wizard to move to the Deployment screen.
5. Select the option to embed the video in the SWF file, and then click Next.
6. From the Symbol type list, select Movie clip.
7. From the Audio track list, select Integrated.
8. Clear the *Place instance on Stage* check box, and select the *Expand timeline if needed* check box.
9. Select to embed the entire video and then click Next.
10. Click Next to use the default encoding options.
11. Click Finish.

Create Video Control Buttons

1. Display the Library panel.
2. Deselect all objects on the Stage, and then create a new button symbol named **Stop**.
3. In the Up keyframe, use the Rectangle tool to draw a black square with no stroke, approximately .25" wide.
4. Insert keyframes in the Over, Down, and Hit frames.
5. Edit the document.

6. Create a new button symbol named **Play**.
7. In the Up keyframe, use the PolyStar tool to draw a black triangle with no stroke pointing right, approximately .25" wide.
8. Insert keyframes in the Over, Down, and Hit frames, and then edit the document.
9. Repeat steps 6 through 8 to create a button symbol named **Rewind** that is a left-pointing triangle.

Insert Video Controls in the Movie Clip

1. Display the Library panel. It should look similar to Illustration A.
2. Right-click the **32BAND** movie clip symbol—not the embedded video file—and click Edit to open it in a new window for editing.

   ✓ *You can preview the video in the movie clip symbol, but you cannot hear the audio.*

3. Rename Layer 1 **Video**.
4. Select frame 1 and insert a stop action so that the video does not automatically play when the movie clip loads in the main Timeline.
5. Insert a new layer named **Stop button**.
6. In frame 1, insert an instance of the Stop button symbol.
7. Position the symbol centered under the video on the Stage.
8. Select the button instance and assign a stop action to it.
9. Insert a new layer named **Play button**.
10. In frame 1, insert an instance of the Play button symbol, and position it to the right of the Stop button.

Illustration A

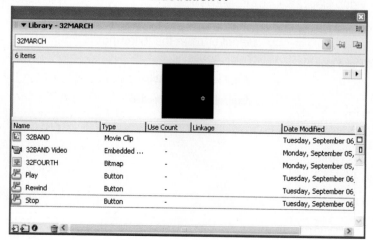

11. Select the Play button instance and assign a Play action to it.

12. Insert a new layer named **Rewind button**, and insert an instance of the Rewind button symbol in frame 1, positioned to the left of the Stop button.

13. Select the Rewind button instance and assign a goto action. Set parameters to go to and play frame 1 of the current scene (these parameters should be the default settings).

14. Lock all layers in the movie clip symbol and save all changes.

15. Select to edit the document to exit symbol editing mode.

Insert the Movie Clip and Test the Document

1. In the **32MARCH** document, insert a new layer named **Video**.

2. Select frame 1 of the Video layer and insert an instance of the **32BAND** movie clip.

3. Align the instance with the left side of the Stage, centered vertically.

4. Resize the instance so it is approximately 3.75" wide. The Stage should look similar to Illustration B. If necessary, adjust the position or size of the movie clip instance so you can see the text.

5. Save the document.

6. Test the movie. When it displays in the Flash Player window click the Play button to start the video.

7. Click the Stop button to stop the video, then click the Play button again. Click the Rewind button to go back to the beginning of the video.

8. When you are finished testing the video controls, close the Flash Player window.

9. Lock all layers in the document.

10. If requested by your instructor, print frame 1.

11. Close the file, saving all changes.

12. Exit Flash.

Illustration B

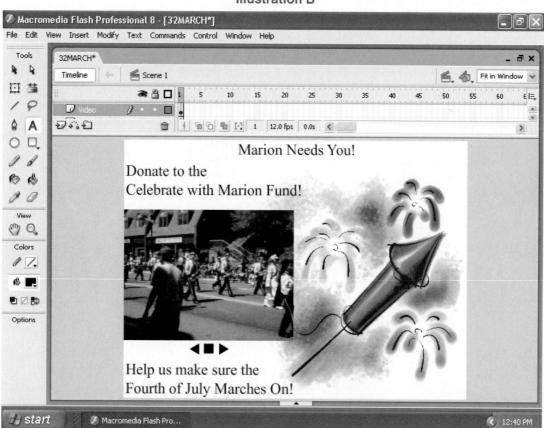

ON YOUR OWN

1. Think of an organization such as a club, team, or volunteer association that might need to recruit members. Create or locate a video clip that represents the organization. For example, for a health club you could use a video of people using the facilities, for a team you could use video of a game, or for a volunteer association you could use video of a fund-raising event.

   ✓ *The organization may have a video clip you could use, or you could use a digital video camera to record a clip and then up load the file to your computer. There are even one-time use video cameras available for a reasonable price at some stores.*

2. Start Flash and create a new document. Save the document as **32MYPIC**.

3. Create a membership drive document you could use on a Web page for the organization. Include graphics and text.

   ✓ *You may use the ◯32DRUM.wmf graphic file and the ◯32JOIN.mov video file provided with this book to create a membership drive document for a marching band.*

4. Import the video file as a movie clip symbol.

5. Create video control buttons to include in the movie clip.

6. Insert the movie clip into the document, and position and align it with the other elements on the Stage.

7. Test the movie and the video control buttons. Make adjustments, if necessary.

8. When you are satisfied with the results, save the changes and lock the layers.

9. If requested by your instructor, print the document.

10. Close the document, and exit Flash.

End of Lesson Projects

- ■ Summary Exercise
- ■ Application Exercise
- ■ Curriculum Integration Exercise
- ■ Critical Thinking Exercise

Exercise | 33

Summary Exercise

Software Skills Castle Gate Productions is promoting a new theater company. In this exercise, you will expand the animation you worked on in Exercises 21 and 22 by adding a scene, importing graphics and sound, and creating text blocks.

DIRECTIONS

Import a Graphic

1. Start Flash and open 💿**33DATA** or open **22CASTLE**. Save the file as **33CASTLE**.
2. Display the Scene panel and rename Scene 1 **Main**.
3. Add a scene and name it **Theater**.
4. Move the Theater scene below the Main scene in the Scene panel so that it plays at the end of the animation.
5. Make the Theater scene active and rename Layer 1 **Stage**.
6. Select frame 1 of the Stage layer.
7. Import the graphic file 💿**STAGE.jpg** provided with this book to the Stage.
8. Resize the graphic to 7" wide—the height should adjust automatically—and center it horizontally and vertically.
9. Select frame 50 and insert a frame to extend the animation.
10. Save the changes and lock the Stage layer.

Import a Sound

1. Insert a new layer named **Applause**.
2. Import the sound file 💿**CLAP.wav** provided with the book to the library.
3. Select frame 1 of the Applause layer and insert an instance of the **CLAP** file.

4. Select frame 50 of the Applause layer and insert a keyframe.
5. Select frame 1 of the Applause layer and, in the Property Inspector, set the sound Effect to Fade out, and set the Sync to Stream.
6. Preview the animation to hear the sound.
7. Save the changes and lock the Applause layer.

Create and Animate a Text Block

1. Insert a new layer named **Text1**, and select frame 1.
2. Select the Text tool and select a serif font such as Times New Roman in 24 points, black.
3. Create a horizontal, extendable text block and type **Introducing...**
4. Center the text block horizontally on the Stage, and position it approximately 3.25" from the bottom of the Stage.
5. Convert the text block to a graphic symbol named **Text1**.
6. Select frame 50 of the Text1 layer and insert a keyframe.
7. Increase the size of the Text1 instance so it is approximately 3" wide and 1" high, and move it up so its top is approximately 2" from the top of the Stage.
8. Select frame 20 of the Text1 layer and create a motion tween. Keep the Scale check box selected.

9. Preview the animation and make adjustments as necessary.

10. Save the changes and lock the Text1 layer.

Create and Animate a Second Text Block

1. Insert a new layer named **Text2**.

2. Select frame 15 of the Text2 layer and insert a keyframe.

3. Select frame 15 and use the Text tool with the same text formatting to create a new horizontal, extendable text block. Type **Theater in the Round**.

4. Center the text block horizontally on the Stage and position it approximately 3.25" from the bottom of the Stage.

5. Convert the text block to a graphic symbol named **Text2**.

6. Select frame 50 of the Text2 layer and insert a keyframe.

7. Increase the width of the Text2 text block to approximately 4". Center it horizontally on the Stage and move it up so its top is approximately 3" from the top of the Stage.

8. Select frame 25 and create a motion tween. Keep the Scale check box selected and set the instance to rotate clockwise 2 times.

9. Preview the animation and make adjustments as necessary.

10. Save the changes and lock the Text2 layer.

Preview All Scenes

1. Make the Main scene active and rewind it to frame 1.

2. Enable the Play All Scenes command.

3. Preview the animation.

4. At the end of the animation, the Stage should look similar to Illustration A.

5. Print the final frame, or, if requested by your instructor, print the Theater scene animation.

6. Close the document and exit Flash, saving all changes.

Illustration A

Application Exercise

Software Skills In this exercise, you continue work on the Castle Gate animation. You will create a movie clip symbol using the sun object and its motion guide. You will also create button symbols and you will insert actions to control the flow of your animation.

DIRECTIONS

Create a Movie Clip Symbol

1. Open ●34DATA or 33CASTLE and save the document as 34CASTLE.

2. Make the Main scene active and unlock the Sun and the Sun motion guide layers.

3. Select all frames on the Sun and the Sun motion guide layers, and select the command to copy the frames.

4. Deselect all frames, and create a new movie clip symbol named **Sunset**.

5. Select frame 1 in the movie clip Timeline and paste the frames.

6. If necessary, move the Sun layer above the guide layer, and then back under the guide layer in order to be certain the motion guide works correctly.

7. Select the Sun guide layer and insert a new layer named **Stop clip**.

8. Insert a keyframe in frame 30 of the Stop clip layer, and then insert a stop action in the keyframe. Preview the animation.

9. Return to editing the document.

Insert and Preview a Movie Clip Symbol

1. In the Main scene, delete the Sun and the Sun motion guide layers.

2. Select the Crown layer and insert a new layer named Stop Scene.

3. Insert a keyframe in frame 30 of the Stop Scene layer, and then insert a stop action in the keyframe.

4. Insert another new layer and name it **Sun Clip**.

5. Select frame 1 of the Sun Clip layer.

6. Display the Library panel and insert an instance of the Sunset movie clip onto the Stage.

7. If necessary, insert a frame in frame 30 of the Sun Clip layer to extend the animation.

8. Use the Test Movie command to preview the animation. The animation should stop at the end of the Main scene.

9. Close the Flash Player window.

Create Buttons Symbols

1. Make sure nothing is selected on the Stage, and create a new, blank button symbol named **Next**.

2. In the Up keyframe, use the Text tool to create a text block and type the word **Next**, using a 36-point sans serif font such as Arial, in black.

3. Use the Rectangle tool to draw a rectangle with no fill and a black stroke approximately 1.25" wide by .5" high around the text block.

4. Insert a keyframe in the Over frame, and another in the Down frame.

5. In the Down keyframe, change the font of the word *Next* to bold.

6. Insert a keyframe in the Hit frame, and then return to editing the document.

7. Deselect all objects on the Stage and create a new button symbol named **Restart**.

8. In the Up keyframe, use the Text tool to create a text block and type the word **Restart**, using the same font as in step 2. Remember to remove the bold formatting.

9. Use the Rectangle tool to draw a rectangle with no fill and a black stroke approximately 1.75" wide by .5" high around the text block.

10. Insert a keyframe in the Over frame, and another in the Down frame.

11. In the Down keyframe, change the font of the word *Restart* to bold.

12. Insert a keyframe in the Hit frame, and then return to editing the document.

13. Save the changes.

Insert Button Instances and Actions

1. Insert a new layer named **Next button**.

2. Select frame 30 and insert a keyframe.

3. In the keyframe, insert an instance of the Next button.

4. Center the instance horizontally and position it approximately .5" from the top of the Stage.

5. Select the instance and insert a goto action.

6. Set the action parameters so the action goes to the first frame of the Theater scene and plays. With the Library panel open, your screen should look similar to Illustration A.

7. Make the Theater scene active and insert a new layer named **Stop Scene**.

8. Copy the frames from the Stop Scene layer in the Main scene to the Stop Scene layer in the Theater scene. Insert or remove frames as necessary so the stop action is in frame 50.

9. Insert a new layer named **Restart**.

10. Select frame 50 of the Restart layer and insert a keyframe.

11. Insert an instance of the Restart button and center the instance horizontally, and position it about .5" from the top of the Stage.

12. Select the instance and insert a goto action, setting parameters so the action goes to the first frame of the Main scene and plays. With the Library panel collapsed, your screen should look similar to Illustration B.

13. Save the changes.

Preview the Animation

1. Use the Test Movie command to preview the animation.

2. At the end of the Main scene, the animation should stop. Click the Next button to play the Theater scene.

3. At the end of the Theater scene, the animation should stop again. Click the Restart button to play the Main scene.

4. If necessary, make adjustments to the document.

5. Lock all layers.

6. Print the last frame in each scene.

7. Close the document and exit Flash, saving all changes.

Illustration A

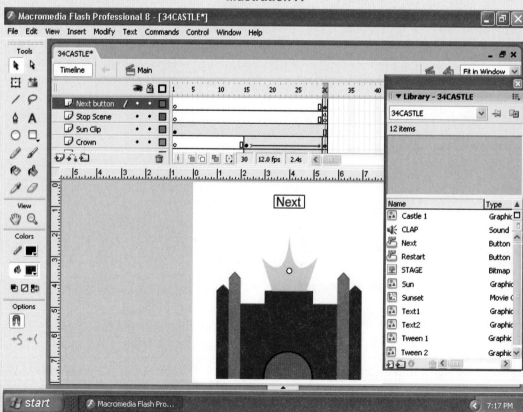

Illustration B

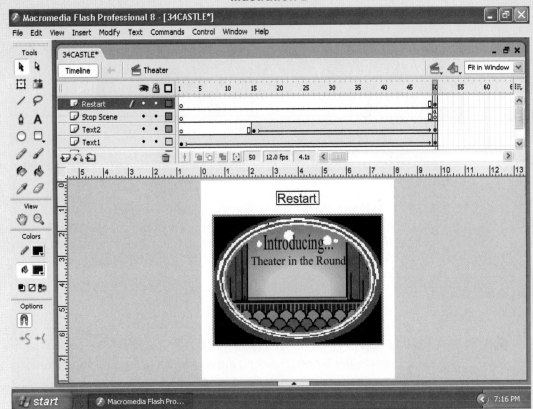

Exercise | 35

Curriculum Integration Exercise

Software Skills For a social studies project, use Flash to create an animation advertising a location as a travel destination. Individually or as a group, select and then research a location. You might use your home town, a nearby city, or any place you would like to visit. The animation should include at least three scenes. You can highlight three aspects of the location on each scene. You should incorporate imported graphics, such as pictures of the location, text, sound, actions, and symbols. If possible, include video as well. The following illustrations are samples of how three scenes might look.

DIRECTIONS

Start a new document and save it as **35TRAVEL**.

Prepare the Stage by setting the ruler units to inches, and displaying visual tools you may find useful, such as the grid or guides.

Create and name three scenes.

Import graphics to illustrate each scene.

Try to locate a sound file that you might be able to incorporate, and import it into the library. For example, if the location has a river, you may be able to locate the sound of running water that you could add to the scene. If the location has a zoo, you might use animal sounds. You could even use a song that plays throughout all scenes.

Use the Text tool to create a text block containing the name of the location, and then animate it. Convert the animation into a movie clip symbol. Insert the movie clip on at least one scene. Use a stop action at the end of the clip so that it doesn't play in a continuous loop.

Create buttons and insert instances in each scene. Add actions to the button instances that users can click to control the flow of the animation. For example, create a button the user can click to view the next scene and one for the previous scene.

Preview the animation using the Test Movie command. Make adjustments as necessary.

Print the completed animation.

Save your changes and close the document.

First Scene Timeline

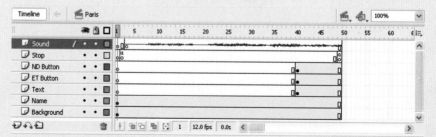

First Scene Preview

Second Scene

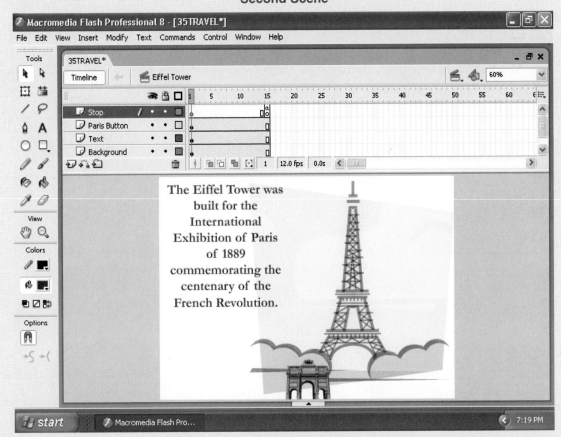

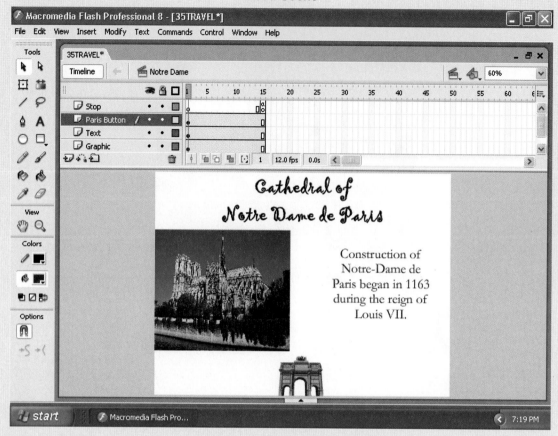

Critical Thinking Exercise

Software Skills The Brighter Than Bright tooth-whitening franchise is expanding to offer other cosmetic dentistry services, such as veneers. In this exercise, you will create an animation using multiple scenes, imported graphics, text, actions, and symbols. You will create one scene, named Menu, from which the user may click a button to go to the other two scenes. On each of the other scenes you will include buttons to go back to the menu or to the other scene. In addition, you will create a logo for the company in a movie clip symbol using animated text blocks. You will insert the logo clip on each scene.

DIRECTIONS

- Create a new Flash document. Save the document as **36BRIGHT**.
- Insert layers and create an animation of the company name: Brighter Than Bright. Create the text in text blocks. You may then want convert it to symbols so that you can use it in animations. For example, you can color tween an instance of a graphics symbol to make text fade in. You may want to break it apart so you can animate each individual character, or so you can transform the characters as shapes.
- When the animation is complete, create a movie clip named **LOGO** and move the animation into it. Add a stop action to its last frame so it does not run in a continuous loop.
- Delete the animation from the main Timeline, and insert the movie clip on a layer named **Logo** in its place.
- Insert a layer named **Text** and create a text block instructing the user to click a button below.
- Rename Scene 1 **Menu**. See the illustration on page 164 for a sample Menu scene.
- Add two new scenes: Veneers and Brighten.
- In the Veneers scene, insert the logo clip on its own layer. In addition, create an animation using text and graphics explaining that Brighter Than Bright now offers veneers using the latest technology. See the illustration at the top of page 165 for a sample Veneers scene.
- In the Brighten scene, insert the logo clip on its own layer. In addition, create an animation using text and graphics explaining that Brighter Than Bright still offers the best teeth-whitening services. (You may want to use the animation you created in Exercise 24 to illustrate this scene. If so, convert it to a movie clip so you can easily insert it into the Timeline.) See the illustration at the bottom of page 165 for a sample Brighten scene.
- Locate two graphic pictures that have something to do with dentistry, and one for a menu. Import them into the Library panel. You will use these pictures as buttons linking to each scene. If you cannot locate suitable pictures, use the files ⚫VENEER.wmf, ⚫MENU.wmf, and ⚫BRIGHT.wmf, provided with this book.
- Convert each graphic to a button symbol. In the Up frame, size the picture so it is about 1" high. Insert a text block beneath it with the appropriate scene name.

- For example, type **Veneers** below one, **Brighten** below one, and **Menu** below the other. Use the same content in the Up, Over, and Down keyframes. In the Hit keyframe, insert a rectangle large enough to cover both the graphic and the text.
- On separate layers, insert the Veneers and Brighten buttons on frame 1 in the Menu scene. Position them in the lower corners of the Stage.
- Insert actions for each instance to go to and play the appropriate scene. For example, when the user clicks the Veneers button, Flash should go to and play the Veneers scene.
- In the Veneers scene, insert the Brighten and Menu buttons, and insert actions to go to and play the appropriate scenes.
- In the Brighten scene, insert the Veneers and Menu buttons, and insert actions to go to and play the appropriate scenes.
- Add stop actions at the end of each scene.
- Test all scenes and test all buttons. Make adjustments as necessary. For example, you may need to extend the animations.
- If requested by your instructor, print the animation.
- Close the document, saving all changes, and exit Flash.

Menu

Veneers

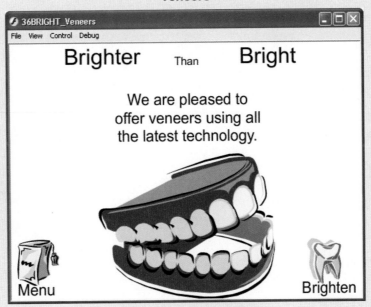

Brighten

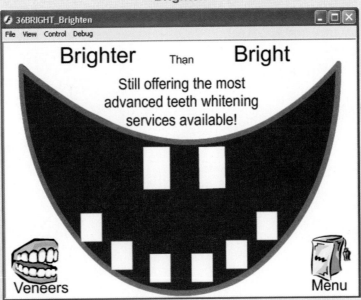

Lesson | 4

Publishing an
Application

Skills Covered

■ **Test a Movie**

■ **Test Download Performance**

Software Skills Use the Test Movie command to see how an animation will look to a user viewing it in a Web browser. Test download performance to identify problems with speed and flow.

Application Skills In this exercise, you will test an application for the Green Space Partnership Web site, thanking patrons for participating in the golf tournament. You will also test the download performance, and modify frames as necessary to ensure a smooth replay.

TERMS

Publish To create a Web-compatible version of a Flash document file, which can then be stored on a Web server and accessed by users on the Web.

NOTES

Test a Movie

■ Before you **publish** your Flash application, it's important to test how it will look to a user on the Internet.

■ Not every feature in a Flash document can be viewed on the Flash stage. For example, you cannot play a movie clip instance.

■ To view the application as it would look on the Internet, you must use the Test Movie command to export the application to a Flash Player file and display it in a Flash Player window.

■ The Flash Player file has the same name as the Flash file, but the three-character file name extension changes from .fla to .swf. For example, a Flash file named Dance.fla would become Dance.swf.

■ The .swf Flash Player file is stored in the same folder as the .fla Flash file.

■ In the Flash Player window, the entire animation plays from the first frame to the last frame. If there are multiple scenes, they play in consecutive order.

■ You may choose to test just the current scene instead of the entire animation.

■ If you test a single scene, the frames from that scene only are exported as a Flash Player file. The

Flash Player file has the same name as the Flash .fla file, with an underscore and the scene name added. For example, Scene 1 in a Flash file named Dance.fla would become Dance_Scene 1.swf.

■ By default, the application loops continuously in the Flash Player window. You can use the Control menu options to rewind, play, stop, and forward an animation in the Flash Player window.

Test Download Performance

■ To play smoothly over the Internet, each frame in a Flash application must download before the animation reaches that frame.

■ If an application reaches a frame that has not yet been downloaded the movie pauses until the download is complete.

■ The speed of the download depends on the data transfer rate and the amount of data stored in each frame.

■ Use the Flash Bandwidth Profiler to test your animation to locate frames where pauses might occur.

■ The Bandwidth Profiler displays a graphic representation of the amount of data that is sent from each frame in the movie.

Bandwidth Profiler in Streaming Graph View

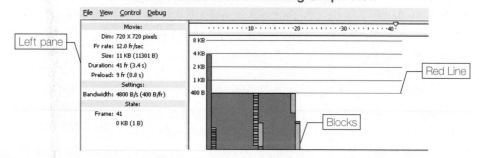

Bandwidth Profiler in Frame by Frame Graph View

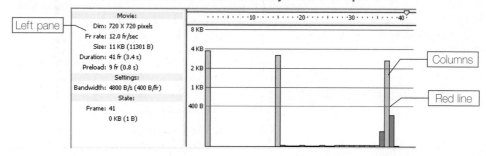

- The left pane of the profiler has three sections:
  - Movie, which includes information about the dimensions, frame rate, frame size, duration, and preloaded frames by number of seconds.
  - Settings, which has bandwidth information.
  - State, which includes information on the number of frames and loading.
- The right pane of the Profiler shows the Timeline header and a graph.
- The red horizontal line in the graph marks the point at which a frame streams in real time with the selected modem speed.
- You can view a Streaming Graph or a Frame by Frame Graph (see the illustrations above).
  - In the Streaming Graph, frames are represented by alternating light and dark gray blocks, stacked in columns. The height of each block indicates its relative byte size.

- In the Frame by Frame Graph, each column represents one frame; any frame extending above the red line might cause a pause in the animation.
- Change the Bandwidth Download settings to see how the animation will play at different modem speeds. For example, you may test the animation as it would play using a 56K modem, a DSL line, or a T1 line.
- If a frame is large enough to impact performance, you can try to optimize it to make it smaller so that it will load faster.
- Typical optimization methods include substituting device fonts for embedded fonts, inserting instances instead of graphics, using vector graphics instead of bitmaps, and deleting unnecessary content.

PROCEDURES

Test a Movie (Ctrl+Enter)

1. Open the document in Flash.

   ✓ *If the document contains multiple scenes, be sure the Play All Scenes command is selected on the Control menu.*

2. Click **Control**..............[Alt]+[O]
3. Click **Test Movie**..................[M]

Test the Current Scene (Ctrl+Alt+Enter)

1. Open the document in Flash.
2. Display the desired scene.
3. Click **Control**..............[Alt]+[O]
4. Click **Test Scene**......................[S]

Control a Movie in Flash Player

1. Open the document in Flash.
2. Click **Control**..............[Alt]+[O]
3. Click **Test Movie**...................[M]
   OR
   Click **Test Scene**......................[S]
4. Click **Control**..............[Alt]+[C]
   in Flash Player window.

5. Click one of the following:

  • **P**lay .... P
  • **R**ewind .... R
  • **L**oop L

  ✓ *A check mark next to the command indicates it is selected.*

  • Step **F**orward One Frame .... F
  • Step **B**ackward One Frame ...... B

  ✓ *If the Controller toolbar is displayed in the Flash window, you can use it to control the movie in the Flash Player window. See Exercise 12 for information on using the Controller toolbar.*

Display the Bandwidth Profiler

1. Open the document in Flash.
2. Click **Control** .... Alt + O
3. Click Test **M**ovie .... M
4. Click **V**iew .... Alt + V
5. Click **B**andwidth Profiler .... B

  ✓ *A check mark next to the command indicates it is selected.*

6. Click **V**iew .... Alt + V
7. Click one of the following:
  • **S**treaming Graph .... S
  • **F**rame by Frame Graph .... F

Change Bandwidth Download Settings

1. Open the document in Flash.
2. Click **Control** .... Alt + O
3. Click Test **M**ovie .... M
4. Click **V**iew .... Alt + V
5. Click **D**ownload Settings .... D
6. Click desired download speed.

Close the Flash Player Window (Ctrl+W)

■ Click **Window Close** button .... ☒
  OR
1. Click **F**ile .... Alt + F
2. Click **C**lose C

EXERCISE DIRECTIONS

Test an Animation

1. Start Flash and open ◉**37DATA**. Save the file as **37GOLF**.
2. Use the Test Movie command to play the animation in a Flash Player window.
3. Disable the Loop command on the Control menu to stop the animation from playing over and over.
4. In the Flash Player window, display the Bandwidth Profiler.
5. If necessary, change the display to the Streaming Graph.
6. If necessary, set the Download Settings to 56K.
7. Rewind and play the animation.
8. Change the display to Frame by Frame Graph. It should look similar to Illustration A. Notice that three frames extend above the red line: frame 1, frame 15, and frame 37.
9. Change the Download Settings to DSL to see how a faster download speed affects performance.
10. Change the Download Settings back to 56K.
11. Close the Bandwidth Profiler.
12. Close the Flash Player window.

Optimize Frames for Download Performance

1. In the Timeline, notice that a lot of content is added to the animation in frames 1, 15, and 37. Having content load in frame 1 is not a problem, but you can improve the download performance by optimizing frames 15 and 37 by converting the animation into a movie clip.
2. Select all frames in the Golfer, Sound, Drop, Guide: Ball, Ball, and Green layers (all layers except Text1 and Text2), and copy the frames.
3. Deselect all content on the Stage, and then create a new movie clip symbol named **Putter**.

4. Select frame 1 on Layer 1 of the movie clip symbol and paste the frames. If necessary, move the Ball layer above its guide layer in the list, and then back down to link it to the guide.
5. At the top of the layer list, insert a new layer named **Stop**.
6. Select frame 41 of the Stop layer and insert a keyframe. Insert a stop action on the keyframe.
7. Lock all layers.
8. Return to editing the main animation and delete the Golfer, Sound, Drop, Guide: Ball, Ball, and Green layers (all layers except Text1 and Text2).
9. Insert a new layer, named **Putter Clip**.
10. Select frame 1 of the Putter Clip layer and insert an instance of the Putter movie clip symbol. Center the instance horizontally and vertically.
11. Save the changes.

Test an Animation

1. Test the animation in the Flash Player window.
2. Disable the Loop control.

  ✓ *The movie clip will not loop because of the stop action in the last frame; disabling the Loop control stops the main animation from looping.*

3. Display the Bandwidth Profiler in Frame by Frame Graph view. It should look similar to Illustration B. Notice that now only frame 1 extends above the red line.
4. Close the Bandwidth Profiler, and then close the Flash Player window.
5. Print frame 15, or, if requested by your instructor, print the entire animation sequence.
6. Lock all layers.
7. Close the file, saving all changes, and exit Flash.

Illustration A

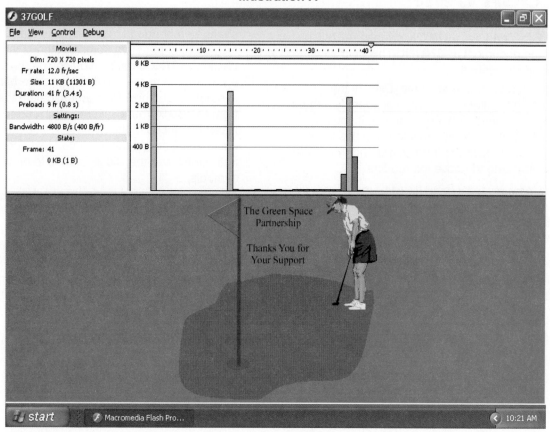

Illustration B

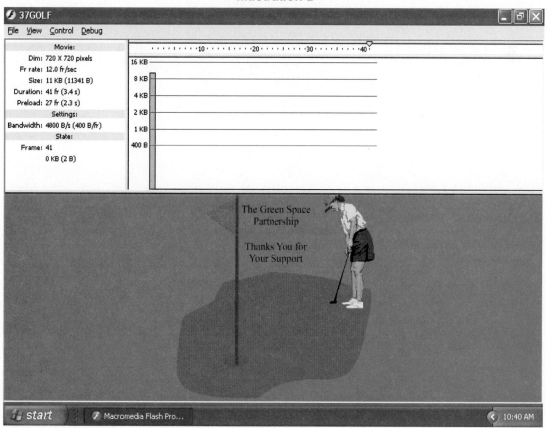

ON YOUR OWN

1. Start Flash and open **31MYPIC** or open **⊙37PIC**. Save the document as **37MYPIC**. This animation has multiple scenes.

2. Test each scene, one at a time. Display the Bandwidth Profiler so that you can identify frames that need optimization. For example, if you are using the **37PIC** data file provided with this book, there are frames in the Intro scene and the Close scene that extend above the red line.

   ✓ Note: When you test a scene, the frame numbering in the Bandwidth Profiler starts at frame 1. When you test the entire movie, the frame numbering continues consecutively through all scenes.

3. Close the Flash Player window and try optimizing frames to improve download performance. You may be able to convert graphics to symbols, or animations to movie clips. You may be able to

change embedded fonts to display fonts, or you may be able to delete some content. For example, in the **37PIC** data file, you could convert the background image (**25FLOWERS**) from a bitmap to a symbol. To optimize the frames, delete the bitmap from the Background layer in each scene, and insert instances of the symbol in its place. You could also convert the animated text sequences in the Intro and the Close scenes to movie clip symbols.

4. After optimizing frames, test the scenes or the entire animation. You should have fewer frames extending above the red line.

5. When you are satisfied with the animation, print the final frame.

6. Save the file and close it, and then exit Flash.

Skills Covered

- **Publish a Flash Application**
- **Publish Settings**
- **Preview a Published Application**

Software Skills When you are ready to distribute a Flash application, you must publish it. Publishing prepares the files required to play the application correctly on a Web page. Select publish settings to control the way the application displays, then preview the published application to make sure you like the results.

Application Skills In this exercise, you will publish an application for the Green Space Partnership. You will select Flash and HTML settings, and then preview the animation in your browser.

TERMS

HTML The acronym for Hypertext Markup Language, which is the programming language used to define and format data for display on the Word Wide Web.

Projector A published Flash document in which a version of Flash Player is stored. The projector plays as a stand-alone video even if the user's computer does not have Flash Player installed.

Web browser A software program such as Microsoft Internet Explorer that displays Web pages and allows the user to navigate from one page to another.

NOTES

Publish a Flash Application

- Publish a complete Flash .fla file in Flash Player format so you—and others—can play it on the Web in the Flash Player program.

- When you publish an application, you select options in the Publish Settings dialog box and Flash generates the files required to display the animation correctly.

- By default, when you publish a file, Flash generates an .swf (Flash Player) version of the original .fla file and an **HTML** document that provides the instructions for inserting the Flash application in a **Web browser** window.

- Alternatively, you can publish the .fla file as a Flash stand-alone **projector** or in alternative file formats that display if there is no Flash Player installed on the user's computer. Available formats include .gif, .jpg, .png, and QuickTime.

- If you edit or modify a Flash file that you have published, you must publish it again in order to update the Flash Player file.

Publish Settings

- Select publish settings in the Publish Settings dialog box (see the illustration on page 174).

Publish Settings Dialog Box

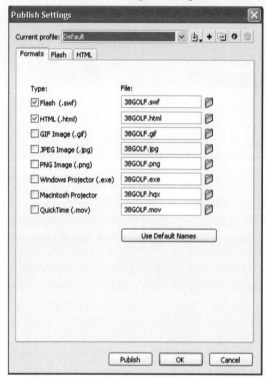

- Options that you select in the Publish Settings dialog box override options that are set in the application file. For example, if you select red as the background color in the Publish Settings dialog box, then red will display, even if you selected gray in the Document Properties dialog box.

- On the Formats tab in the Publish Settings dialog box you select the type of files you want to generate. By default, Flash (.swf) and HTML (.html) are selected.

- By default, published file names are the same as the original .fla file name, with the appropriate file name extension added, and published files are stored in the same location as the original .fla file.

- You can change the default file name and select a different storage location, if desired.

- In the Publish Settings dialog box, Flash displays a tab for each selected file format so you can select options such as dimensions, color settings, and image control settings.

- On the Flash tab, set image, sound compression, debugging, and file protection options; and select to generate a text file listing the amount of data in each frame of the final Flash Player file, if desired.

- On the HTML tab, select an HTML template, and set parameters specifying options such as how to align the application onscreen, what size window to use, and the background color, as well as playback and quality options.

  ✓ By default, Flash uses the basic HTML template which embeds the Flash Player file as an object in the HTML page.

Preview a Published Application

- Use the Publish Preview command to see how your published movie will look in a Web browser.

- Flash creates a file that you can open in your default Web browser.

- You can also test all interactive options, such as buttons.

- The file may launch automatically in your Web browser, or you may have to use Windows to open it.

PROCEDURES

Display Publish Settings Dialog Box (Ctrl+Shift+F12)

1. Open the document in Flash.
2. Click **File**.................... Alt + F
3. Click **Publish Settings**............. G

Set File Type Options

1. Display Publish Settings dialog box.
2. Click Formats tab, if necessary.
3. Click to select or deselect file types:
   - **Flash (.fla)**................. Alt + F
   - **HTML (.html)**............. Alt + H
   - **GIF Image (.gif)**.......... Alt + G
   - **JPEG Image (.jpg)**........ Alt + J

   - **PNG Image (.png)**........ Alt + P
   - **Windows Projector (.exe)**...................... Alt + W
   - **Macintosh Projector**...... Alt + M
   - **QuickTime (.mov)**.......... Alt + Q

4. Replace default file name(s) with new file name(s), if desired.

   ✓ You must include the correct file name extension.

5. Click **Select Publish Destination** icon.................................... to change storage location, if desired, then locate and select desired location and click **Save**.

   ✓ The default location is the same as the storage location for the original .fla file.

6. Click **OK**........................ Enter to save the settings and close the dialog box.

Select Flash (.swf) Publish Settings

1. Display Publish Settings dialog box.
2. Click Formats tab, if necessary.
3. Click to select **Flash (.fla)**, if necessary............. Alt + F

4. Replace default file name(s) with new file name(s), if desired.

   ✓ *You must include the correct file name extension.*

5. Change storage location, if desired.

   ✓ *The default location is the same as the storage location for the original .fla file.*

6. Click **Flash** tab........ Ctrl + Tab⇆

7. Click **Version** drop-down arrow and click Flash Player version to use.

   ✓ *If you select version 6, you may select the option to optimize for Flash Player 6.*

8. Click **Load order** drop-down arrow, and then click one of the following:

   • **Bottom up** to load layers from the bottom of the layer list to the top.

   • **Top down** to load layers from the top of the layer list to the bottom.

9. Click **ActionScript version** drop-down arrow and click ActionScript version to use.

10. Select or deselect options to control debugging as desired:

    • **Generate size report** to create a text file listing amount of data in each frame of the published Flash Player file.

    • **Protect from import** to prevent unauthorized users from converting the .swf file back to a .fla file.

      ✓ *You may enter a password to protect the file.*

    • **Omit trace actions** to prevent the Output panel or tab from displaying comments.

    • **Debugging permitted** to allow remote debugging.

      ✓ *You may enter a password to protect the file.*

    • **Compress movie** to reduce file size.

11. Adjust the **JPEG quality** slider to control bitmap compression.

    ✓ *The lower the quality, the smaller the published file.*

12. Click **Audio Stream Set** button to set compression, bit rate, and quality options for streaming audio.

    ✓ *Click OK to return to Publish Settings dialog box.*

13. Click **Audio Event Set** button to set compression bit rate and quality options for event sounds.

    ✓ *Click OK to return to Publish Settings dialog box.*

14. Select **Override sound settings** check box to override .fla file sound settings.

15. Select **Export device sounds** check box to export sounds suitable for devices.

    ✓ *Available for Flash Professional only.*

16. Click **Local playback security** drop-down arrow and then click one of the following:

    • **Access local files only** to let the published files interact with files on the local system, but not on the network.

    • **Access network only** to let the published files interact with files on the network, but not on the local system.

17. Click **OK** .... ↵Enter to save the settings and close the dialog box.

Select HTML (.html) Publish Settings

1. Display Publish Settings dialog box.

2. Click Formats tab, if necessary.

3. Click to select **HTML (.html)** .... Alt + H, if necessary.

4. Replace default file name(s) with new file name(s), if desired.

   ✓ *You must include the correct file name extension.*

5. Change storage location, if desired.

   ✓ *The default location is the same as the storage location for the original .fla file.*

6. Click **HTML** tab........ Ctrl + Tab⇆

7. Click **Template** drop-down arrow and then click desired template.

   ✓ *Flash Only is the default.*

   ✓ *Click Info to display a description of selected template.*

8. Select **Detect Flash Version** check box to have published file automatically send user to an alternative HTML page if the installed Flash Player version does not match the version selected on the Flash tab of the Publish Settings dialog box.

9. Click **Dimensions** drop-down arrow and then click one of the following:

   • **Match Movie** to use the current document size.

   • **Pixels** to specify width and height in pixels.

     ✓ *Enter values in Width and Height boxes.*

   • **Percent** to specify size as a percentage of browser window.

     ✓ *Enter values in Width and Height boxes.*

10. Select desired playback options:

    • **Paused at start** to pause animation until user action such as a click.

    • **Loop** to repeat animation continuously.

    • **Display menu** to display shortcut menu when user right-clicks browser screen.

    • **Device font** to substitute device fonts for embedded fonts not available on user's system.

11. Click **Quality** drop-down arrow, and then click desired Quality option:
    - **Low**
      to set a low quality and a high processing speed.
    - **Auto Low**
      to automatically increase quality if possible without slowing processing speed.
    - **Auto High**
      to automatically sacrifice image quality to improve processing speed.
    - **Medium**
      to set an intermediate quality and processing speed.
    - **High**
      to set a high quality even if it means slowing processing speed.
    - **Best**
      to display the highest possible quality without regard to processing speed.

12. Click **Window Mode** drop-down arrow and then click desired transparency option:
    - **Window**
      to play animation in its own window on Web page.
    - **Opaque Windowless**
      to display animation over HTML background, without letting the background show through.
    - **Transparent Windowless**
      to display animation over HTML background, letting the background show through transparent areas of the animation.

13. Click **HTML alignment** drop-down arrow and then click desired option for aligning Flash

Player window within browser window:
    - **Default**
      to center animation in browser window.
    - **Left**
      to left-align animation in browser window.
    - **Right**
      to right-align animation in browser window.
    - **Top**
      to align animation at top edge of browser window.
    - **Bottom**
      to align animation at bottom edge of browser window.

14. Click **Scale** drop-down arrow and then click desired scale options:
    - **Default (Show all)**
      to fit animation within specified dimensions without distortion.
    - **No border**
      to fit animation within specified dimensions without distortion, cropping if necessary.
    - **Exact fit**
      to fit within specified dimension with distortion.
    - **No scale**
      to prevent the animation from scaling even if the Flash Player window is resized.

15. Click **Flash alignment Horizontal** drop-down arrow and then click desired option for aligning animation horizontally in Flash Player window:
    - **Left**
    - **Center**
    - **Right**

16. Click **Flash alignment Vertical** drop-down arrow and then click desired option for aligning animation vertically in Flash Player window:
    - **Top**
    - **Center**
    - **Bottom**

17. Select **Show warning messages** check box to display error messages if HTML settings conflict.

18. Click **OK** ....⏎Enter
    to save the settings and close the dialog box.

Preview a Flash Application in a Web Browser

1. Open your browser.
2. Open the document in Flash.
3. Click **File** ....Alt + F
4. Click **Publish Preview** ....R
5. Click file format to preview:
    - **Default (HTML)** ....D
    - **Flash** ....F
    - **HTML** ....H

    ✓ *Other formats may be available, depending on the options selected in the Publish Settings dialog box.*

6. Change to your Web browser to view the application.
7. Click Web browser's **Close** button ⊠ to close window when finished.

Publish an Application Using Current Publish Settings (Shift+F12)

1. Open the document in Flash.
2. Click **File** ....Alt + F
3. Click **Publish** ....B

EXERCISE DIRECTIONS

Select Publish Settings and Preview the Application

1. Start your Web browser.
2. Start Flash and open ●38DATA. Save the file as **38GOLF**. This is a version of the file you worked with in Exercise 37, with a Replay button added.
3. Display the Publish Settings dialog box.
4. On the Formats tab, verify that Flash and HTML are selected, and that the default file names and storage locations are entered.
5. Click the Flash tab.
6. Verify that the default settings are selected:
   - Version: Flash Player 8
   - Load order: Bottom up
   - ActionScript version: ActionScript 2.0
   - Compress movie: Enabled
   - JPEG quality: 80
7. Click the HTML tab and verify the following settings:
   - Template: Flash Only
   - Detect Flash Version: Disabled
   - Dimensions: Match Movie

      ✓ *If necessary, select this option from the Dimensions list.*

   - Loop: Enabled
   - Display menu: Enabled
   - Quality: High
   - Window Mode: Window
   - HTML alignment: Default
   - Scale: Default (Show all)
   - Horizontal alignment: Center
   - Vertical alignment: Center
   - Show warning messages: Enabled
8. Click OK to save the settings and close the dialog box.

9. Select the Publish Preview command from the File menu, and then select the Default format (HTML).
10. Switch to your Web browser to view the file published with the current default publish settings. You may have to scroll down in the browser to view the bottom of the window.

Change Publish Settings, Preview, and Publish the Application

1. Switch to Flash and display the Publish Setting dialog box.
2. Click the HTML tab.
3. From the Dimensions drop-down list, select Percent. Verify that the Width and Height are set to 100%.
4. Click OK to save the settings and close the dialog box.
5. Select the Publish Preview command from the File menu, and then select the Default format (HTML).
6. Switch to your Web browser to view the file published with the current default publish settings. It should look similar to Illustration A on page 178.
7. When the animation stops, click the Replay button.
8. When the animation stops, right-click anywhere in the browser window to display a shortcut menu.
9. On the shortcut menu, click Play.
10. When the animation stops, close your browser window.
11. Publish the application file.
12. Close the file, saving all changes, and exit Flash.

Illustration A

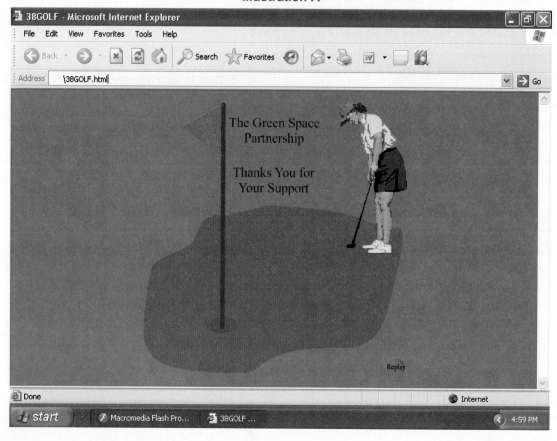

ON YOUR OWN

1. Start Flash and open **37MYPIC** or open **38PIC**. Save the document as **38MYPIC**.

2. Preview the application in your browser using the current Publish Settings. Test all buttons. Test the shortcut menu.

3. Change the publish settings and preview the application again. For example, change the dimensions, the alignment, or the scale.

4. Use the Publish Preview command to preview the application in Flash. It should play in a Flash Player window, similar to when you use the Test Movie command.

5. Change the publish settings to display the animation at 50% of its actual size, aligned on the right side of the browser window, and then preview the application in your browser.

6. Publish the application.

7. Save the file and close it, and then exit Flash.

Exercise | 39

Skills Covered

- ■ **Export Flash Content**

Software Skills Export an entire Flash document so you can display it in a program other than Flash, or if you want to generate a sequence of still images of frames. For example, you can export an animation to create an animated GIF file to embed in a Web page. You can also export the content of a single frame or even a selected object so you can use it in a different program. For example, export a single frame as a JPEG file to insert as an illustration in a report or brochure.

Application Skills The owner of the Grace Notes stationery boutique wants to make use of content you created in a Flash file in a slide presentation for potential investors. In this exercise, you will export a frame from the animation to save an image in JPEG format. You will also export the entire animation to create an animated GIF file. Finally, you will view the exported files in your Web browser.

TERMS

Animated GIF A .gif-formatted file in which two or more images display in sequence, creating the appearance of animation.

Export To save a file or object created in one program in a format that can be used by a different program.

NOTES

Export Flash Content

- ■ **Export** the content of an entire Flash document so you can use it in another program.

- ■ With the Export Movie command, you can save a complete Flash document file in a different movie file format, or as a sequence of still image files.

- ■ You name the exported file and select the file format in the Export Movie dialog box.

- ■ In an exported sequence, each frame is saved as a separate file. That means that if there are 50 frames in an animation, there will be 50 exported files. Numbers are added to the file names to indicate the sequential order.

- ■ Some Flash features may not be supported by the export file type. For example, a movie clip may not display when exported in **animated GIF** format, but may display when exported in QuickTime format.

- ■ Likewise, actions such as those assigned to buttons may not work in all exported file formats.

- ■ You can export a document to the file formats shown in the opposite column.

File Format	File Extension
Flash Movie	.swf
Windows AVI	.avi
QuickTime	.mov
Animated GIF	.gif
WAV Audio	.wav
Enhanced Metafile Format sequence	.emf
Windows Metafile sequence	.wmf
Encapsulated Postscript 3.0 sequence	.eps
Adobe Illustrator sequence	.ai
AutoCad DXF sequence	.dxf
Bitmap sequence	.bmp
JPEG sequence	.jpg
GIF sequence	.gif
PNG sequence	,png

- ■ Use the Export Image command to save a single frame as an image file, or to save a selected object as an image file.

- ■ You name the exported file and select the file format in the Export Image dialog box.

- ■ You can export a frame or an object to the following file formats:

179

File Format	File Extension
Flash Movie	.swf
Enhanced Metafile	.emf
Windows Metafile	.wmf
Encapsulated Postscript 3.0	.eps
Adobe Illustrator	.ai
AutoCad DXF	.dxf
Bitmap	.bmp
JPEG Image	.jpg
GIF Image	.gif
PNG	,png

Export GIF Dialog Box

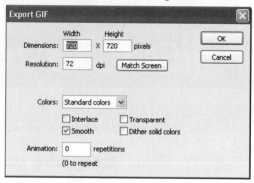

- Some file formats display an Export *file type* dialog box before exporting the file so that you can set export options. For example, when you export to a .gif file, the Export GIF dialog box displays so you can set options for dimensions, color settings, and image control settings (see the illustration at the top of the opposite column).

- Many options in the Export dialog boxes are similar to those you set on the different format tabs in the Publish Settings dialog box. In some cases, the export command may use the settings currently selected in the Publish Settings dialog box.

- Some file formats do not have export options and therefore do not display an Export dialog box.

PROCEDURES

Export a Flash Document
(Ctrl+Alt+Shift+S)

1. Open the document in Flash.
2. Click **File** .... Alt + F
3. Click **Export** .... E , ↵Enter
4. Click **Export Movie** .... M
5. Type new file name.
6. Click **Save as type** drop-down arrow.
7. Click **Export** *file type*.
8. Select storage destination, if necessary.

9. Click **Save** .... ↵Enter
10. Select export options and click **OK** .... ↵Enter as necessary.

Export a Flash Frame or Object

1. Open the document in Flash.
2. Select frame or object to export.
3. Click **File** .... Alt + F
4. Click **Export** .... E , ↵Enter
5. Click **Export Image** .... E

6. Type new file name.
7. Click **Save as type** drop-down arrow.
8. Click **Export** *file type*.
9. Select storage destination, if necessary.
10. Click **Save** .... ↵Enter
11. Select export options and click **OK** .... ↵Enter as necessary.

EXERCISE DIRECTIONS

Export a Single Frame

1. Start Flash and open **39DATA**. Save the file as **39NOTES**. This is a version of a file you worked with in earlier exercises.
2. Select frame 20.
3. Select the Export Image command.
4. In the Export Image dialog box, name the file **39FRAME**, and select the JPEG Image (*.jpg) file type.
5. Click Save to export the frame. The Export JPEG dialog box displays.
6. Click OK to export the file using the default settings.

Export a Document

1. In the **39NOTES** document, select the Export Movie command.
2. In the Export Movie dialog box, name the file **39MOVIE**, and select the Animated GIF (*.GIF) file type.
3. Click Save to export the frame. The Export GIF dialog box displays.
4. Click OK to export the file using the default settings.

View the Exported Files in Your Browser

1. Use Windows to navigate to the folder or disk location where you stored the files for this exercise.

Illustration A

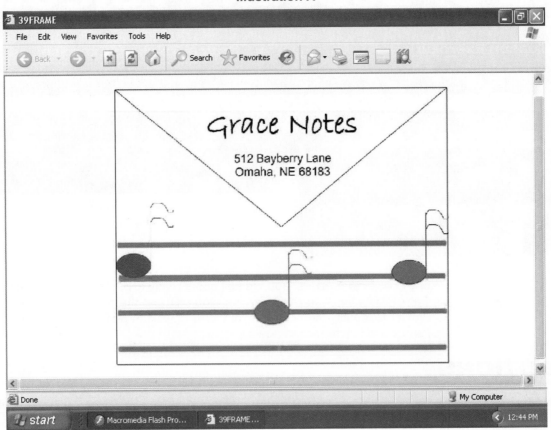

2. Right-click the **39FRAME.jpg** file, click Open with, and then click the name of your Web browser. The JPEG file should open in your browser and look similar to Illustration A.

   ✓ *You may have a different program available for viewing JPEG files, such as Microsoft Windows Picture and Fax Viewer, Paint, Adobe Illustrator, or Macromedia Fireworks.*

3. Close your Web browser.

4. Right-click the **39MOVIE.gif** file, click Open with, and then click the name of your Web browser.

The animated GIF file should open in your browser, looping through the animation.

   ✓ *You may have a different program available for viewing animated GIF files, such as Microsoft Windows Picture and Fax Viewer.*

5. Close your Web browser.

6. Close the Flash file, saving all changes, and exit Flash.

ON YOUR OWN

1. Start Flash and open **38MYPIC** or open ⊘**39PIC**. Save the document as **39MYPIC**.

2. Select one frame and export it with the file name **39XPORT1** in GIF format.

3. Export the entire document with the name **39XPORT2** in Animated GIF format.

4. View the exported files in your Web browser, or a different program. Close the program when you are finished.

5. If you have a video program installed, such as QuickTime or Windows Media Player, export the document to a compatible video format. For example, for QuickTime, export it to .mov format, or for Windows Media Player, export it to .avi format. Use the file name **39XPORT3**.

6. View the exported video file in the appropriate program. Close the program when you are finished.

7. Save the Flash file and close it, and then exit Flash.

End of Lesson Projects

- Summary Exercise
- Application Exercise
- Curriculum Integration Exercise
- Critical Thinking Exercise

Exercise | 40

Summary Exercise

Software Skills You are just about ready to publish the animation for Castle Gate Productions. In this exercise, you will test the movie using the Bandwidth Profiler to identify frames that might slow download performance. You will optimize frames and test the movie again.

DIRECTIONS

Test a Movie

1. Start Flash and open **40DATA** or open **34CASTLE**. Save the file as **40CASTLE**.

2. Test the entire movie.

3. In the Flash Player window, display the Bandwidth Profiler in Frame by Frame Graph view. Note that frame 31—the first frame in the Theater scene—is 45 KB in size, which is larger than the others (see Illustration A). You may be able to reduce its size using optimization techniques.

4. Close the Flash Player window.

5. In the **40CASTLE** document, make the Theater scene active, unlock all layers, and select frame 1 on the Stage layer.

   ✓ Remember, when you play the entire movie, the frames are numbered consecutively, but when you play a single scene, the first frame in the scene is frame 1. Therefore, frame 1 in the Theater scene corresponds to frame 31 in the entire movie.

6. Select the bitmap graphic in frame 1 of the Stage layer and convert it to a graphic symbol named Theater. Using symbols in place of bitmap graphics may reduce the size.

7. Select frame 1 of the Text1 layer, and then move the keyframe to frame 10.

8. Select frame 1 of the Applause layer, and then move the keyframe to frame 10. This moves some

of the content out of frame 1, which should make it smaller.

9. Test the movie again. Notice that frame 31, which corresponds to frame 1 of the Theater scene, is a little bit smaller—42 KB—but that frame 40, which corresponds to frame 10, is larger than it was before. You could reduce the size of the frames containing text by using display fonts instead of embedded fonts.

10. Close the Flash Player window.

Replace Embedded Fonts with Display Fonts to Optimize Frames

1. Remove all frames in the Text1 layer and then insert a keyframe in frame 10.

2. Select the Text tool, select the _sans font (top of the font list) in 42 points, black, and insert an extendable text block. Type the text **Introducing...**

3. Align the text block in the horizontal center of the Stage, about 2.5" from the top.

4. Select frame 50 of the Text1 layer and insert a frame to extend the animation.

5. Remove all frames in the Text2 layer and then insert a keyframe in frame 15.

6. Select the Text tool, change the font size to 24, and insert an extendable text block. Type the text **Theater in the Round**.

7. Select frame 50 in the Text2 layer and insert a keyframe. Align the text block on frame 50 in the horizontal center, about 3.25" from the top (under the Text1 text block).

8. Select frame 15 in the Text2 layer, and resize the text block to about 1" wide by .26" high. Align the text block in the horizontal center of the Stage, about 3.25" from the bottom.

9. Select frame 40 in the Text2 layer and create a motion tween. Select the Scale check box.

10. Select frame 1, and then use the Control Play command to preview the Theater scene in the Flash window. Make adjustments if necessary.

11. Test the movie in the Flash Player window. Frame 31 may still be 42 KB, but frame 30 should now be close to the red line.

12. Close the Flash Player window.

13. Print frame 15 of the Theater scene, if requested by your instructor.

14. Lock all layers, close the document, and exit Flash, saving all changes.

Illustration A

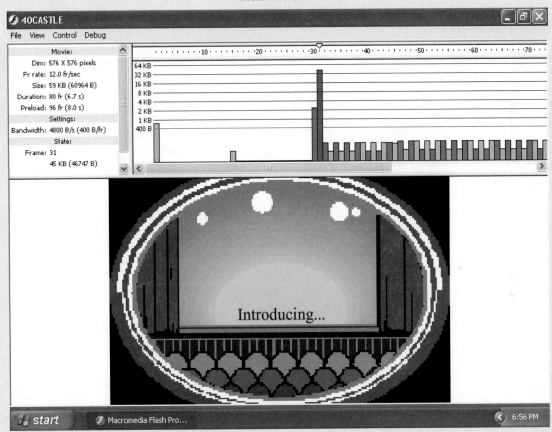

Exercise | 41

Application Exercise

Software Skills In this exercise, you continue work on the Castle Gate animation. First, you will select publish settings for the animation and preview the animation in your Web browser. Next, you will publish the document. You will export content that the manager of Castle Gate wants to use on a postcard mailing into JPEG format, and you will export the entire document to an animated GIF file.

DIRECTIONS

Select Publish Settings

1. Open ●41DATA or 40CASTLE and save the document as 41CASTLE.
2. Open the Publish Settings dialog box.
3. On the Formats page, make sure only the Flash and HTML check boxes are selected.
4. Click the Flash tab and verify the default settings:
   - Version: Flash Player 8
   - Load order: Bottom up
   - ActionScript version: ActionScript 2.0
   - Compress movie: Enabled
   - JPEG quality: 80
5. Click the HTML tab and apply the following settings:
   - Template: Flash Only
   - Detect Flash Version: Disabled
   - Dimensions: Percent
   - Width: 80
   - Height 80
   - Paused at start: Disabled
   - Loop: Enabled
   - Display menu: Enabled
   - Device font: Enabled
   - Quality: High
   - Window Mode: Window
   - HTML alignment: Right
   - Scale: Default (Show all)
   - Horizontal alignment: Center
   - Vertical alignment: Center
   - Show warning messages: Enabled.
6. Click OK to save the settings and close the Publish Settings dialog box.

Preview the Document in Your Web Browser and Publish It

1. Start your Web browser.
2. In Flash, select the Publish Preview command from the File menu, and then select the Default format (HTML).
3. Switch to your Web browser to view the file published with the current publish settings. At the end of the Main scene, click the Next button to go to the Theater scene. At the end, it should look similar to Illustration A.
4. Close your Web browser.
5. In Flash, select the Publish command to publish the file with the selected settings.

Export Flash Content

1. In the 41CASTLE document, make the Main scene active and select frame 30.
2. Select the Export Image command, and export the frame with the file name 41FRAME in JPEG format.
3. In the Export JPEG dialog box, set the dimensions to match the screen, and increase the quality to 80.
4. Click OK to export the file.
5. In Flash, select the Export Movie command, and export the document with the file name 41MOVIE in Animated GIF format, using the default Export GIF options.
6. Open the 41FRAME.jpg file in your Web browser. It should look similar to Illustration B.
7. Open the 41MOVIE.gif file in your Web browser. It should play the animation from beginning to end, without stopping.

✓ *Animated GIF does not support actions. To export the Flash document to a video format that does support actions, use QuickTime (*.mov).*

8. Close your Web browser.

9. Close the document and exit Flash, saving all changes.

Illustration A

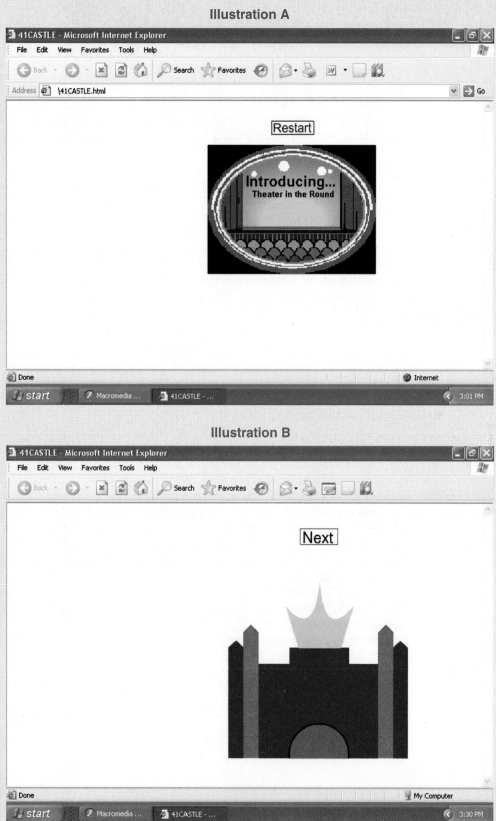

Illustration B

Exercise | 42

Curriculum Integration Exercise

Software Skills For a health and wellness project, develop a public service announcement supporting healthy behavior, such as good nutrition, exercise, not smoking, or safe driving. Use Flash to create an animation that could be used on a Web site or in a presentation for the announcement. Individually or as a group, select and then research the healthy behavior. You might also want to research other public service announcements that are displayed in magazines, on billboards, or on TV to get a sense of how you want to organize and present your announcement. Write text and plan the Flash document, deciding how you want to use it and the types of information you want to include. For example, you might include graphics, text, sound, and video. When the document is complete, select publish settings and preview it in your Web browser (refer to the illustration on page 187 for an example). Publish the document. Export one frame in a graphic file format so that you can include it in a document such as a brochure or mailing.

DIRECTIONS

Start a new document and save it as **42HEALTH**.

Prepare the Stage by setting the ruler units to inches, and displaying visual tools you may find useful, such as the grid or guides.

Create or import the media you need to compile the animation, such as graphics, sounds, text blocks, and video.

Insert all static images, such as backgrounds, extending them to the end of the animation as necessary.

Create animations using tweens or frame-by-frame techniques.

Use actions to control the flow of the animation, if appropriate. For example, include a button to replay the animation or to skip the animation.

Preview the document on the Stage as your work, making adjustments as necessary.

You may want to print the animation so you can discuss it with your group or teacher. The printed animation can help you view the overall organization and flow of the Flash document.

Use the Test Movie command to preview the application in the Flash Player window. Use the Bandwidth Profiler to see if any frames need optimization. Again, make adjustments as necessary.

When you are satisfied with the application, select publish settings and preview it in your browser. Publish the application.

Export at least one frame to a graphics file format so you can use it to illustrate a handout, presentation, or other document.

Present your announcement to the class.

Preview in Your Web Browser

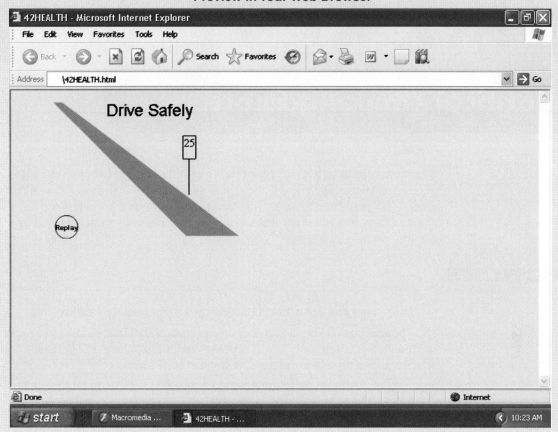

Exercise | 43

Critical Thinking Exercise

Software Skills Brighter than Bright, the tooth-whitening franchise, wants a more sophisticated animated logo. Once completed, they can use it as a movie clip in other Flash applications, in an ad banner on a Web page, or in any presentation. In this exercise, you will open an existing file that contains three graphic symbols and use the symbols to create a flying logo.

DIRECTIONS

- Start Flash and open **⊛43DATA**. Save the document as **43BRIGHT**.
- Rename layer 1 **Oval** and insert an instance of the Oval symbol in frame 1. Size the instance to about 7" by 5" and center it horizontally and vertically on the Stage. Set the Alpha Amount for the instance to 0%.
- Insert a keyframe on frame 40 and set the Alpha Amount for the instance to 100%. Scale the instance to about 4" by 3" and center it horizontally and vertically.
- Create a motion tween from frame 1 to frame 40, with Scale selected and the easing set to 25. Preview the tween on the Stage and then lock the layer.
- Create a new layer named **Tooth 1** and insert an instance of the Tooth symbol in frame 1. Align the instance in the upper-left corner of the Stage and set the Alpha Amount to 0%.
- Insert a keyframe in frame 10 and set the Alpha Amount for the instance to 50%. Move the instance to the bottom center of the Stage. Insert a keyframe in frame 20 and set the Alpha Amount for the instance to 100%. Move the instance to the upper-right corner of the Stage. Insert a keyframe in frame 30 and center the instance horizontally and vertically. Insert a keyframe in frame 40 and position the instance so its X coordinate is approximately 1.5 and its Y coordinate is approximately 2.7. This should place it along the left edge of the oval, centered approximately on the 3" mark on the vertical ruler.
- Create motion tweens between the keyframes along the Tooth 1 layer, disabling the Scale check box and setting the easing to 25. Preview the animation on the Stage, and then lock the layer. Save your work.
- Create a new layer named **Tooth 2** and insert an instance of the Tooth symbol in frame 1. Align the instance in the upper-right corner of the Stage and set the Alpha Amount to 0%.
- Insert a keyframe in frame 10 and set the Alpha Amount for the instance to 50%. Move the instance to the bottom center of the Stage. Insert a keyframe in frame 20 and set the Alpha Amount for the instance to 100%. Move the instance to the upper-left corner of the Stage. Insert a keyframe in frame 30 and center the instance horizontally and vertically. Insert a keyframe in frame 40 and position the instance so its X coordinate is approximately 5.6 and its Y coordinate is approximately 2.3. This should place it along the right edge of the oval, centered approximately on the 3.5" mark on the vertical ruler.

- Create motion tweens between the keyframes along the Tooth 2 layer, disabling the Scale check box and setting the easing to 25. Preview the animation on the Stage, and then lock the layer.

- Create a new layer named **Text** and insert an instance of the Text symbol on frame 1. Center the instance on the bottom of the Stage and set the Alpha Amount to 0%.

- Insert a keyframe in frame 40 and set the Alpha Amount for the instance to 100%. Scale the instance to approximately 3.75" wide and 1" high. (You may have to disable the Constrain check box so that Flash does not try to maintain the original proportions.) Center the instance horizontally and vertically.

- Create a motion tween on the Text layer, select the Scale check box, set the easing to 25, and set the instance to rotate three times clockwise. Preview the animation on the Stage and then lock the layer.

- Insert a new layer named **Actions**, insert a keyframe in frame 40, and insert a stop action.

- Test the movie and then close the Flash Player window.

- Select publish settings to publish the animation in Flash and HTML formats. Set the HTML dimensions to 50%. Preview the animation in your Web browser (refer to the following illustration for an example). Make adjustments if necessary, and then publish the document.

- Using the default settings, export the entire document to an animation GIF file named **43LOGO**. Open the GIF file in a graphics program, or import it back into a new Flash document to see how it looks.

- If requested by your instructor, print the animation.

- Close the document, saving all changes, and exit Flash.

Preview in Your Web Browser

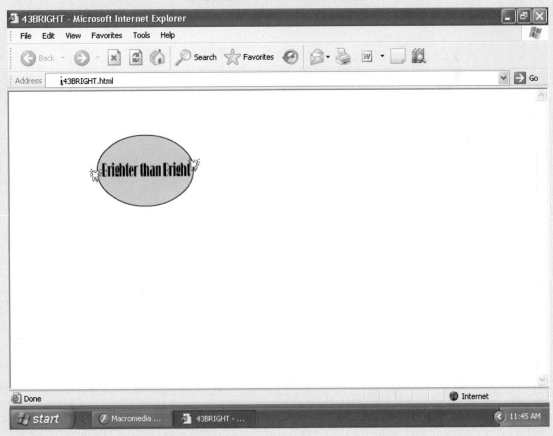

Lesson | 5

Using Advanced Features

Exercise | 44

Skills Covered

- **Use the Movie Explorer**

Software Skills Use the Movie Explorer to examine the contents of an application to quickly locate specific elements such as instances. For example, you can use the Movie Explorer to select all instances of a specific symbol or to select a symbol in the library. You can even use it to print a flowchart of a scene or of the entire application.

Application Skills The president of a community senior softball league started working on an animation for its Web site, recruiting new members. He has asked you to help complete the application. In this exercise, you will use the Movie Explorer to examine the existing document and to print a flow chart of the document's contents.

TERMS

Collapse To change the view to hide items. For example, collapse a hierarchical display to hide sub-elements and show only the main element.

Expand To change the view to show hidden items. For example, expand a hierarchical display to show sub-elements branching off the main element.

Hierarchical list A diagram in which elements branch from a main element—the root—to other elements. It is usually used to show how the elements relate to each other. Sometimes called a tree diagram.

Symbol definition The content that comprises a symbol.

NOTES

Use the Movie Explorer

- Use the Movie Explorer to view and organize the contents of a document, to locate an element by name, to locate all instances of a specific symbol, or to select elements in the document.

- The Movie Explorer opens in a panel and displays a **hierarchical list** of elements currently used in the document. **Expand** or **collapse** the display to show or hide elements that branch off of other elements (see the following illustration).

Movie Explorer

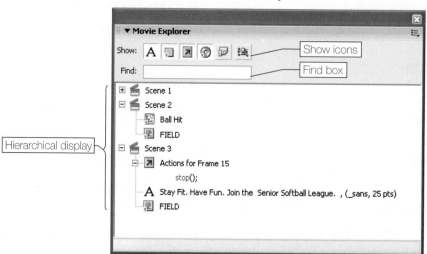

- By default, Flash displays the elements one scene at a time. You may choose to display all scenes.
- You may also choose to display **symbol definitions** in place of movie elements, or you may display both.
- Customize the display by selecting the specific elements you want to view: text; graphics; buttons;

movie clips; actions; and imported files, such as sounds, bitmaps, and videos.

- You can also print the Movie Explorer to generate a diagram of the document structure.
- The Movie Explorer is particularly useful for managing large applications and familiarizing yourself with a document created by someone else.

PROCEDURES

Show/Hide Movie Explorer (Alt+F3)

1. Click **Window**............... `Alt` + `W`
2. Click **Movie Explorer**............... `M`, `M`, `↵Enter`

   ✓ *A check mark next to the Movie Explorer command indicates it is already displayed.*

Show/Hide Elements in Movie Explorer

1. Display Movie Explorer.
2. Click button to show or hide element:
   - **Show text** `A`
   - **Show movie clips, buttons, and graphics** `☐`
   - **Show ActionScript** `↗`
   - **Show video, sounds, and bitmaps** `⊙`
   - **Show frames and layers** `▦`

Customize Movie Explorer Display

To Select Elements to Display

1. Display Movie Explorer.
2. Click **Customize which items to show** button `▾`.
3. Click to select or deselect elements to show:
   - **Text**............................ `T`
   - **Buttons**.......................... `B`
   - **Movie clips**....................... `M`
   - **Video**............................ `V`
   - **ActionScript**..................... `A`
   - **Bitmaps**.......................... `I`
   - **Graphics**......................... `G`
   - **Sounds**........................... `S`
   - **Layers**........................... `L`
   - **Frames**........................... `F`
4. Click **OK**........................ `↵Enter`

To Change Display Category

1. Display Movie Explorer.
2. Click **Customize which items to show** button `▣`
3. Click to select or deselect category for organizing display:
   - Movie **elements**................. `E`
   - **Symbol definitions**............... `Y`
4. Click **OK**........................ `↵Enter`
   OR
   a. Right-click in Movie Explorer panel.
   b. Click desired option:
   - Show Movie Elements
   - Show Symbol Definitions
   - Show All Scenes

     ✓ *A check mark next to an option indicates it is already selected.*

Expand or Collapse the Movie Explorer List

1. Display Movie Explorer.
2. Do one of the following:
   - Click **plus sign** to expand list.
   - Click **minus sign** to collapse list.
   OR
1. Right-click element in Movie Explorer list.
2. Click one of the following:
   - **Expand Branch** to expand current element.
   - **Collapse Branch** to collapse current element.
   - **Collapse Others** to collapse all except current element.

Resize Movie Explorer Panel

- Drag a panel border.

Find an Element in Movie Explorer Panel

1. Display Movie Explorer.
2. Click in **Find** box.
3. Type element to find.

   ✓ *Flash displays matching element(s) and hides other elements.*

To Display All Elements

- Delete all text from Find box.

Use Movie Explorer Options

1. Display Movie Explorer.
2. Right-click element in list.
3. Select option:
   - **Go to Location** to display frame containing current element.
   - **Go to Symbol Definition** to display symbol definition for current element.
   - **Select Symbol Instances** to select all instances of current symbol.
   - **Find in Library** to select current symbol in Library panel.
   - **Rename** to rename current element.
   - **Edit in Place** to edit current element in place on Stage.
   - **Edit in New Window** to edit current element in symbol editing mode.

Print the Movie Explorer List

1. Display Movie Explorer.
2. Right-click in panel.
3. Click **Print**.
4. Select print options in Print dialog box.
5. Click **OK**........................ `↵Enter`

EXERCISE DIRECTIONS

1. Start Flash and open 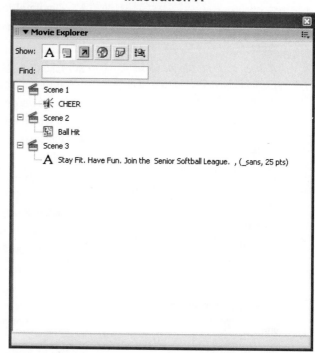44DATA. Save the file as **44LEAGUE**.

2. Use the Test Movie command to play the animation, and then close the Flash Player window.

3. Display the Movie Explorer.

4. Display all scenes in the Movie Explorer panel.

   ✓ *Increase the size of the Movie Explorer panel by dragging the panel borders, if necessary.*

5. Collapse all scenes by clicking the minus sign next to the scene name.

6. Customize the display to show text, sounds, and movie clips.

7. Expand all scenes by clicking the plus sign next to the scene name. The window should look similar to Illustration A.

8. Customize the display to show all elements, including layers and frames.

9. Collapse Scene 1 and Scene 2, leaving Scene 3 expanded.

10. Select the Text1 layer. Notice that it displays on the Stage in the Flash window.

11. Expand Scene 1 and then type **Bat** in the Find box. The Movie Explorer displays layers containing instances of the Bat symbol.

12. Right-click any one of the Bat instances and then click Find in Library. Flash opens the Library panel and selects the Bat symbol.

13. Close the Library panel.

14. Delete the word *Bat* from the Find box.

15. Display all elements except frames and layers, and expand all scenes.

16. Print the Movie Explorer.

17. Close the Movie Explorer.

18. Close the file, saving changes if necessary, and exit Flash.

Illustration A

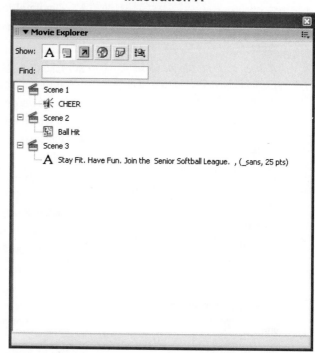

ON YOUR OWN

1. Start Flash and open **39MYPIC** or open ⬤**44PIC**. Save the document as **44MYPIC**.

2. Use the Movie Explorer to look carefully at the composition of the animation.

3. Show and hide different elements. For example, show text, buttons, and ActionScript, but hide movie clips.

4. Display all elements in all scenes, and print the display.

5. Use the Movie Explorer to find and display one particular element, such as a graphic symbol or a button.

6. When you have finished exploring the movie, save the file and close it, and then exit Flash.

Exercise | 45

Skills Covered

- **Organize the Contents of a Library**
- **Make Library Items Available in Different Documents**

Software Skills Use libraries to organize and manage symbols and imported files, such as bitmaps, sounds, and videos. You can sort items in a library, group them into folders, rename them, and delete them. In addition, you can make items stored in one library available for use in other documents.

Application Skills In this exercise, you will use the library to organize the elements in the animation for the senior softball league.

TERMS

Shared library A library that is stored on a network and is available to Flash documents via links.

Use count The number of times a symbol or file has been inserted in a movie.

NOTES

Organize the Contents of a Library

- In addition to simply storing elements, you can use a document's library to organize and view symbols and imported files.

  ✓ *For a refresher on using the Library panel, see Exercise 14.*

- By default, Flash displays the following information about each element in columns in the Library panel (see the illustration on page 196):
  - Name—the symbol or file name.
  - Type—the symbol or file type.
  - **Use Count**—the number of times that the element has been inserted.
  - Linkage—whether or not the element is linked to a **shared library**.
  - Date Modified—the date the item was last edited.
- You can sort the items in the Library panel by the information in any column. For example, you can sort alphabetically by name or type, chronologically by date modified, or numerically by use count.

- You can also organize the items into folders, which may help you locate specific items. For example, you may want to place all bitmaps into a folder named Bitmaps, or all sounds into a folder named Sounds.
- You can rename, delete, copy, and move items in the Library panel. Keep in mind that if you delete a symbol, all instances of that symbol are also deleted.
- Other options available in the library include selecting all unused items and updating the use count.
- Selecting unused items is handy for identifying items you may want to delete. Updating the use count keeps you informed on the number of times an instance or file is used in a document.

195

Library Panel

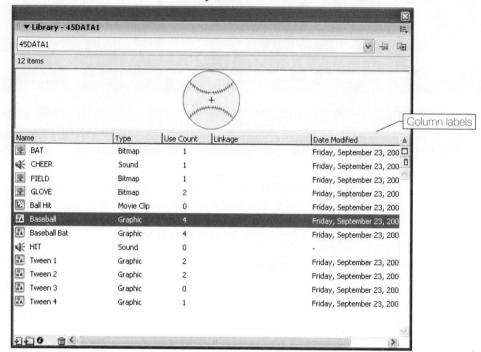

Make Library Items Available in Different Documents

- If you want to use an item stored in one document's library in a different document, simply open both documents at the same time.

- When multiple documents are open, all of the libraries are available from the File name drop-down list in the Library panel (see the illustration on page 197). Simply click a file name on the list to display that file's library.

- You can switch back and forth between the open documents by clicking a file name tab above the Timeline in the Flash document window.

- Once you insert an item from a different document's library, Flash adds the item to the current document's library.

- Alternatively, use the Open External Library command to open the library from the other document without opening the entire document.

- You may also copy an item from one library to another.

Make Multiple Libraries Available

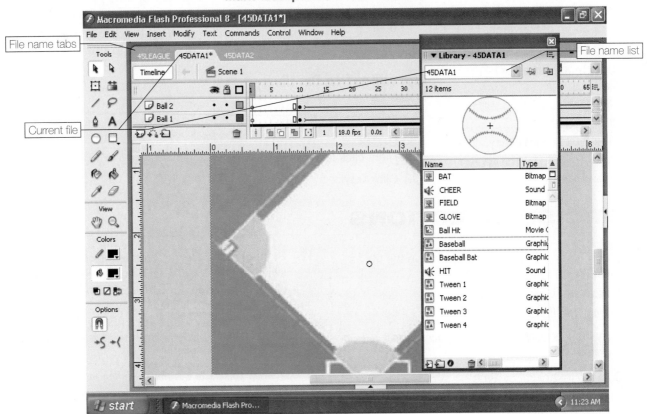

PROCEDURES

Open Library Panel (Ctrl+L)

1. Click **Window**..............Alt +W
2. Click **Library**.........................L

   ✓ *A check mark next to the Library command indicates the panel is already displayed.*

Sort Library Items

1. Open Library panel.
2. Click column header to sort by that column.
3. Click **Toggle Sorting Order** button ▴▮ to reverse sort order.

Update Use Count

1. Open Library panel.
2. Click **Options** menu button ▤.
3. Click **Update Use Counts Now**.

   To Keep Use Counts Updated

1. Open Library panel.
2. Click **Options** menu button ▤.
3. Click **Keep Use Counts Updated**.

   ✓ *A check mark next to the command indicates it is already selected.*

Select Unused Items

1. Open Library panel.
2. Click **Options** menu button ▤.
3. Click **Select Unused Items**.
   OR
   a. Right-click in Library panel.
   b. Click **Select Unused Items**.

Delete an Item from the Library

1. Open Library panel.
2. Click item to delete.
3. Click **Delete** button 🗑.
   OR
   a. Right-click item to delete.
   b. Click **Delete**.

Rename an Item in the Library

1. Open Library panel.
2. Right-click item to rename.

3. Click **Rename**.
4. Type new name.
5. Press **Enter**..................↵Enter

Create a New Library Folder

1. Open Library panel.
2. Click **New Folder** button 📁.
3. Type new folder name.
4. Press **Enter**..................↵Enter

Move an Item into a Folder

1. Open Library panel.
2. Drag item on to folder.
3. Release mouse button.

Access Multiple Libraries

1. Open first Flash document.
2. Open additional Flash document(s).
3. Open Library panel.

4. Click File name drop-down arrow in Library panel.

5. Click name of file whose library you wish to display.

Open An External Library (Ctrl+Shift+O)

1. Click **File**..................... `Alt` `+` `F`

2. Click **Import**....................... `I`

3. Click **Open External Library**....... `O`

   ✓ *Flash displays the Open as Library dialog box.*

4. Locate and select document containing library you wish to open.

5. Click **Open**..................... `↵Enter`

Copy an Item from One Library to Another

1. Open library containing item to copy.

2. Right-click item to copy.

3. Click **Copy**.

4. Open library to which you wish to copy the item.

5. Right-click in Library panel.

6. Click **Paste**.

EXERCISE DIRECTIONS

1. Start Flash and open ●**45DATA1**. Save the file as **45LEAGUE**.

2. Display the Library panel.

3. Display the library in wide view.

   ✓ *For more information on using the Library panel, refer to Exercise 14.*

4. Sort the library list by Type.

5. Reverse the sort order. The Sound files should be at the top of the list.

6. Update the use count, and then sort by use count. Notice that some elements are not used, including Tween 3.

   ✓ *Some elements that have no use count may be used by other symbols, such as in a movie clip. Before deleting an element make sure you do not need it for the animation. If you delete an element that you need, use the History panel or the Undo command to restore it.*

7. Select Tween 3 and delete it.

8. Create a new folder named **Sounds**.

9. Move the two sound files into the Sounds folder. Expand the folder

10. In Flash, open the file ●**45DATA2**. Notice that its library displays in the Library panel.

11. In the Library panel, select the Replay button. A preview displays in the Preview area.

12. Right-click the Replay button and click Copy, then switch to the 45LEAGUE library. Right-click a blank area in the 45LEAGUE Library panel and click Paste to copy the Replay button from the 45DATA2 library to the 45LEAGUE library. The 45LEAGUE Library panel should look similar to Illustration A.

    ✓ *When you paste the Replay button into the 45LEAGUE library, be sure not to select the Sounds folder. Right-click a blank area of the library window, and then click Paste. If you paste it into the Sounds folder, you can drag it out into the main library window.*

13. Change the Library panel to narrow view, and then close the **45DATA2** file without saving changes.

14. In the **45LEAGUE** file, make Scene 3 active, and select frame 1 on the Background layer.

15. Insert an instance of the Replay button, and align it in the lower-right corner of the Stage.

16. Select the Replay button on the Stage and insert a goto and play action, set to play the first frame of Scene 1.

17. Test the movie. At the end of the animation, click the Replay button. It should replay the animation from the beginning.

18. Close the Flash Player window.

19. Close the Flash file, saving all changes, and exit Flash.

Illustration A

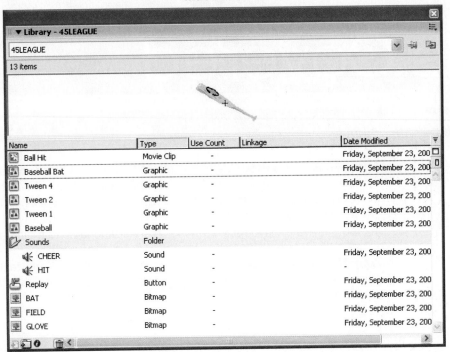

ON YOUR OWN

1. Start Flash and open **44MYPIC** or open ⬤**45PIC**. Save the document as **45MYPIC**.

2. Use the Library panel to organize the elements used in the animation.

3. Update the use count, and delete any elements that you do not need.

4. Sort the elements by type.

5. Create folders for storing different types of symbols and files, and then move the elements into the new folders.

6. If possible, add an element from a different library to the **45MYPIC** file. For example, you may add the Replay button from the **45LEAGUE** file.

7. Save the Flash file and close it, and then exit Flash.

Exercise | 46

Skills Covered

- **Create Selectable Text**
- **Link a Text Block to a URL**

Software Skills Create selectable text in a text block so that users can select the text onscreen while viewing a Flash application. Users may then copy and paste the text into a different document, such as a word processor or text editor. For example, a user may want to copy directions from a Web site. You can also link text to a URL in order to create a hyperlink that users can click to jump to a different page or file.

Application Skills In this exercise, you will add one text block containing selectable text to the animation for the senior softball league, and another text block linking to a Web site.

TERMS

Hyperlink Text or graphics that is linked to a destination location, such as a Web page, so that when you click the link, the destination displays.

URL Uniform Resource Locator. The address of a page or document on the Internet, an intranet, or World Wide Web.

NOTES

Create Selectable Text

- Set text block properties in the Property Inspector to make text in a static, horizontal text block selectable.

  ✓ *For a refresher on creating text blocks, refer to Exercise 27.*

- Users viewing a Flash application in a Web browser or in the Flash Player can select the text on the screen in order to copy it to the Windows Clipboard.

- When a user positions the mouse pointer over selectable text in a Web browser or the Flash Player window, the pointer resembles an I-beam.

- Drag the I-beam across the text to select it.

- All text in the text block becomes selectable.

Link a Text Block to a URL

- Use options in the Property Inspector to create a **hyperlink** between a static text block and a **URL** (see the illustration at the top of page 201).

- Flash formats the linked text with a dotted underline; when the mouse pointer rests over the linked text in a Web browser or Flash Player window, the pointer resembles a hand with a pointing finger.

- When a user clicks the text, the destination page or file listed in the URL displays.

- All text in the text block becomes part of the link.

- You must have a connection to the Internet to access pages on the Internet or Web.

Creating Linked Text

PROCEDURES

Make Text Selectable

1. Create a static, horizontal text block.
2. Select text block.
3. Click **Selectable** button 🆎 in Property Inspector.

Test Selectable Text

1. Click **Control**.................Alt+O
2. Click **Test Movie**.....................M
3. Move mouse pointer over selectable text.

   ✓ *The mouse pointer should change to an I-beam.*

4. Drag pointer across text.

   ✓ *The selected text should appear highlighted.*

Link a Text Block to a URL

1. Create a static text block.
2. Select text block.
3. Click URL link box in Property Inspector.
4. Type destination URL.

Test Linked Text

1. Click **Control**.................Alt+O
2. Click **Test Movie**.....................M

3. Move mouse pointer over linked text.

   ✓ *The mouse pointer should change to a hand with a pointing finger.*

4. Click linked text.

   ✓ *The destination page or file should display.*

EXERCISE DIRECTIONS

Create a Text Block with Selectable Text

1. Start Flash and open **45LEAGUE** or open **●46DATA**. Save the file as **46LEAGUE**.
2. Make Scene 3 active and insert a keyframe on frame 10 of the Text1 layer.
3. Align the text block with the top of the Stage and center it horizontally.
4. Create a motion tween with no Scale option and a 25 Ease setting to move the text block to the top of the Stage.
5. Insert a new layer and name it **Text2**.
6. Select frame 10 of the Text2 layer and insert a keyframe.
7. Create a static, horizontal, fixed-width text block approximately 2.5" wide. Using the _sans device font in 18 points, black, type **For more information contact Jerry Dupree, 555-1234.**
8. Center the text in the text block, and align the text block horizontally and vertically in the center of the Stage.
9. Select the text block and click the Selectable button in the Property Inspector.

Create a Text Block Linked to a URL

1. Create a new layer named **Text3**.
2. On frame 1 of the new layer, insert a static, horizontal, fixed-width text block approximately 1.25" wide. Using the _sans device font in 12 points, black, type **Click here for information about softball.**
3. Left align the text within the text block, and align the text block in the lower-left corner of the Stage.
4. Select the text block.
5. Deselect the Selectable option, if necessary, and then, in the URL link box in the Property Inspector, type **http://www.softball.org**.

Test the Scene

1. Use the Text Scene command to test the scene in the Flash Player window.
2. In the Flash Player window, select the text *Jerry Dupree, 555-1234*.
3. Move the mouse pointer over the linked text in the lower-left corner of the animation. Your screen should look similar to Illustration A.

Illustration A

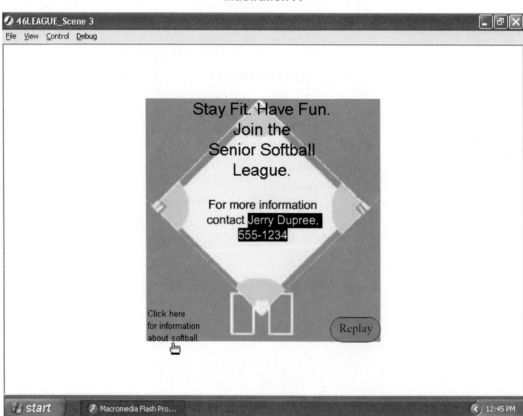

4. If you have an Internet connection, click the linked text. Your Web browser should start and display the home page for the Amateur Softball Association.

5. Close your Web browser.

6. Close the Flash Player window.

7. If requested by your instructor, print frame 15 of Scene 3.

8. Close the file, saving all changes.

9. Exit Flash.

ON YOUR OWN

1. Start Flash and open **45MYPIC** or open ⬤**46PIC**. Save the document as **46MYPIC**.

2. Select an existing text block and make the text in it selectable, or insert a new text block containing selectable text. For example, create a new text block on a new layer containing an address that viewers can select if they want to copy it to a word processing document.

3. Link an existing text block to a URL, or insert a new text block and link it to a URL. For example, create a link to an organization's home page, such as http://www.garden.org, the home page for the National Gardening Association.

4. Test the scene containing the text blocks and test them in the Flash Player window.

5. Print the frame(s) containing the text blocks.

6. Save the Flash file and close it, and then exit Flash.

Skills Covered

- **Create Printable Applications**
- **Disable Printing**

Software Skills Make an application printable so that users may print frames while viewing the animation in a Web browser or the Flash Player window. You may also specify frames that you do not want users to print. For example, make it possible for users to print text information or a coupon, but disable printing for copyrighted images.

Application Skills In this exercise, you will enable the shortcut menu so users can use it to print from their browser or the Flash Player window. You will also label a frame as printable, so that users can print a registration form.

TERMS

Frame label A name or designation you can use to identify a frame instead of using the frame number.

Print range An area that will print. The print range may or may not include all content in a window.

NOTES

Create Printable Applications

- Set options to allow users on the Web or in the Flash Player to print content displayed in a Flash application.
- By default, all frames in the Timeline print. To limit the number of frames that print, you enter the **frame label** #p in each frame you want printable. Unlabeled frames will not print.
- When you label a frame, a red flag displays in the frame in the Timeline.
- There are two basic methods for making Flash content printable:
  - Enable a shortcut menu so users can right-click the content and select the Print command.
  - Assign a Print action to a button, frame, or movie clip.
- In either case, the Print dialog box displays so the user may select printing options, such as the number of copies to print.

- Even if all frames are printable, if you select the Selection option button in the **Print Range** area of the Print dialog box, only the displayed frame prints.
- The Flash Player uses the HTML settings entered in the Publish Settings dialog box to control the dimension, scale, and alignment of printed frames.
- You can test a print action from the Flash Player or from your Web browser, but you can only test the shortcut menu from your Web browser.

Disable Printing

- To make an entire application nonprintable, enter the frame label !#p in any frame. This dims the Print command on the Flash Player shortcut menu so it cannot be selected.
- Disabling printing in Flash does not affect a user's ability to print using browser commands.

PROCEDURES

Designate Printable Frames

1. Open Flash document.
2. Select frame to make printable.
3. Insert a keyframe.
4. Click the **Frame Label** box in Property Inspector.
5. Type **#p**.
6. Repeat steps 2–5 for each frame you want to make printable.

Enable/Disable Printing from the Shortcut Menu

1. Open Flash document.
2. Click **File**....................Alt +F
3. Click **Publish Settings**...............G
4. Click **HTML** tab.
5. Click to select or clear **Display menu** check box...........Alt +M
6. Click **OK**........................↵Enter

Use the Shortcut Menu to Print

1. Open Web browser.
2. Open Flash document.
3. Click **File**....................Alt +F
4. Click **Publish Preview**..............R
5. Click **Default**.........................D
6. Switch to Web browser.
7. Right-click content to print.
8. Click **Print**.

   ✓ *The Print dialog box displays, with the Selection option in the Range area selected.*

9. Click **Print**.....................↵Enter

   ✓ *Only the current frame prints. To print all frames, select the All option button in the Range area.*

Assign a Print Action

1. Open Flash document.
2. Label frames as printable.

3. Select element to which you will assign the Print action.
4. Display Actions panel.
5. Enable ScriptAssist.
6. Click **Global Functions**.
7. Click **Printing Functions**.
8. Double-click **Print**.

Disable Printing

1. Open Flash document.
2. Select first keyframe in Timeline.
3. Click the **Frame Label** box in Property Inspector.
4. Type **!#p**.

EXERCISE DIRECTIONS

Print Using the Shortcut Menu

1. Start Flash and open ●47DATA. Save the file as **47LEAGUE**. This is a version of the file you have been working with in the previous exercises.
2. Open the Publish Settings dialog box.
3. Verify that the HTML and Flash file formats are selected.
4. On the HTML tab, set the dimensions to 100% and deselect the Loop check box.
5. Verify that the Display menu check box is selected, and that the Scale is set to Show All.
6. Click OK, and then preview the animation in your Web browser.
7. When the animation stops, right-click anywhere in the Web browser window to display the shortcut menu. Your screen should look similar to Illustration A on page 206.
8. Click Print on the shortcut menu, and then click Print in the Print dialog box to print the current frame only.
9. Close your Web browser.

Label a Frame as Printable

1. In the **47LEAGUE** document, select frame 16 of the Registration layer.
2. In the Property Inspector, click in the Frame box, type **#p**, and press Enter. A red flag displays in frame 16 in the Timeline.

Use a Print Action to Create a Print Button

1. Create a new layer named **Print**, and insert a keyframe on frame 16.
2. From the library, insert an instance of the Print button on frame 16 of the Print layer.
3. Select the Print button and align in the lower-left corner of the Stage.
4. Test the movie in the Flash Player window.
5. When the animation stops, click the Register button to display the registration form. The Flash Player window should look similar to Illustration B on page 206.
6. Click the Print button.
7. In the Print dialog box, click Print to print the frame.
8. Close the Flash Player window.
9. Close the Flash file, saving all changes, and exit Flash.

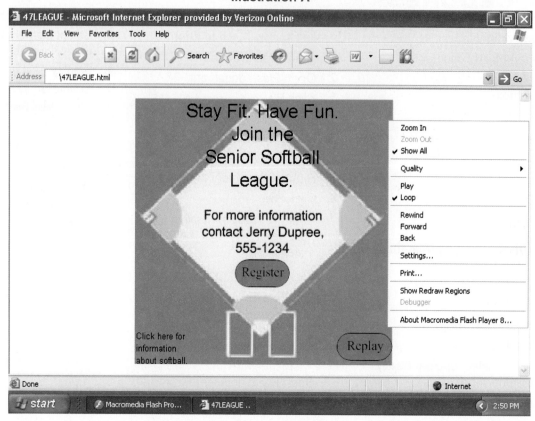

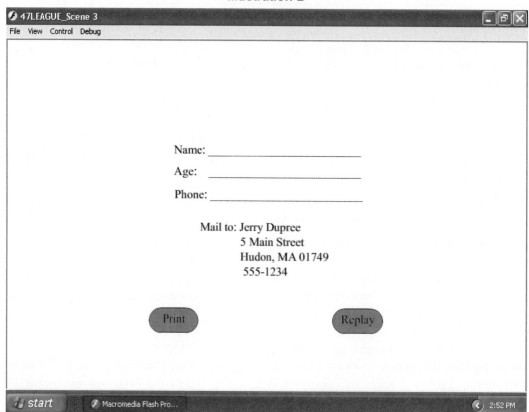

ON YOUR OWN

1. Start Flash and open **46MYPIC** or open ◉**47PIC**. Save the document as **47MYPIC**.

2. Set publish settings so that viewers will be able to use the shortcut menu to print content from their Web browser.

3. Preview the animation in your browser, and use the shortcut menu to print a frame.

4. In the Flash document, designate at least one frame as printable.

5. Create a Print button symbol that uses a Print action to print the current frame upon release.

   ✓ *Remember, you can copy a button from one library to another.*

6. Use the Print button to print the frame.

7. Save the Flash file and close it, and then exit Flash.

Skills Covered

- **About Timeline Effects**
- **Use Timeline Effects**

Software Skills Apply a Timeline effect to an object in a Flash document to create a complex animation without using a lot of time or effort. For example, use a Timeline effect to add a drop shadow or blur to a circle, or to cause an object on the Stage to appear to explode. Timeline effects may be applied to text, graphics, bitmaps, and button symbols.

Application Skills To improve the animation for the senior softball league, you would like to make the ball in Scene 2 explode when the bat makes contact. In this exercise, you will remove the existing tween, and then apply a Timeline effect to make the ball explode.

TERMS

Timeline effects Predefined animations that come with Flash that you can apply to objects on the Stage.

NOTES

About Timeline Effects

- **Timeline effects** are built-in animations that you can apply to text blocks, graphics, bitmap images, or button symbols.
- When you apply an effect to an element, Flash moves the element to a new layer or, if there is no other content on the current layer, renames the current layer. The layer name reflects the type of effect you apply.
- Flash also creates a folder in the library for storing the elements required for the effect.
- When you apply a Timeline effect to an object, Flash may convert the object to a symbol. For example, if you animate a drawn circle, Flash converts the circle to a symbol.
- The Timeline effects are divided into three submenus:
  - Assistants
  - Effects
  - Transform/Transition
- On the Assistants submenu, you can select either Copy to Grid or Distributed Duplicate.
  - Copy to Grid duplicates a selected object to create a grid of columns and rows.

- Distributed Duplicate duplicates a selected object by a specified number of times. Each additional object is modified incrementally to achieve a desired result.
- On the Effects submenu, you can select from the following:
  - Blur, which creates a motion blur effect by changing the alpha value, position, or scale of an object over time.
  - Drop shadow, which creates a shadow below the element.
  - Expand, which expands, contracts, or expands and contracts objects over time.
  - Explode, which causes elements of text or a group of objects to break apart, spin, and arc outward.
- On the Transform/Transition submenu, you can select either Transform or Transition:
  - Transform adjusts the position, scale, rotation, alpha, and tint of the selected elements.
  - Transition wipes in or wipes out selected objects by fading, wiping, or a combination of both.
- Not all effects are available for all objects. For example, you cannot apply the Expand effect to drawn objects, but you can apply it to button symbols.

Use Timeline Effects

▪ When you select an effect from the Timeline Effects menu, Flash displays a settings window in which you preview the animation and select settings and options.

▪ For example, when you select the blur effect, you may specify options such as the duration in frames and the direction of movement (see the illustration below).

▪ Update the preview after making changes to see the animation with the new settings.

▪ On the Timeline, the frames containing the effect are gray. Use the Play command to preview the animation on the Stage.

▪ You can edit a Timeline effect to change the selected settings, or you can remove the effect completely.

Blur Effect Settings Window

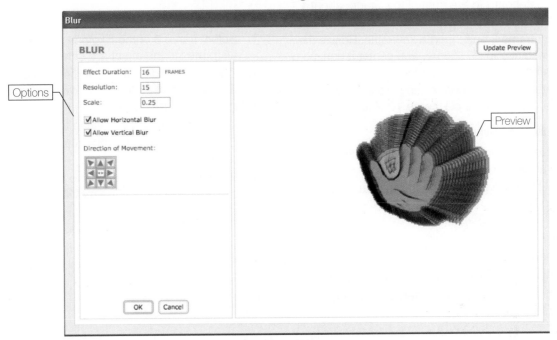

PROCEDURES

Apply a Timeline Effect

1. Right-click object to animate on Stage.

   OR

   a. Select object to animate on Stage.
   b. Click **Insert**..............Alt + I
2. Click **Timeline Effects**..............E
3. Click one of the following:
   ● Assistants
   ● Effects
   ● Transform/Transition
4. Click desired effect.

   ✓ *The settings window displays. The options depend on the selected effect.*

5. Select options as desired.
6. Click **Update Preview** to view animation with new settings.
7. Click **OK**.........................↵Enter

Edit a Timeline Effect

1. Right-click object to edit on Stage.

   OR

   a. Select object to edit on Stage.
   b. Click **Modify**.............Alt + M
2. Click **Timeline Effects**..............E
3. Click **Edit Effect**.....................D
4. Change settings as desired.
5. Click **Update Preview**.
6. Click **OK**.........................↵Enter

Remove a Timeline Effect

1. Right-click object to edit on Stage.

   OR

   a. Select object to edit on Stage.
   b. Click **Modify**.............Alt + M
2. Click **Timeline Effects**................E
3. Click **Remove Effect**.................R

View a Timeline Effect on the Stage

1. Click **Control**................Alt + O
2. Click **Play**............................P

EXERCISE DIRECTIONS

Remove the Existing Animation

1. Start Flash and open ●48DATA. Save the file as **48LEAGUE**. This is a version of the softball league file you worked with in earlier exercises.
2. Make Scene 2 active.
3. Remove all frames from the Ball layer.
4. In Frame 1 of the Ball layer, insert a keyframe, and then insert an instance of the Ball graphic symbol.
5. Size the instance to .25" square, and position it in the Pasteboard to the right of the Stage, about 1" from the bottom.
6. Select frame 5 and insert a keyframe. Resize the Ball instance to .5" square, and center it horizontally about 2" from the top of the Stage.
7. Create a motion tween, setting the instance to scale, and to rotate clockwise 10 times.

Apply the Explode Timeline Effect

1. On the Ball layer, select frame 6 and insert a keyframe.
2. Select the Ball instance on frame 6, and apply the Explode Timeline Effect. The Explode effect settings window displays.
3. Edit the settings as follows:
   - Change the Effect Duration setting to 30 frames.
   - Change the Direction of Explosion to upper right.
   - Change the Rotate Fragments by setting to 90 degrees.
   - Set the X: value of the Change Fragments Size by setting to 100.
4. Click the Update Preview button to view the changes. The settings window should look similar to Illustration A.
5. Click OK to close the window and apply the effect. Notice that Flash renames the Ball layer to Explode 1.
6. Rewind and play the scene to view the animation on the Stage.

Edit the Timeline Effect

1. Select frame 6 of the Explode 1 layer. Notice that all frames in the effect are selected.
2. Choose the Edit Effect command to display the Explode effect settings window.
3. Change the Effect Duration to 35 frames and change the Arc Size X: value to 75.
4. Click OK to apply the changes and close the window.
5. Rewind and play the scene to view the animation on the Stage, or test the movie in the Flash Player window.
6. If requested by your instructor, print frame 15 of Scene 2, or print the entire scene.
7. Close the Flash file, saving all changes, and exit Flash.

Illustration A

ON YOUR OWN

1. Start Flash and create a new document. Save the document as **48MYPIC**.

2. Create an animation using your name and Timeline effects. You might apply the effect to a whole text block, or break apart the block and animate the individual characters.

3. Try different effects and settings until you achieve a result you like.

4. Draw or import a graphic of something you like, or something that you feel represents you well. Try using one of the Assistants effects to create a background using the imported graphic. For example, import or draw a picture of your pet, or any animal you like, and copy it to a grid to create a background. You may import the ⊕**48CAT.jpg** file supplied with this book if desired.

5. Apply any other animations, features, or effects that you want to enhance the animation. For example, you might want to import sounds, or apply shape or motion tweens. You may import the ⊕**48MEOW.wav** sound file supplied with this book if desired.

6. Test the scene and make adjustments as necessary.

7. Print a frame, or, if requested by your instructor, print the animation.

8. Save the Flash file and close it, and then exit Flash.

Exercise | 49

Skills Covered

- ■ Break Apart a Bitmap
- ■ Use the Magic Wand
- ■ Use a Bitmap Image as a Fill
- ■ Transform a Bitmap Fill

Software Skills Editing and modifying bitmaps increases your ability to edit and modify imported images. You can break the bitmaps apart so you can edit the pixels. For example, you can erase portions of the image or change the color. You can create interesting effects by using a bitmap as a fill for a different object.

Application Skills You think it will improve the softball league animation if the background ball field has a different color green in each scene. In this exercise, you will break apart the bitmap image in each scene and change the colors. You will then use a bitmap image as a fill to create a background for the printable registration form.

TERMS

Smoothing A technique used to adjust the edges of shapes and lines so that they appear smoother onscreen.

Threshold A value that defines where a change will occur.

Tile To repeat an image to fill a defined space.

NOTES

Break Apart a Bitmap

- ■ Use the Break Apart command to separate a bitmap image into its defining pixels.

    ✓ You can use the Break Apart command to convert vectors to bitmaps as well; simply select the command multiple times until the graphic is broken down into its defining pixels.

- ■ Once the image is broken apart, you can modify it using Drawing tools.

    - • Use the Eraser ⬭ to delete areas.
    - • Use the Selection tool ▶ to select areas.
    - • Use the Lasso ⟳ with or without the Magic Wand modifier ⬩ to select areas.
    - • Transform selected areas.
    - • Change the fill color of selected areas.

Use the Magic Wand

- ■ The Lasso with the Magic Wand modifier ⬩ is useful for selecting areas in a bitmap that has been broken apart.

- ■ The Magic Wand allows you to select areas of pixels based on color.

- ■ Use the Magic Wand Settings dialog box to specify a **Threshold** setting between 1 and 200 to determine how closely the color of adjacent pixels must match in order to be included in the selection (see the following illustration).

Magic Wand Settings Dialog Box

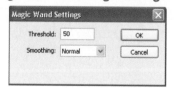

- ■ The lower the value, the more selective the result. For example, if you enter a value of 1, only adjacent pixels that are very, very similar in color to the pixel you click are selected. If you enter a value of 99, pixels that are not closely matched will be selected as well.

- ■ You may also specify a **Smoothing** setting to determine how much the edges of the selected area will be smoothed. The options include Pixels, which applies no smoothing; Rough; Normal; and Smooth.

Use a Bitmap Image as a Fill

- Use a bitmap image as a fill for new or existing objects on the Stage. For example, you may fill a shape with a bitmap image, or use the brush to paint with the bitmap image.
- Use the Color Mixer panel to select any bitmap image in the current document's library as a fill (see the following illustration).

Color Mixer Panel

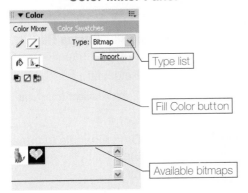

- Alternatively, if you break apart a bitmap on the Stage, you can use the Eyedropper tool to select the image as a fill.

- In either case, the image displays on the Fill Color tool, just like a solid color or gradient.
- Apply the fill as you would any fill color.

Transform a Bitmap Fill

- You can use the Gradient Transform tool to transform the bitmap fill.
- When you click the Gradient Transform tool, a bounding box with editing handles displays around the selected object.
- Each editing handle controls a specific transformation. Drag a handle to apply the transformation.
- Starting at the top center of the bounding box and moving clockwise, the available transformations include skew horizontal, rotate, skew vertical, resize height, scale, and resize width (see the illustration below).
- You may also drag the center point to reposition the bitmap within the object.
- To **tile** the bitmap within the object, reduce the scale of the fill.

Transform a Bitmap Fill

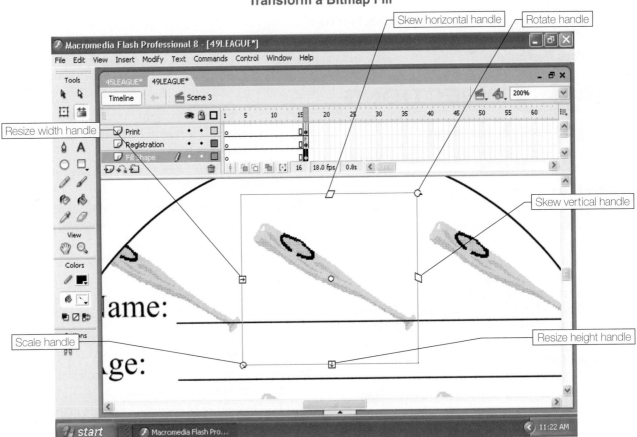

PROCEDURES

Break Apart a Bitmap (Ctrl+B)

1. Select bitmap image on Stage.
2. Click **Modify** .... `Alt`+`M`
3. Click **Break Apart** .... `K`

Select Magic Wand Settings

1. Click **Lasso** tool 🔍 .... `L`
2. Click **Magic Wand Settings** button 🪄 .
3. Click **Threshold** box ...... `Alt`+`T`
4. Replace current value with a value between 1 and 200.
5. Click **Smoothing** drop-down arrow .... `Alt`+`S`+`↓`
6. Click one of the following:
   - Pixels
   - Rough
   - Normal
   - Smooth
7. Click **OK** .... `↵Enter`

Use the Magic Wand

1. Click **Lasso** tool 🔍 .... `L`
2. Click **Magic Wand** button 🪄 .

---

3. Click a spot on the image where you want to select.

Use a Bitmap Image as a Fill
To Use the Eyedropper

1. Break apart bitmap on Stage.
2. Click **Eyedropper** 🖊 .... `I`
3. Click bitmap image.
4. Apply the fill to objects as desired:
   - Use **Paint Bucket** tool 🪣 to apply fill to existing objects.
   - Use **Brush** tool 🖌 to paint with fill.
   - Use **Oval** tool ⬭, **Rectangle** tool ▢, or **PolyStar** tool ⬠ to draw a new object using fill.

To Use the Color Mixer Panel

1. Open document.
2. Select object on Stage.
3. Click **Window** .... `Alt`+`W`
4. Click **Color Mixer** .... `X`
5. Click **Fill Color** button 🎨▪ in Color Mixer panel.

---

6. Click **Type** drop-down arrow in Color Mixer.
7. Click **Bitmap**.
8. Click bitmap image to use as fill.

   ✓ Fill is applied to selected object.

9. Apply fill to additional objects as desired.

Transform a Bitmap Fill

1. Apply bitmap fill.
2. Select fill.
3. Click **Gradient Transform** tool 🔳 .
4. Drag a handle to transform the fill.

   OR

   Drag the center point to reposition the fill.

EXERCISE DIRECTIONS

Break Apart and Modify Bitmap Images

1. Start Flash and open 🌀**49DATA** or open **48LEAGUE**. Save the file as **49LEAGUE**.
2. Make Scene 1 active and select frame 1 of the Background layer.
3. Break apart the bitmap, and then deselect all items on the Stage.
4. Select the Lasso tool, with the Magic Wand option. Display the Magic Wand Settings dialog box, and set the Threshold to 50 and the Smoothing to Normal. Click anywhere in the green around the edges of the graphic. All pixels that are similar in color to the one you click are selected.
5. Click the Fill color palette and select a dark green (#006600). Flash changes the color of the selected pixels. Your screen should look similar to Illustration A.

   ✓ If not all of the green area is changed, use the Lasso with the Magic Wand to repeat the steps to change the color.

6. Make Scene 2 active and select frame 1 of the Background layer.
7. Break apart the bitmap, and then deselect all objects on the Stage.
8. Select the Lasso tool with the Magic Wand option, and click anywhere in the green around the edges.
9. Click the Fill color palette and select a bright green (#00CC00).

   ✓ If not all of the green area is changed, use the Lasso with the Magic Wand to repeat the steps to change the color.

10. Make Scene 3 active, and select frame 1 of the Background layer.
11. Repeat the steps to change the color of the field to a pale green (#99CC66).
12. Test the movie to view the changes in the Flash Player window.

Illustration A

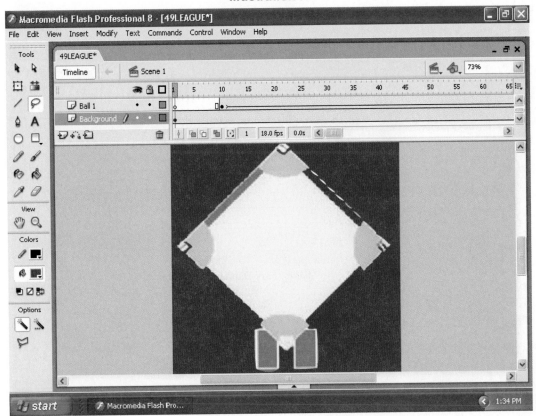

Use a Bitmap as a Fill

1. In Scene 3, select the Stop layer and insert a new layer, named **Fill Shape**.

2. Select frame 16 and insert a keyframe.

3. Select the Oval tool, make Object Drawing active, and draw a circle with no fill and a black stroke approximately 4.75" in diameter. Center it horizontally and align it with the top of the Stage.

   ✓ You do not have to use Object Drawing to apply a bitmap as a fill.

4. With the circle shape selected on the Stage, display the Color Mixer panel.

5. Click the Fill Color button, and then select Bitmap from the Type drop-down list. The bitmap images available in the file display in the panel.

6. Click the image of the ball field. Notice that it displays as the fill in the circle on the Stage.

7. Click the image of the bat to make it the fill for the circle.

8. Close the Color Mixer panel and then click the Gradient Transform tool.

9. Drag the Scale handle—the arrow in the circle in the lower-left corner—in to decrease the size of the bats until you can see three rows. Your screen should look similar to Illustration B on page 216.

   ✓ The Gradient Transform tool can be a bit sensitive. If it does not work at first, try clicking a different bat in the bitmap fill and increasing the zoom so you can get a more accurate position with the mouse pointer.

10. Print the frame.

11. Close the Flash file, saving all changes, and exit Flash.

Illustration B

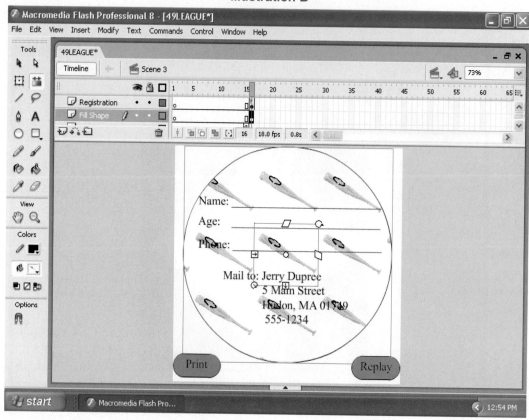

ON YOUR OWN

1. Start Flash and open **48MYPIC** or open ◐**49PIC**. Save the document as **49MYPIC**.

2. Add to the animation using an imported bitmap graphic. For example, you might import a digital photograph of yourself. Or, use a graphic that is already part of the animation.

3. Break the bitmap apart and modify it. For example, delete part of it or change the color of selected areas.

4. If you want, add a shape to the animation and fill it with a bitmap image.

5. Print a frame that shows the modified bitmap, or print the entire animation.

6. Save the Flash file and close it, and then exit Flash.

Exercise | 50

Skills Covered

- ■ Use a Mask Layer

Software Skills A mask layer lets you hide areas of the Stage, leaving selected areas showing. A mask layer is useful for creating a spotlight effect or for highlighting content.

Application Skills In this exercise, you will create an opening scene and use a mask layer animated with a shape tween to reveal a background image.

TERMS

Masked layer A layer underlying and linked to a mask layer, containing the content that is visible through the mask.

Mask item A shape or instance through which the content on the underlying masked layer is revealed. The area outside the mask item remains hidden.

Mask layer A layer used to overlay other layers, hiding all but one area of the Stage.

Opaque Not transparent.

NOTES

Use a Mask Layer

- ■ Create a **mask layer** to simulate the effect of a spotlight or to create sophisticated transition effects.
- ■ A mask layer requires at least two layers: the mask layer and the underlying, linked **masked layer**.
- ■ On the Timeline, a mask layer is marked by a mask symbol. The masked layer(s) are indented below the mask layer, and are marked with a masked symbol (see the illustration at the top of page 218).
- ■ To create the mask, you insert a **mask item** on the mask layer. The mask item may be a filled shape, an instance of a graphic symbol or a movie clip, or a text block.
- ■ In the completed animation, the mask item displays as transparent, while everything outside the item displays as **opaque**, in the color currently set as the Stage background.

- ■ The result is that the viewer sees through the mask item to the underlying layer(s), while the opaque area hides all other content on the Stage.
- ■ You can have only one mask item on a mask layer, but you can have more than one masked layer underlying the same mask layer.
- ■ You can animate a mask layer using any method except a motion path. For example, you can use a motion or shape tween to move the object across the Stage, thereby moving the spotlight effect, or to increase the size of the object in order to increase the size of the area visible on the Stage.
- ■ You cannot use a mask layer in a button and you cannot apply a mask to a mask layer.
- ■ To display the mask in Flash, the mask layer and the masked layer(s) must be locked.

Using a Mask Layer

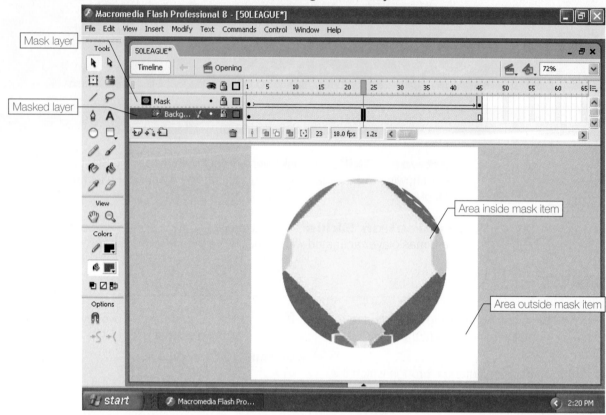

Mask layer | **Masked layer** | **Area inside mask item** | **Area outside mask item**

PROCEDURES

Create a Mask Layer

1. Select layer to be masked.
2. Insert new layer.
3. In keyframe on new layer, insert mask item through which you want content on masked layer to be visible.

   ✓ *You may draw a filled shape, insert an instance of a graphic symbol or movie clip, or create a text block.*

4. Right-click layer name in Timeline.
5. Click **Mask**.

   ✓ *Flash creates the mask layer and the masked layer, and locks both.*

Link Additional Masked Layers to an Existing Mask Layer

■ Drag existing layer directly below existing mask layer in Timeline.

   OR

   Insert new layer directly below existing mask layer in Timeline.

OR

1. Right-click layer to mask.

   ✓ *The layer must not be above the existing mask layer in the Timeline.*

2. Click **Properties**.
3. Click **Masked** option button.
4. Click **OK**..........................⤶Enter

OR

1. Select layer to mask.

   ✓ *The layer must not be above the existing mask layer in the Timeline.*

2. Click **Modify**................Alt ＋ M
3. Click **Timeline**........................M
4. Click **Layer Properties**..............L
5. Click **Masked** option button.
6. Click **OK**..........................⤶Enter

Unlink Masked Layers

1. Unlock layers.
2. Drag masked layer above mask layer in Timeline.

OR

1. Right-click masked layer.
2. Click **Properties**.
3. Click **Normal** option button.
4. Click **OK**..........................⤶Enter

OR

1. Select masked layer.
2. Click **Modify**................Alt ＋ M
3. Click **Timeline**........................M
4. Click **Layer Properties**..............L
5. Click **Normal** option button.
6. Click **OK**..........................⤶Enter

EXERCISE DIRECTIONS

Prepare a New Scene

1. Start Flash and open **49LEAGUE** or open ⬤**50DATA**. Save the file as **50LEAGUE**.

2. Display the Scene panel and create a new scene named **Opening**. Position the new scene at the top of the scene list so that it plays at the beginning of the animation.

3. Rename Layer 1 **Background**.

4. Make Scene 2 active and select frame 1 of the Background layer.

5. Click Edit and then click Copy to copy the content from frame 1 to the Windows Clipboard.

6. Make the new Opening scene active and select frame 1 of the Background layer.

7. Click Edit and then click Paste in Place to paste the content from the Clipboard to the Stage. Insert a frame in frame 45 to extend the background.

Create a Mask Layer

1. Insert a new layer and name it **Mask**.

2. On the new layer, use the Oval tool to draw a circle, using a dark green fill (#006600) and a black stroke.

3. Size the circle to .25" in diameter, and position in the center horizontally and vertically.

4. Select frame 45 of the Mask layer and insert a keyframe.

5. Resize the circle to 7" in diameter and position it in the center horizontally and vertically. It should completely cover the Stage.

6. Select frame 20 of the Mask layer and create a Shape tween to scale the circle from small to large. Your screen should look similar to Illustration A.

7. Rewind and play the animation. The green circle grows to hide the background content on the Stage.

8. Right-click the Mask layer and click Mask.

9. Rewind and play the animation. The content on the Stage begins masked by all but a small transparent circle. As the circle shape increases in size, the Stage is revealed.

10. Test the movie in the Flash Player.

11. Close the Flash file, saving all changes, and exit Flash.

Illustration A

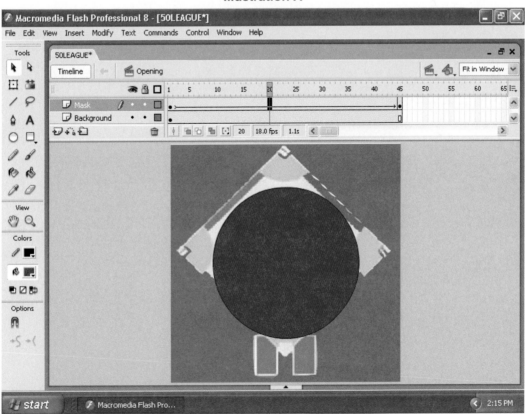

ON YOUR OWN

1. Start Flash and open **49MYPIC** or open **50PIC**. Save the document as **50MYPIC**.

2. Use a mask layer to create an opening or introductory scene. For example, create a new scene, add content, and then use a mask layer to spotlight the content. If the animation includes a Timeline effect such as Copy to Grid, you can copy the frames from the Copy to Grid layer to the new scene, and then use a mask to reveal the graphics in the grid. Use frame-by-frame animation or a tween to cause the mask item to change shape, size, and move around the Stage. As it moves and changes, it can reveal more, or different, objects on the underlying masked layer.

3. Preview the scene, and the entire animation.

4. Print the new scene.

5. Save the Flash file and close it, and then exit Flash.

Skills Covered

■ **Use User Interface Components**

Software Skills Components provide you with tools to create complex Flash applications even if you do not have a thorough understanding of ActionScript. For example, insert user interface components to quickly create elements such as check boxes that viewers can use to interact with your animation.

Application Skills In this exercise, you will complete the animation for the senior softball league by replacing the Age text block with radio buttons on the print-able registration form. That way, viewers will be able to select from a list of age range options. You will also change the stroke color of the circle shape and modify the action for the Replay button so it goes to the first frame in the first scene.

TERMS

Component In Flash, a prewritten object defined as a movie clip with parameters that allow you to mod-ify its appearance and behavior.

Radio button A user interface object that a user clicks to select an option. Radio buttons are gener-

ally grouped, but only one button in the group may be selected at a time.

User Interface objects Elements that someone viewing an application can use to interact with the application.

NOTES

Use User Interface Components

■ Flash 8 includes a powerful feature called **components**, which are built-in objects you use to provide complex functionality to your Flash applica-tions, even without a thorough knowledge of ActionScript.

■ Many components are **user interface objects** that someone viewing a Flash application in a Web browser or Flash Player window can use to interact with the application. For example, there are **radio button**, check box, and text input field components.

■ The components are created as movie clip objects that include ActionScript code. You simply insert the component into your Flash document by dragging it from the Components panel to the Stage.

■ If necessary, you use the Parameters tab in the Property Inspector to set parameters to control the appearance and behavior of the component (see the illustration at the top of page 222).

■ Once you insert a component into a Flash docu-ment, the component is added to the document's library, so you can insert additional instances directly from the Library panel.

Using a Check Box Component

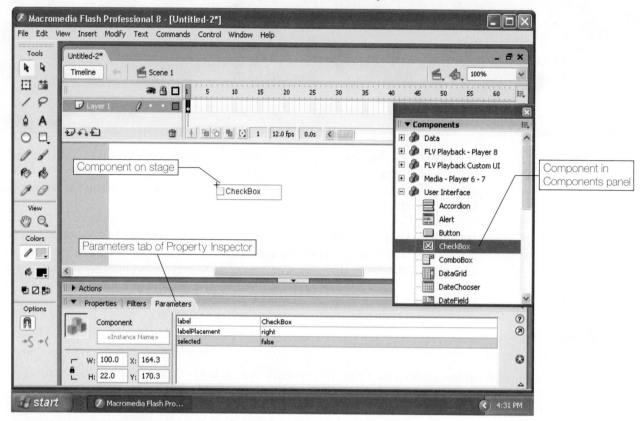

Labels pointing to the screenshot:
- Component on stage
- CheckBox
- Parameters tab of Property Inspector
- Component in Components panel

PROCEDURES

Apply a User Interface Component

1. Select keyframe where you want to insert component.
2. Click **Window**..............Alt + W
3. Click **Components**......C, ↵Enter
4. Double-click **User Interface** in Components panel.

5. Drag desired component from Components panel to Stage.
6. Click **Parameters tab** in Property Inspector.
7. Set parameters as necessary.

Delete a Component

1. Select component on Stage.
2. Press **Delete**......................Del

EXERCISE DIRECTIONS

Prepare the Stage

1. Start Flash and open **50LEAGUE** or open ⊘**51DATA**. Save the file as **51LEAGUE**.
2. Make Scene 3 active and select frame 16 on the Fill Shape layer.
3. Change the stroke color to light beige (#FFCC99). This will make it easier to view all of the text.
4. Select frame 16 on the Registration layer and then select and delete the text block containing the text *Age*.
5. Move the Name text block down a bit, so its top edge is aligned approximately 1" from the top of the frame, and then move the Phone text block up so its top edge is aligned approximately 1.5"

from the top of the frame. Center both text blocks horizontally.

6. Select the Mail to text block and align it with the bottom of the Stage, centered horizontally.

Insert Components

1. Select the Fill Shape layer and insert a new layer named **Age Range**. Select frame 16 on the new layer and insert a keyframe.
2. Display the Components panel.
3. Double-click the User Interface category in the Components panel, and then scroll down—or enlarge the panel—until you see the RadioButton component.

4. Drag the RadioButton component from the Components panel to frame 16 of the Age Range layer, dropping the component somewhere between the Phone and Mail to text blocks. When you release the mouse button, your screen should look similar to the one in Illustration A.

5. With the RadioButton component selected, display the Property Inspector and click the Parameters tab.

6. In the left column of the Parameters tab, click the groupName text *radioGroup* and replace the default name (radioGroup) with the group name **Age**.

   ✓ *Radio buttons must be part of a group so that only one option in the group can be selected. In this case, you are naming the group Age.*

7. Click the label text *Radio Button* and replace it with the label **Age: 55-60**. Press Enter. Notice on the Stage that the RadioButton component label changes to show the label you just entered.

8. Select frame 16 of the Age Range layer and drag another RadioButton component from the Components panel to the Stage, dropping it to the right of the first button.

9. On the Parameters tab, change the groupName to **Age**, and change the label to **Age: 61-65**.

10. Insert a third RadioButton component to the right of the others, and change the groupName to **Age** and the label to **Age: 66+**.

11. Close the Components panel.

12. Align the three radio buttons so their bottom edges are about 2" from the bottom of the Stage. Position them horizontally across the width of the circle shape so they appear evenly spaced (see Illustration A).

Complete the Animation

1. Select frame 16 of the Registration layer and then select the Replay button instance.

2. Display the Actions panel.

3. Edit line 2 of the script to change the Scene parameter to Opening. You want the button to go to and play frame 1 of the Opening scene.

4. Close the Actions panel.

5. Test the movie in the Flash Player window.

6. When it displays, click the Register button to display the form, and then click the Age: 55-60 button. Your screen should look similar to Illustration B on page 224.

7. Print the form.

8. Click the Replay button. The animation should start again from the beginning.

Illustration A

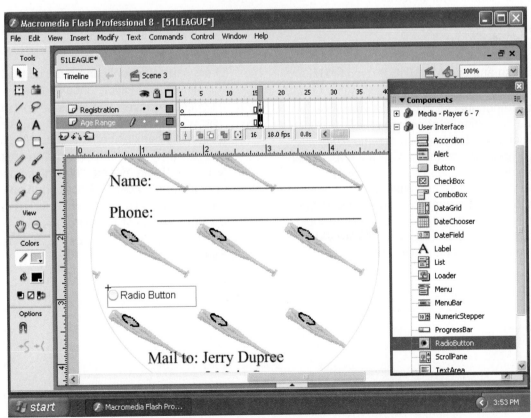

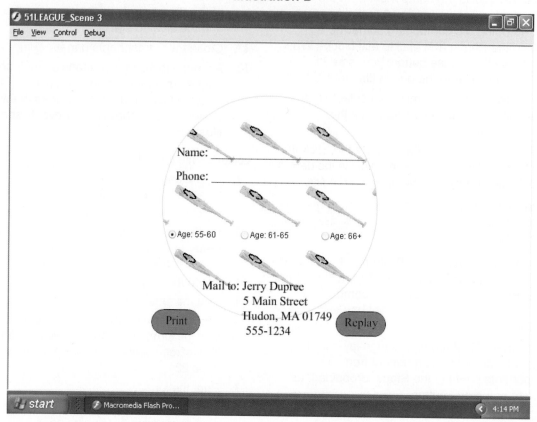

9. This time, click the Age: 66+ button on the Registration form, and then print it.

10. Close the Flash Player window.

11. Close the Flash file, saving all changes, and exit Flash.

ON YOUR OWN

1. Start Flash and open **50MYPIC** or open **⊘51PIC**. Save the document as **51MYPIC**.

2. Insert components so that viewers can interact with the animation to provide feedback about the animation itself. Use a group of radio buttons to solicit a response on the quality of the animation. For example, one button could be labeled Excellent, one Good, and one Poor. Use check boxes to solicit information about elements they would like more of. For example, one box could be labeled Sound, one could be labeled Video, and one could be labeled Graphics. Remember,

users can select only one radio button in a group, but can select multiple check boxes.

3. If necessary, insert text to explain or prompt the user on how to use the component. For example, insert a text box asking the question, How would you rate this animation? (select an option below).

4. Make the frame that contains the components printable, and create a Print button on it.

5. View the animation in Flash Player, use the components, and print the frame.

6. Save the Flash file and close it, and then exit Flash.

End of Lesson Projects

- Summary Exercise
- Application Exercise
- Curriculum Integration Exercise
- Critical Thinking Exercise

Exercise | 52

Summary Exercise

Software Skills Managers from Castle Gate Productions have asked you to make enhancements and changes to the animations. In this exercise, you will use the Movie Explorer and the library to locate and organize elements in the animation. You will also change colors in some bitmap graphics in the animation, and add a mask to draw attention to important content.

DIRECTIONS

Use the Movie Explorer and the Library

1. Start Flash and open ✸52DATA or open 41CASTLE. Save the file as 52CASTLE.
2. Display the Movie Explorer.
3. In the Movie Explorer, display only movie clips, buttons, and graphics.
4. Display frames and layers and click the plus sign to expand the Main Scene.
5. In the Find box, type **Castle**.
6. In the Movie Explorer, right-click any one of the Castle 1 graphics and click Find in Library to display the document's library.
7. Change to Wide Library View, and then right-click in the library and select to update the use count. Notice that the Castle 1 graphic is used 17 times in the animation.
8. Sort the items in the library by type. The library should look similar to Illustration A on page 226.
9. Close the library, or change to Narrow View.
10. Right-click in the Movie Explorer and select to view all scenes.
11. Display all available elements.
12. Delete the text Castle from the Find box.
13. Click the minus sign to collapse the Main scene, and then click the plus sign to expand the Theater scene.

14. Click the Plus sign to expand the Restart layer and frame 50, and the Applause layer and Frame 10. The Movie Explorer should look similar to Illustration B.
15. Expand the Main Scene and then print the Movie Explorer.
16. Close the Movie Explorer panel.

Break Apart and Modify Bitmaps

1. In the 52CASTLE document, make the Theater scene active and unlock all layers, if necessary.
2. Select frame 1 of the Stage layer and select the Break Apart command twice—first to restore the instance to a bitmap, and again to break the bitmap apart.
3. Deselect all elements on the Stage, and then select the Lasso tool with the Magic Wand option.
4. Click the Magic Wand Settings button to display the dialog box, change the Threshold to 40, and select Normal Smoothing. Click OK to close the dialog box.
5. With the Magic Wand, click an area on the brick red curtains to select it. Adjacent areas that match the color you click should be selected. Press and hold Ctrl and click to select additional brick red areas.

   ✓ Don't worry if you cannot select the edges of the curtains. You may leave them unchanged.

225

Illustration A

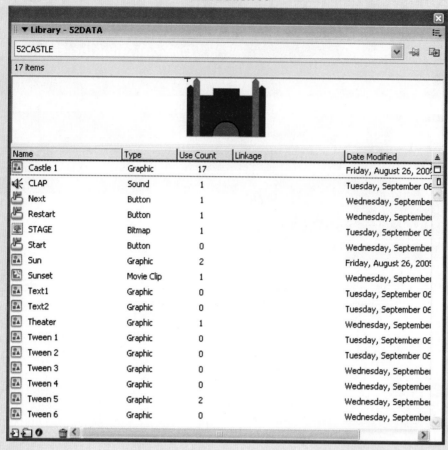

Illustration B

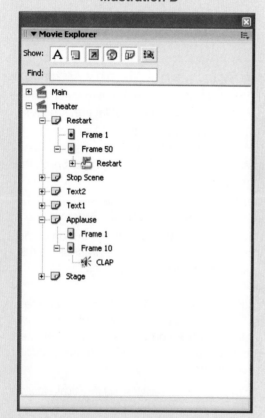

6. Click the Fill Color button and click purple (#9900CC) to change the color of the selected areas.

7. Deselect all elements on the Stage. With the Magic Wand, select the black area in the upper-left corner of the image and then delete it.

8. Repeat step 7 to delete the black areas from the other three corners.

9. Use the Eraser tool to delete any traces of the black from the corners on the Stage.

10. Select frame 1 of the Stage layer to select all of the bitmap, and then click Modify, Group. Your screen should look similar to Illustration C (on page 227).

Create a Mask Layer

1. In the Theater scene, insert 20 frames at the beginning of the Text1, Text2, Stop Scene, and Restart layers. This should make frame 70 the last frame of the animation.

2. Select frame 70 of the Stage layer and insert a frame, and then select frame 70 of the Applause layer and insert a frame.

3. Select the Stage layer and insert a new layer, named **Mask**.

226

Illustration C

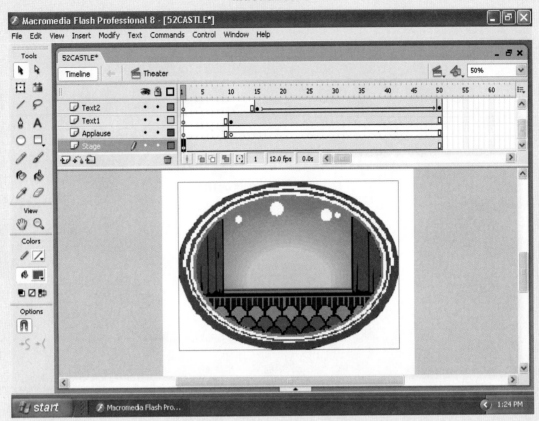

4. Select frame 1 of the Mask layer and use the Oval tool to draw a circle 1.5" in diameter. The fill and stroke color do not matter, because the shape is a mask item. Position the circle along the upper-left arc of the Stage bitmap, so the X coordinate is 1.0 and the Y coordinate is 2.0.

5. Insert a keyframe in frame 10 and move the circle diagonally down and to the right to position it along the lower-right arc of the bitmap, so both the X and Y coordinates are 5.0.

6. Insert a keyframe in frame 20 and move the circle up to position it along the upper-right arc of the bitmap so the X coordinate is 5.0 and the Y coordinate is 2.0.

7. Insert a keyframe in frame 27 and scale the circle to 10" in diameter and center it horizontally and vertically on the Stage.

8. Insert motion tweens between frames 1 and 10 and frames 10 and 20. Deselect the Scale check box and set the Ease to 100.

9. Insert a motion tween between frames 20 and 27, and set to Scale the object.

10. Right-click the Mask layer and click Mask.

11. Display the Library panel, right-click the Next button, and click Edit. Change the color of the text from black to yellow in all four stages, and then exit symbol editing mode.

12. Edit the Restart button to change its text color from black to yellow in all four stages. Exit symbol editing mode.

13. Display the Document Properties dialog box, and change the background color to Black.

14. Test the movie in the Flash Player window. The final frame should look similar to Illustration D on page 228.

15. Close the Flash Player window.

16. If requested by your instructor, print frame 35 of the Theater scene.

17. Lock all layers, close the document, and exit Flash, saving all changes.

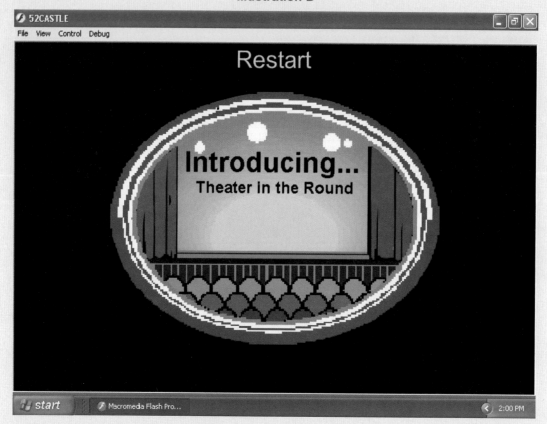

Application Exercise

Software Skills In this exercise, you continue work on the Castle Gate animation. You will add a new scene in which you create a printable frame. The frame will include selectable text, a link to a URL, and check box components. You will complete the animation by inserting buttons and actions to control the flow. Finally, you will preview and publish the animation.

DIRECTIONS

Add a New Scene

1. Open ⬤53DATA or 52CASTLE and save the document as **53CASTLE**.
2. Display the Scene panel and add a new scene after the Theater scene, named **Info**.
3. Close the Scene panel.
4. Rename Layer 1 **Background** and use the Rectangle tool to draw a rectangle with no stroke and a white fill exactly the size of the Stage.

   ✓ *Because the Stage Background is black, this shape ensures that the content you enter on the Stage can be seen.*

5. Create a new layer named **Text**. Use the Text tool to create a static, fixed-width text block approximately the same width as the Stage. Using a sans serif font in 15 points, bold, black, and centered, type the text **Theater in the Round, 6 Forum Street, Hudson, MA 01759, 978-555-0987**.
6. Select the text block and then click the Selectable button in the Property Inspector. Position the text block about .5" from the top of the Stage, centered horizontally.
7. Create another text block approximately 5.5" wide and use the same font in 32 points. Type **Information Request Form**. If necessary, expand the width of the text block so that the text fits on a single line. Position this text block about .25" below the first block, centered on the Stage. Click the Selectable button to turn off the feature.
8. Create another text block, approximately 5" wide, and use the same font in 18 points, left aligned, to type the name, address, city, state, ZIP, phone, and e-mail lines, as shown in Illustration A on page 230. Position the text block about .25" below the previous block, centered on the Stage.
9. Create a fourth text block about 5.75" wide, and use the same font in 18 points, center-aligned, to type **First Production: Shakespeare's Twelfth Night!**

10. Position this block approximately 1.25" below the previous block, centered on the Stage.
11. Create a final text block approximately 6" wide and, use the same font in 16 points, center-aligned, to type **Click here to learn more about this wonderful comedy.** Position the block directly below the previous block, centered on the Stage.
12. Select the last text block and in the URL link box in the Property Inspector, type **http://www.allshakespeare.com/twelfth/**.

Insert Components

1. Create a new layer named Components and select frame 1.
2. Display the Components panel and expand the User Interface category, if necessary.
3. Drag the CheckBox component from the panel to the Stage.
4. Click the Parameters tab in the Property Inspector and replace the default label text with the text **Send information**.
5. On the Stage, resize the component to approximately 2.5" wide, or wide enough so all of the label text is visible onscreen.
6. Drag another CheckBox component on to the Stage and change its label to **Add to mailing list**.
7. Resize the component to approximately 2.5" wide, or wide enough so all of the label text is visible onscreen.
8. Drag another CheckBox component on to the Stage and change its label to **Add to e-mail list**, and size the component to approximately 2.5" wide. Close the Components panel.
9. Position the three components across the width of the Stage, approximately 2.0" from the bottom of the Stage (refer to Illustration A on page 230).

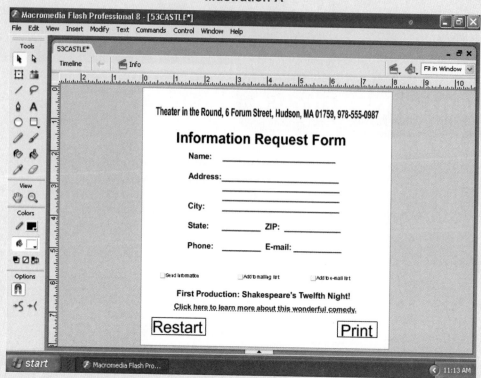

Make the Frame Printable

1. Insert a new layer and name it **Buttons**.
2. Select frame 1. In the Property Inspector, click in the Frame box and type **#p**.
3. Insert an instance of the Restart button and position it in the lower-left corner of the Stage. In the Property Inspector, click the Color button and then click Tint. Select black from the color palette, and set the tint level to 100%.
4. In the Library panel, right-click the Next button symbol and click Duplicate. Change the button name to **Print**.
5. Edit the Print button symbol to change the text on all four stages to Print, also changing the text color to black.
6. Return to the document and insert an instance of the Print button on frame 1 of the Buttons layer and position it in the lower-right corner of the Stage.
7. Select the Print button and insert a Print action.
8. Select the Restart button and insert a goto and play action, setting parameters so that Flash goes to the first frame of the Main scene.
9. Insert a new layer named **Stop scene**. Insert a stop action on frame 1. The frame should look similar to Illustration A.

Complete and Preview the Animation

1. Make the Theater scene active, and unlock all layers.

2. Display the Library panel if necessary, right-click the Next button symbol and click Duplicate. Change the button name to Info.
3. Edit the Info button symbol to change the text on all four stages to Info, and return to the document.
4. Rename the Restart layer in the Theater scene **Buttons**.
5. Select frame 70 on the Buttons layer and insert an instance of the Info button.
6. Center the Info button horizontally and position it about .25" from the bottom of the Stage.
7. Select the Info button on the Stage, and insert a goto and play action, setting parameters so that Flash goes to the first frame of the Info scene.
8. In the Publish Settings dialog box, on the HTML tab, set the dimensions to 100%, and use all other default settings.
9. Preview the animation in your browser, testing all buttons. Test the link to the URL, and make sure you can select the selectable text. Make adjustments in Flash as necessary.

   ✓ *When you test the URL, you may receive a security warning message from Macromedia Flash Player.*

10. Publish the animation.
11. Close the document and exit Flash, saving all changes.

Curriculum Integration Exercise

Software Skills For an English class, use Flash to illustrate a climactic scene from a short story, novel, or poem. For example, for Ernest Hemingway's *The Old Man and the Sea*, you could animate the old man fishing; for a Harry Potter book, you could animate Harry casting a spell; or for the poem *Stopping by the Woods on a Snowy Evening* by Robert Frost, you could animate a horse and buggy in a snowy forest. Working alone or in a group, select the scene you want to illustrate and then plan the animation. For example, plan the flow of the animation from start to finish and decide what elements you will need. Locate graphics to import, or draw your own. If you want sound or video, create or locate the files.

When you are ready, create the Flash document. Include the title of the work as well as the author, and text from the work that identifies the scene. When the animation is complete, present it to the class. A sample document illustrating *The Old Man and the Sea* is shown on page 232.

DIRECTIONS

Start the project by selecting the work and deciding which scene you want to animate. Plan the animation, including gathering the elements you will need to complete the document.

Start a new document and save it as **54ENGLISH**.

Prepare the Stage by setting the ruler units to inches, and displaying visual tools you may find useful, such as the grid or guides.

Create or import the media you need to compile the animation, such as graphics, sounds, text blocks, and video.

Insert all static images, such as backgrounds, extending them to the end of the animation as necessary. If you want, break apart bitmaps to modify them. Use a mask layer to spotlight content, if desired.

Create animations using tweens or frame-by-frame techniques. Try to incorporate a Timeline Effect, such as a Blur, Drop Shadow, or Explode.

Include buttons and actions to control the flow of the animation and to make one or more frames printable.

Preview the document on the Stage as you work, making adjustments as necessary.

You may want to print the animation so you can discuss it with your group or teacher. The printed animation can help you view the overall organization and flow of the Flash document.

When you are satisfied with the application, select publish settings and preview it in your browser. Publish the application.

Present the animation to the class.

Critical Thinking Exercise

Software Skills The owner of a pet store has asked you to design an animation for its birthday celebration. In this exercise, you will break apart a bitmap image of a dog and manipulate the pixels to make it appear that the dog's mouth is moving. You will synchronize the movement with a sound file so it will appear that the dog is singing the Happy Birthday song!

DIRECTIONS

- Start Flash and create a new file. Save the document as **55DOG**.
- Rename Layer 1 **Dog** and import a bitmap image of a dog, or draw a dog using the drawing tools. It will be easier to use a drawing rather than a photograph. If you cannot locate an image, use the ✺**DOG.jpg** graphics file provided with this book.
- Size and position the image on the Stage, and then break apart the bitmap.
- Use the Lasso to select an area that includes the lower jaw of the dog and then convert the selection into a graphic symbol named **Mouth**.
- Insert a new layer named **Song** and import the file ✺**SONG.wav** provided with this book. Alternatively, use any song file you want. Insert a frame as far out on the Timeline as necessary to accommodate the length of the song.
- On the Dog layer, create a frame-by-frame animation where the Mouth graphic moves to make it appear that the dog is opening its mouth. To do this, rotate the graphic a small amount, and then move it so that its end appears to stay hinged to the dog (refer to the illustration on page 234). Repeat this as necessary to make the mouth open and then close. Insert frames where nothing moves to simulate the mouth holding a note for an instant, or where the mouth moves up a small amount, and then back down. By varying the movements you will achieve a more realistic appearance.
- When you complete a frame-by-frame sequence where the dog's mouth opens and then closes again, copy the frames and paste them as many times as necessary to fill the frames until the end of the song. An alternative method would be to create a movie clip, and then insert the movie clip multiple times.
- Preview the animation. Adjust the movement as necessary to match the song. For instance, you want the dog's mouth to close at the end of the song. Also, make necessary changes to the bitmap, such as erasing lines or adding color. You may want to enhance the animation with other effects, such as making the dog wink.
- Insert a stop action at the end of the animation so that it does not loop.
- Select publish settings to publish the animation in Flash and HTML formats. Set the HTML dimensions to 100%. Preview the animation in your Web browser. Make adjustments if necessary, and then publish the document.
- If requested by your instructor, print the animation.
- Close the document, saving all changes and exit Flash.

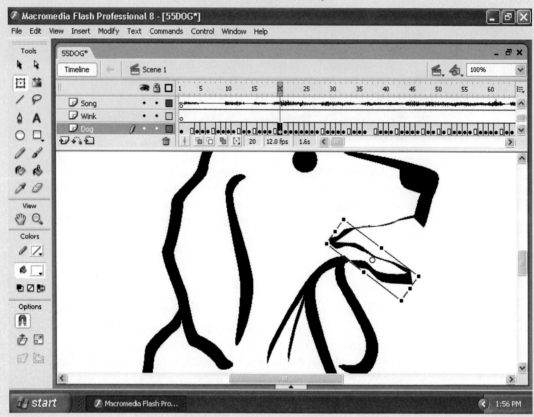

INDEX

SINGLE PC LICENSE AGREEMENT AND LIMITED WARRANTY